DATE DUE

IN CONFIDENCE

Ronald Goldfarb

IN CONFIDENCE

WHEN TO PROTECT SECRECY AND WHEN TO REQUIRE DISCLOSURE

Yale University Press New Haven & London

Published with assistance from the Louis Stern Memorial Fund.

Set in Galliard type by The Composing Room of Michigan, Inc.
Printed in the United States of America by Sheridan Books, Ann Arbor, Michigan.

Library of Congress Cataloging-in-Publication Data

Goldfarb, Ronald L.
In confidence : when to protect secrecy and when to require disclosure / Ronald Goldfarb.
p. cm.
Includes bibliographical references and index.
ISBN 978-0-300-12009-7 (cloth : alk. paper) 1. Confidential communications—United States. 2. Privileges and immunities—United States. I. Title.
KF8958.G65 2009
342.7308′58—dc22

2008038670

A catalogue record for this book is available from the British Library.

This paper meets the requirements of ANSI/NISO Z39.48-1992 (Permanence of Paper). It contains 30 percent postconsumer waste (PCW) and is certified by the Forest Stewardship Council (FSC).

10 9 8 7 6 5 4 3 2 1

FOR ANABEL, CAITLIN, JOANNA, AVA, MILES, NATHANIEL, AND OTHERS WHO MAY JOIN THEM

CONTENTS

PREFACE

To communicate in confidence is a common experience. One may lower one's voice, perhaps looking around to ensure privacy. This might happen in an informal moment, over a drink with a friend or a meal with one's spouse, or in a private conversation with a business associate. Or the setting might be more formal, in an office with an attorney or doctor, in a confessional booth, on a psychiatrist's couch, or in a secret meeting with a reporter. It could be a guarded confession or an unintended slip. It may be in writing, signed, or anonymous.

In that moment of disclosure, two conflicting phenomena occur: invariably, the revealing of a secret; and often, the hopeful—naive might be a better adjective—understanding that it will remain a secret. The terms *confidential* or *in confidence* are a plea, not a statement of fact. For reasons that have been explored by analysts and novelists as well as jurists, people have an impulse to share secrets, sometimes revealing embarrassing or even incriminating information about themselves or others. In contrast to that common compulsion for candor and openness is the competing—and equally common—impulse to attempt to confine and control the access to and disclosure of this now un-private information.

Intelligence agents and law-enforcement officials, employees in sensitive business positions, government officials, families, school officials, friends, all seek to share information on a confidential basis; but at the same time, they expect (unrealistically) or hope that their disclosures can be contained.

Our legal system has historically protected communications with certain classes of people—doctors, lawyers, clergy, spouses—from enforced exposure on the ground that those relations are important to protect for practical and humane reasons. But even the professional secrets for which the law provides privileged status must be disclosed in specific situations, as subsequent chapters will make clear.

The search for truth and legitimate needs for public information are regularly balanced against competing needs for censorship and requirements for privacy and secrecy, which, even when legitimate, are inherently jeopardized by human nature and evolving technology. What is the role of revelation?

This book examines the question of confidentiality—its justifications, its rationales, its virtues, and its complexities. It explores conundrums of personal secrecy and judicial notions about the search for truth. These ruminations reveal interesting conflicts between competing needs for privacy and transparency and the corresponding values of confidentiality and exposure, whose balancing and resolutions define the state of democracy in our society as a new century begins.

INTRODUCTION

Everything is confidential. Nothing is confidential. We all want privacy at the same time that we clamor for openness. People have strong impulses to share even their most private information, but they also unrealistically expect their shared conversations to be kept private. The disclosure of information is impossible to control, yet people have always attempted and will forever attempt to control it.

The late Supreme Court justice William O. Douglas, in a dissenting opinion in a 1973 case, wrote that the authors of the Bill of Rights believed that "every individual needs both to communicate with others and to keep his affairs to himself." Thus, the jurist opined, "the individual should have the freedom to select for himself the time and circumstances when he will share his secrets with others and decide the extent of that sharing."[1] The fact is that Justice Douglas was unrealistic; once information is disclosed, its subsequent dissemination cannot be controlled.

Confidentiality aspires to be perpetual. But this hope goes against human nature. Confidentiality is elusive, if not impossible, in a time and world of immediate and pervasive information access and disclosure. How can these two realities—openness and privacy—coexist?

There are no permanent and inviolate secrets. Benjamin Franklin, a founding father of our country in the eighteenth century, and Carlos Marcello, a founding father of the American Mafia in the twentieth century, have both been quoted as stating, "Three may keep a secret if two of them are dead."

Gossip and secrets are the stuff of novels and drama—and of ancient considerations. The Bible refers to the keeping of confidences. In Ecclesiastes 3:1–7, we read, "For everything there is a season, and . . . a time to keep silence and a time to speak." Proverbs 11:12–13 states, "The man of broad discernment is one that keeps silent," and Proverbs 25:9–10 warns, "Do not reveal another man's secrets, or he will reproach you when he hears of it and your indiscretion will then be beyond recall."

Keeping a secret is a virtue all people admire and few can claim to honor absolutely. There is a common appetite for secrets to be shared. The most honorable and sophisticated citizens frequently begin a conversation with words such as "I'm not supposed to say anything, so promise you won't tell anyone" before they break their vow of secrecy. We all receive documents marked "Confidential" and doubt their actual confidentiality. We all have heard the admonition "Let me tell you confidentially" or "off the record," knowing that these words are used in a less than pure and absolute sense.

The nineteenth-century Italian novelist Alessandro Manzoni perceptively noted: "When a friend . . . indulges in the joy of unburdening a secret on to another friend's bosom, he makes the latter, . . . feel the urge to taste the same joy himself. He implores him . . . not to tell a soul; but if such a condition were taken absolutely literally, it would at once cut off the flow of these joys at their very source. The general practice is for the secret to be confided only to an equally trustworthy friend, the same conditions being imposed on him. And so from trustworthy friend to trustworthy friend the secret goes moving on round that immense chain, until finally it reaches the ears of just the very person . . . whom the first talker had expressly intended it never should reach."[2]

All people possess powerful competing impulses both to maintain secrets and to reveal them. Dr. Samuel Johnson wondered "whether a secret has not some subtle volatility by which it escapes imperceptibly, at the smallest vent, or some power of fermentation, by which it expands itself, so as to burst the heart that will not give it away."[3] The need to possess secrets and the desire to reveal them compete within us all.

Secrecy is part of a universal value system that ranges from innocent children who cross their hearts and hope to die before they share secrets to thieves and murderers who observe their own "honor system" in which snitching is considered a dishonorable sin warranting swift and summary sanctions.

Confidentiality plays a part in literature and films, as in life. In Anton Chekhov's short story "A Trifle from Life," a young boy was devastated when his mother's lover betrayed a secret he swore to keep "on my honor." The young boy was horrified to be so deceived: "You promised on your word of honor." Chekhov explained that there are "a great many things for which the language of children has no expression." Children are not competent enough to give their consent concerning confidentiality, some psychoanalysts believe; their secrets are family secrets. "The secret of childhood is perhaps more a poetic secret than a scientific one."[4] An older and more worldly André Malraux concluded that man is "a miserable little pile of secrets."[5]

From the innocence of children to the profane world of vice and crime, expectations of confidentiality prevail. A former madam, Xaviera Hollander, famous for her revealing book *The Happy Hooker, My Own Story,* reported that "there is a code of ethics in prostitution. . . . People go to prostitutes to keep their secrets. My father was a doctor; I know the rules. You don't talk about your patients, and as a prostitute, you don't talk about your Johns."[6]

The "professions," even the illegal ones, understand the need for confidentiality. An amateur analyst, Ms. Hollander noted the psychic power of confidential secrets. "Keeping such secrets provides an adrenaline rush."[7] Hollander says that she "would never name names," a profoundly moral position that divided this country during the McCarthy era, when people anguished about the morality of betraying their friends' and colleagues' confidences.

The Mafia has a cardinal rule of *omertà,* popularized in fiction and by the famous *Godfather* movies. "Omerta became the religion of the people," author Mario Puzo noted. Former Mafia member Joseph Valachi's televised testimony in 1963 before the U.S. Senate about the Mafia in America was called by the late attorney general Robert F. Kennedy "the greatest intelligence breakthrough in the history of organized crime in the United States."[8] Secrecy is the fundamental rule of criminals and prisoners.

The Mafia is only one example of a secret society; there are many more, some innocuous, others deadly. Secrecy is the oxygen they all demand. They may be international and ominous, like the Japanese Mafia (*yakuza*) and al-Qaeda; fraternal, like the Freemasons; religious, like the Knights of Columbus; social, like the Bohemian Club or Skull and Bones; historical, like the Priory of Sion; revolutionary and criminal, like the Ku Klux Klan; or even fictional, like the fantasy Elders of Zion. There is an international encyclopedia of secret societies, itself an inherently inconsistent notion.

Secret societies are associations of individuals who share confidences. By joining together, members create a sense of elitism or power. These groups usually have a specific purpose that brings them together, as well as rituals that seem silly to others but are taken very seriously by members. Secret societies are another example of the inconsistent nature of secrets: members are compelled to share secrets exclusively while pledged to keep them from others.

The underworld "morality" of confidentiality has been debated in the modern hip-hop era. Recently, a "stop snitching" campaign appeared on the Internet urging people not to cooperate with law-enforcement officials. At the same time, law-enforcement officials have suggested a "Start Snitching" campaign. Who should be protected, the assaulted or the assailant, is a question that has actually been asked in a twisted moral debate. One writer argued that the morality of snitching is "not easily answerable" and that the "anti-snitching position can be a legitimate and sophisticated response."[9] Criminals have standards; apparently keeping secrets is one of them. One gang member called breaking the rules of criminal confidentiality "such a severe violation of the street code that retaliation is almost inevitable."[10]

In addition to purchasing a "stop snitching" T-shirt, people can subscribe to a Web site called Who's A Rat (http://whosarat.com), which lists names of witnesses who cooperate with the government. The site has photos of them (about forty-three hundred so far), and electronic excerpts from court documents are posted online. The purpose of the site, Justice Department officials complained, is witness retaliation, intimidation, and harassment.[11] Not only are cooperating witnesses outed, but undercover operations are disclosed as well (about four hundred undercover agents have been identified so far), creating dangers to cooperating witnesses and informers as well as law-enforcement officials, impeding investigations, and jeopardizing prosecutions. Defense lawyers argue that the Internet site is protected by the First Amendment, so sealing this information, as critics suggest, is against public policies supporting openness and public access to information. Transparency policies frequently conflict with legitimate needs for secrecy.

Law-enforcement officers protect their anonymous sources as a matter of life and death. The witness protection program is the extreme example. But everyday police practices are premised on the value of anonymous informants. Law-enforcement officials rely on citizen informants ("911, there's a burglar crawling into my neighbor's house"), criminal informants ("reduce my charge or sentence, and I'll tell you what you want to know"), and paid informants ("here's twenty dollars; let me know who is coming and going at apartment 1"). The law-enforcement officer controls the anonymity of these sources. Cooperate and tell the truth or be "burned" (exposed). The value of anonymity in these situations is that it is necessary to induce the source to impart the information, except for the good citizen who is helpful because he or she is motivated by civic responsibility (though he or she may or may not wish to be identified). The identity of the informant, not the information revealed by the informant, is privileged.

There is a psychological aspect to the notions of confidentiality and disclosure. In some cases, people need to disclose facts. They ask traditional professionals and many others for confidentiality because they need to be open about private thoughts. Ms. Hollander described one example of this; academics too have expressed opinions on the subject. In discussing the moral implications of the attorney-client privilege, University of Utah philosophy professor Bruce Landesman suggested that there is a psychological aspect to all confidential communications. "The basis for confidentiality," he wrote, "is that speakers need to express damaging information without losing control over its use." Sometimes the speaker's motive is to make the hearer a "confederate"; "the speaker wishes both to retain the privacy of the information and at the same time to express it to someone else. Confidentiality is the device for doing this." Professor Landesman suggests that the speaker may have "a need to confess, to share . . . the burden of his guilt."[12]

"A guilty conscience needs to confess," Albert Camus wrote.[13] But confessors want their disclosures to go only so far, and not further. Communication provides a release. But after the psychic relief that follows disclosure comes the unsettling worry about preventing that communication from being disclosed to others. Once it is let out, the revelation can no longer be contained under the protection of privacy.

Maintaining secrets can be a way of elevating the importance of that which is hidden. Intimate confidences proceed, the French writer and moralist François, duc de la Rochefoucauld, suggested, "from a desire to be pitied or admired."[14] Johann Wolfgang von Goethe remarked, "Secrecy has many advantages for when you tell someone the purpose of any object right away, they often think there is nothing to it." But if you wrap it in a secret, it "is deemed to possess greater value and credibility." It is more precious. "We guard what we deem to be valuable," a student of secrecy suggests.[15]

There is a sociology of secrecy, one scholar explains, a hide-and-seek of relationships. "The ability to keep secrets implies the ability to disclose secrets selectively. . . . Selective disclosure at one's own discretion is important to individual autonomy. . . . Shared secrets create solidarity. . . . By telling secrets we bring them close to us." The author reminds us, however, that "secrets once revealed cannot be retracted."[16] Another student of the subject suggests that "in a world awash in data, we unconsciously establish trust in each other by selectively sharing information. Intimates are allowed to know a lot, but not everything. Friends are told less. Acquaintances are given mere inklings. And strangers nothing."[17]

Sigmund Freud, the father of psychoanalysis, stated, "He who has eyes to see and ears to hear becomes convinced that mortals can keep no secret. . . . Betrayal forces its way through every pore."[18] There is a push-pull to all secrets. As one commentator wrote: "The more important a secret is the greater the energy charge it acquires and the stronger its push to re-emerge. At the same time the greater is the desire to possess it exclusively. The more dangerous a secret, the greater the desire to give it away, and at the same time the greater the fears of its revelation."[19]

A confidential disclosure may be a cry for help, as in the case of a patient who fears doing damage and wants to be stopped. A Greek Orthodox priest asked a psychiatrist friend in his parish what he should do about a dilemma. The priest had found a job for one of his parishioners, who was subsequently fired for misconduct. In anger, the parishioner told the priest that he was going to burn down his employer's home. Not sure whether this was bluster and hyperbole or a real threat, and not wanting to divulge a pastoral confidence, the priest sought the psychiatrist's advice. Call the police, the psychiatrist advised, if there is any chance that the parishioner might be capable of doing what he threatened. So the priest did. The police gave the man a choice—to be incarcerated for his threats or to commit himself for mental health care. He chose the latter option. When he was released after treatment, he thanked the priest for intervening—it was the help he had needed.

Like the parishioner in this story, troubled people want to keep their inner impulses secret at the same time that they fear doing something they know is wrong. For example, a psychiatric patient may disclose a disposition to commit a crime to a therapist, or a communicant may confess a contemplated wrongful course of action to a pastoral counselor; both seek intervention—despite the confidential setting and their invocation of parochial ground rules surrounding the confidentiality of their communication.

The psychoanalyst George Moraitis has explained the psychoanalytical aspects of confidentiality and revelation. Maintaining secrets is part of everybody's life. It is a form of protection against the revelation of potentially damaging and embarrassing events, ideas, and fantasies. People want to share secrets with people they want to bond with, but they want to conceal their secrets from others.[20]

Society's interest in the dilemmas of confessors may be conflicted. Although there is a public interest in needy people having private solicitude and help from professionals, there is a corresponding public interest in solving and stopping the crimes, misconduct, or mischief that these people may be inclined to commit. The policy question is whether that latter interest should be deemed important enough to override the confessor's expectation of privacy, as in the perplexing cases that are described in the chapters on the pastoral and psychiatric privileges.

Secrecy is not an easy process. It requires a good deal of energy to conceal the presence of forbidden desires and the memory of guilt-provoking behaviors. According to Freud (who died with secrets of his own), we don't hide our secrets only from others. We also hide them from ourselves by developing defenses and by obliterating them from our consciousness through a process he called repression. Our deepest secrets are buried in the unconscious, according to Freud. The secrets we are conscious of are only derivatives of the repressed secrets that we have no memory of without psychoanalytical prodding.

The psychoanalyst Melanie Klein suggested that people have an instinct for knowledge and a need to know the truth.[21] Our unconscious beliefs influence our feelings and actions. We can modify our unconscious beliefs only by making them conscious. Ronald Britton, a British psychoanalyst and one of Klein's students, described the imagination as an "unknowable place," an "other room" that is with us as much as the objective world around us. Perhaps that powerful need to know, and to explore the "other room" of people's imagination, explains the drive to expose secrets.

The importance of secrets is evident in the behavior of both individuals and groups. Beginning in childhood, secrecy becomes an indispensable part of growing up. It facilitates the child's capacity to develop a sense of autonomy and identity. Children guard their secrets with great tenacity and reveal them only partially to a few trusted friends. Anne Frank "told secrets to her diary," one scholar reminded us, as many adolescent girls do.[22]

Children bond through sharing secrets, which enhances human attachments and offers protection.[23] The secret life of adults is a good deal more complex and can be present in all forms of human interaction—marriage, parent-child relationships, friendships, employment—and in the world of fantasy, which cannot exist without secrecy. Wartime resistance movements are based on confidentiality in life-and-death situations.

Secrets not only facilitate autonomy and the sense of identity (it has been said that who we are is determined by our secrets); they create both an intimacy with the secret sharer and a sense of isolation that can be very painful if the secrets are not shared. Police investigators know that suspects share with them a common language of revelation that competes with their self-protective need not to disclose information about their crimes. Investigators are adept at enabling criminal suspects to confess their incriminating information. As one report of confessions to New York City police concludes, "for many people, the urge to explain, if not to confess, is as urgent as it was for Raskolnikov in 'Crime and Punishment.'"[24]

It is not surprising, therefore, that along with the need to hide, there is a compelling need to reveal what one has so carefully concealed. Such revelation generates a sense of intimacy that can be pleasurable. When friends or lovers reveal their secrets to each other, they experience first a sense of dread, which often leads to a sense of relief from "unloading" a heavy and solitary burden. But the German philosopher Friedrich Nietzsche warned that although we forget our guilt when we confess to another, "the other does not usually forget it."[25]

People keep diaries, submit to revelatory biographers, and write autobiographies and memoirs to reveal what they often have kept secret, in an attempt to try to control the presentation and timing of private facts. An insightful reviewer noted that "people lie in letters all the time, and they use diaries to moan and vent"; biographers believe "that the real person is the private person, and the public person is mostly a performance." His conclusion, and my point about the conundrum of confidentiality, is that what everybody wants in life is "to control the narrative."[26]

An artistic businessman in Germantown, Maryland, created an Internet Web site called PostSecret. People send him anonymous postcards with drawings and secret remarks that they wish to publicize. His offbeat project has generated over a dozen postcards a day, mounting in volume over several years to now fill his fifth book of collected secrets. The cards' messages are often affecting, sometimes shocking, occasionally gross. But their ambiguity and secretiveness seems to have a cathartic impact on the senders.[27]

Seldom, if ever, is any whole story revealed. What is left unsaid and what has been altered in the saying creates a new sense of secrecy in this cyclical process. Secret life cannot be extinguished; it can only be modified to meet personal needs and cultural standards.

People not only struggle to maintain or reveal their own secrets. They are also fascinated by the secrets of others. Often they go to great lengths to discover what others try to hide, at times at the expense of established standards of good social behavior. The public's fascination with secrets is evident in what we read and view. Popular magazines, books of biography, memoirs, even fiction, offer readers who are thirsty for revelations a wealth of material to satisfy their sleuth-like instincts. Gossip-magazine and tabloid reporters pursue with ferocity (and uncertain accuracy) the hidden stories of those in power and famous celebrities. The financial success of often scurrilous gossip magazines and the popularity of television's pseudo-exposés are proof of the public's prurient and voyeuristic preferences for probing other people's private stories.

The fascination with secrets has also been manipulated by those in power—political, economic, military—as well as by those who seek it, to advance their own aims. "The euphoria of secrecy goes to the head," wrote C. P. Snow. "I have known men, prudent in other respects, who became drunk with it. It induces an unbalancing sense of power."[28] One major reason for the late J. Edgar Hoover's extraordinary power when he was director of the FBI was that he held information about people, which he concealed or revealed to control and influence those people. Many of them were powerful officials or influential celebrities.

Government organizations, churches, professions, and businesses all deal with secrecy. Legal secrets are strategic tools of power, one legal scholar concluded, that are governed by rules of contract, torts, and ethics.[29]

Can secrets be kept in all circumstances? Is complete confidentiality really possible? Such questions parallel the time-honored philosophical question, Can the truth ever be found? And if so, how? This latter question leads to consideration of the adversarial system, whose rationale is to arrive at the truth when it is contested. This rationale in turn leads to conflicts over claims of confidentiality; if information is allowed to remain secret, how does a trial find the truth in a dispute? In 1911, one court said, regarding a claimed privilege to withhold information by a journalist, that a point-of-honor promise of confidentiality has not been accepted by courts for over two hundred years. The fact that a communication is made in confidence does not create a privilege. "No pledge of privacy, nor oath of secrecy, can avail against demand for the truth, the whole truth, in a court of justice."[30]

A fundamental premise of all litigation is to establish the truth. In order to do so, the courts rely on the sworn testimony of witnesses. There are, however, exceptions to that rule. When the rules of privileged communications are applied, certain classes of individuals—lawyers, doctors, psychotherapists, priests, spouses—are exempt from the obligation to inform the courts of what they know. Their privilege is predicated on the ground that their testimony would cause serious psychological injury to those who shared their secrets, or would violate the sanctity of a church's dicta or professional rules of conduct.

The very nature of these privileged relationships has changed over time, raising questions about the inviolability of the confidentiality of such relationships. If gays may marry, for example, would the traditional spousal privilege extend to them? Other groups have argued—some successfully (psychoanalysts and social workers), others not successfully (journalists and accountants)—that the rationale for protecting their confidential relations is comparable to that for traditionally protected groups, and have claimed that the same privilege should be extended to them.

These historically privileged communications are considered in subsequent chapters dealing with the attorney-client, doctor-patient, spousal, and clerical privileges, and with claims by comparable groups for special protections of their confidentiality.

Hovering over the confidentiality of all these relationships is the effect on them of new technology. For example, is a communication between an attorney and his client confidential if it is sent as an e-mail? Or is an e-mail, as one judge suggested to me, no more private than a postcard?

The variety and pervasiveness of modern confidentiality issues is remarkable. Not a day goes by without some public story or private anecdote concerning confidentiality arising. One recent morning, a perusal of the *Washington Post* and the *New York Times* revealed four exemplary stories: (1) the U.S. government's secret examinations of financial records in a vast international database, including thousands of private banking records; (2) the alleged rape of a U.S. Coast Guard cadet who claimed that she was coerced by a classmate into having sex out of fear that her attacker would reveal a secret about her (according to the article, "she believed that she had to comply to protect her secret"); (3) a story describing how reporters accessed sensitive material that had been electronically "blacked out" in a government brief (regarding a government leak investigation, no less); and (4) a National Science Foundation–funded survey that concluded that a growing number of Americans "have no one in whom they can confide."[31]

Claims of confidentiality are widespread and consequential. In Chief Justice John Roberts's Supreme Court confirmation hearing, the Senate's access to memoranda he wrote when he was working as a government attorney hinged on whether they were deemed to be covered by the attorney-client privilege or executive privilege. The highly publicized special investigation of columnist Robert Novak's outing of a CIA agent and the consequent jailing of *New York Times* reporter Judith Miller raised public questions about the so-called reporter's privilege to refuse to disclose anonymous sources when subpoenaed in legal proceedings. The conservative radio host Rush Limbaugh questioned the right of Florida investigators to subpoena his pharmacist's records, claiming (unsuccessfully) that the traditional doctor-patient privilege protected the confidentiality of such records. The sex-abuse scandal in the Catholic Church was exacerbated when it was disclosed that many of the young parishioners' accusations against priests were known to church officials, who treated the confidential disclosures as privileged. When a court-martial of an air force cadet demanded records from a rape crisis center, the victim's counselor complained that she was forced to choose between the health and privacy of her patient and the needs of the trial system, at the risk of being jailed for contempt. One can rarely turn to the news without seeing some intriguing story about public battles over access to information that is claimed to be private, privileged, and confidential.

People in the book business—publishers, editors, authors, agents—deal with recurring questions of confidentiality. Manuscripts and book proposals commonly are sent to multiple publishers; when the contract is made between the author and the eventual publisher, the competitors all know about the book they won't be publishing. It is a classic example of a widely shared secret. If a proposed book has sensitive features, an author's agent may ask for a confidentiality agreement before showing the author's proposal. By agreeing to it, prospective editors contract not to disclose the contents, regardless of whether they or their competitors become the eventual publisher. Publishers show book galleys to prospective magazines that may be bidding to publish excerpts—first serial rights, they are called. Again, editors see material they may not eventually publish, and they commit not to reveal the contents. Those commitments, however, are frequently breached.

Express or implied circumstances of confidentiality in the publishing world do not include a privilege not to disclose information if that information is required in a legal proceeding. Though participating in conventions of confidentiality, members of the publishing world realize that the prophylactic is not a guarantee against disclosure.

In the seamier world of tabloids, huge fortunes are paid to sources who reveal information (not always facts) obtained in confidential settings—former employees, for example, who tell tales about their celebrity employers who presumed or hoped that their interactions were confidential. Public figures' medical records have been leaked to the press. A New York politician's suicide attempt and a Miami designer's hospitalization made headlines in metropolitan newspapers. The dead body of the model Anna Nicole Smith could not be embalmed for days until a local court ordered it be done, but only after the Aycock Funeral Home and Crematory signed a confidentiality agreement promising not to discuss or photograph her body.[32]

A Los Angeles court enforced a preliminary injunction against a former husband of the actress Jennifer Lopez. The two had entered into a confidentiality agreement barring him from including disparaging information about their brief marriage in his "tell all" memoir, and the court held him to that promise.[33] In addition, an arbitrator awarded Lopez damages. A Connecticut court held the wife of the celebrity dermatologist Dr. Nicholas Perricone to her confidentiality agreement, despite her argument that her promise to keep matters confidential violated her First Amendment right to go public with her spousal complaints.

Which business records are confidential? A litigious spouse subpoenaed a florist's records to prove her husband's infidelity. Should video sales to public officials be confidential? Library records of a celebrity? If such records are confidential, to whom should they be denied? Private confidentiality agreements or understandings like these are considered in chapter 8.

A great many ordinary relationships require confidentiality. Business, government, employment, educational, even private relationships between parents and children and between friends, require participants to honor the confidentiality of communications in order to encourage communal participation. If participants thought that there would be no confidentiality, they might not participate fully and openly. Confidentiality should therefore be encouraged. Only when public disclosure is required for a strong and countervailing public purpose should confidentiality be breached. Society's needs for openness and transparency conflict regularly with its desire for privacy and confidentiality, and striking the right balance is an inexact science.

What may people justifiably expect when they enter into a confidential relationship? The law protects some relationships (those between doctors and patients, for example), but it also requires disclosure in specific situations (for example, in cases of suicide or sexually transmitted diseases). Many laws provide for privileged communications, but others mandate disclosure. People must realize that no secret is truly a secret forever and in every situation. The sources for and sensibility of these crosscurrents of public policy are discussed in later chapters.

Communications in confidential settings can prejudice a third party. Should that innocent third party not have recourse to penetrate the private confidential setting to correct an injustice? A relatively modern institution, a rape crisis center, provides important assistance to crime victims at a particularly traumatic time. The value of rape crisis centers is beyond question. Their clientele needs to know that what they say at these wrenching times will remain confidential. But a defendant who stands trial for a serious crime like rape is presumed innocent and may challenge charges made against him. He may seek access to records of these centers in order to establish, if not his innocence, the infirmities of the case against him.

Courts are called upon regularly to balance two equally important and valuable, but conflicting, rights. How could rape crisis counselors expect their clients to discuss their personal and traumatic experiences if the sanctity of those conversations could not be ensured? Imagine, however, that remarks by a rape victim to one providing solace at the safe haven of a rape crisis center happened to have exculpatory value to a defendant later on trial for her rape. How could a fair system of justice preclude access to such evidence by one facing imprisonment?

In a military court-martial of a cadet charged with raping a classmate, records of a mental-health counselor at a rape crisis center were subpoenaed. The cadet charged argued that his right to a fair trial outweighed the rape victim's right of privacy. The rape counselor argued that she and her client should not be forced to choose between justice and healing. "I'm caught between two ethics here," the counselor pleaded. "We need more clarity. Right now I can't promise people confidentiality." The trial court struck a balance between the victim's privacy and the accused's constitutional rights; exculpatory evidence was to be turned over to the defendant, but nothing else.[34]

Many professions have codes of conduct that mandate confidentiality. Architects, engineers, chiropractors, and accountants are licensed and have professional societies and codes of conduct that address, among other things, the confidentiality of their members' dealings with clients. Their rules describe when they are excused from their duty to maintain confidentiality and when they are mandated to disclose confidential information. The American Anthropological Association has adopted principles of professional responsibility that address confidentiality and the ethical need to protect sources of information in research reports.[35]

Many other nonlicensed professionals also operate under parochial guidelines. When a football coach was questioned by the press about the drug offense of one of his players, he remarked, "We all have a professional responsibility as clubs to live by the confidentiality rules, which are designed to protect players."[36] A tennis pro expressed the same sentiment to me: "I have to protect the confidentiality of my players' habits and behavior." Under Florida's Brokerage Relationship Disclosure Act, real estate agents have nine fiduciary duties to sellers and buyers; third on the list—between "loyalty" and "obedience"—is "confidentiality," though no definition or explanation is offered to guide agents.

The law, so far, does not provide these professionals with the privilege to keep this confidential information from disclosure in litigation.[37]

The reality remains that many people in many business and professional relationships think that they are operating under confidential circumstances, as they should. But whether public policy should protect and ensure the confidentiality of those dealings with a corresponding privilege against forced disclosure, as is the case with doctors and lawyers and priests, is less clear.

The requirements of disclosure of secrets as a matter of contract or tort law are related to standards of confidentiality. Professor Kim Lane Scheppele concludes that "secrets may only be kept in those circumstances where silence alone is the means of maintaining the secret" and lies or half-truths or concealed inside information are not involved. She also warns that "confidential relationships give rise to special duties to disclose information." Other more skeptical observers have concluded that "in entering the workplace, you check your privacy at the door."[38]

Related to confidentiality is the question of classification, the statutory scheme by which government documents and information are classified as confidential and thus kept from public scrutiny. That subject—itself worthy of book-length analysis—is treated in chapter 2, on government secrecy.

There is another perspective that points out the inconsistency of confidentiality claims. Secrecy is essential to journalists, for example, yet their regular sources are leakers who break their promises to keep secrets. Government employees sign nondisclosure agreements requiring them to subject themselves to censorship, yet they often seek exceptions to their pledges in order to write about the very matters they promised to keep confidential. It is a crime to reveal certain confidential information, yet the press generally cannot be prevented from publishing this information if it receives it surreptitiously. The privacy-proclaiming public often roots for these secret-sharers to release their confidential information.

This privacy paradox arises in cases questioning excessive government intrusions predicated on homeland security. We all want to be safe from outside dangers, but we also want to be free from overreaching government behavior.

Although many observers fear the impositions upon privacy posed by modern technology, the corresponding social values of these incursions have been defended. In the medical profession, confidential information that is ordinarily kept private may need to be made public to save lives, to prevent the spread of disease, and to deter criminal activity—for example, a psychotherapist may need to disclose a patient's intention to hurt someone. Sociologist Amitai Etzioni's communitarian view is that some diminutions of privacy are necessary and serve the public—identifying terrorists or exposing AIDS victims or publicizing pedophiles may be necessary for public safety in some situations and thus may override individual needs for privacy. A proper balance is called for, Professor Etzioni argues, between individual rights and social responsibility. His view is that we are not merely rights-bearing individuals but also community members who are responsible for each other. In Professor Etzioni's judgment, civic culture has taken a backseat in the late twentieth century to more vocal claims for privacy.[39]

The conservative federal judge and prolific author Richard Posner chides liberals over this inconsistency, arguing that it is a product of civil-libertarian hostility to national-security interests, distrust of government, and fetishes over what he views as questionable constitutional claims. Judge Posner argues that privacy may be a universal value but that it is not a constitutional right or a uniform practice. It is socially valuable for people to be able to have frank private communications, Judge Posner agrees, with the assurance that they will remain private. But, he adds, for intelligence purposes, at least, it is inconsistent to claim that one may make personal information quasi-public through their library use, book purchases, phone use, and medical records in order to get a job, insurance, or a loan, or to borrow a book or rent a movie, and at the same time to be aghast that the government wants limited access to those records for national-security reasons. Our society, Judge Posner claims, has evolved into "a culture of radically diminished informational privacy" where people value their informational privacy but "surrender it at the drop of a hat," and regularly reveal intimate details of their health, love life, and finances to strangers.[40]

Law professor Alan Westin noted in the late 1960s that the notion that people mind their own business, and let others alone, is "a fantasy of some libertarian's imagination" and not the state of modern (mid-twentieth-century) society, which has an "insatiable craving to discover the secret and forbidden."[41]

A brief time surfing the Internet and television's exhibitionist programmatic smorgasbord is evidence enough of the general public's willingness to display an interest in observing normally private and confidential events: matrimonial escapades, mating habits, surgical and health experiences, worship, litigation, law enforcement, funerals, even other people's sexual exploits. It's all on tape now—ubiquitous, pervasive, and totally at war with any reasonable notion of privacy. We are in a culture where "instruments for recording and disseminating information about people's intimate behavior are cheap and easy to use, and . . . newspapers and magazines and television programs and Web sites purvey that kind of information without restraint, and . . . even ordinary people apparently can't do enough to tell the world everything about themselves," a perceptive critic wrote recently.[42]

We give our privacy away, one law professor noted (in the context of a discussion of credit cards), for frequent-flyer miles. The current generation of young people uses the Internet to share personal information casually, at least by the standards of older generations. Some of these younger exhibitionists have been shocked by the exploitation of their shared personal information and have regretted providing it.

With modern data-gathering techniques, much of everyone's personal history is recorded and public—motor-vehicle, voting, birth, death, marriage, real estate, and court records are available. They include more information about us than most people would prefer was known publicly. Social-welfare, tax, military, and school library records are generally not public but may be accessed in specific situations. Point-of-sale data allows marketers to profile customers. Toll booths record where travelers are. Genetic profiling could soon tell employers, insurance companies, and prospective spouses prejudicial information about us, and arguments can be made that it should. The results of an analysis of the Nobel Prize winner James D. Watson's genome—which revealed that he had an unusually high percentage of genes of African origin—was published by the *Times* of London and picked up by the international press. The reason offered for the publicity was that Watson had made controversial remarks suggesting that black Africans are not as intelligent as whites. As the *New York Times* sarcastically stated, "His own brilliant DNA seems to blur the lines."[43]

What confidential information remains, one might wonder, to protect? It is this protectable category of confidential information that this book considers: privileged communications in professional relationships and private agreements contracted for or imposed by law. In examining these subjects, I examine the inevitable and confounding compromises between openness and secrecy, between the search for truth and the need to protect privacy. When it is feasible to do so, I suggest solutions. The analysis of confidentiality recalls the proverb "To whom you tell your secrets, to him you resign your liberty."

1

PRIVACY, CONFIDENTIALITY, AND PRIVILEGED COMMUNICATIONS

The History of Privacy

The jurisprudential rationales for confidentiality and privilege, and their conflicts with the adversary system, derive from the broader concept of privacy. The overall concept of privacy covers many subjects: immunity from physical intrusion, the right to be let alone, the right to be free from physical invasion of one's person and property, the right to have "a room of one's own" (as Virginia Woolf described the need for personal autonomy). Third and Fourth Amendment rights to be free in one's home and to be free from illegal searches and seizures are examples of this kind of privacy. Civil rights to protect against the commercialization of one's person (for example, the sale of unauthorized photographs) are another.

A different form of privacy concerns private information about oneself—personal facts uncovered and publicized or disclosed conditionally but later made public. Evolving notions of privacy arose in modern Ninth Amendment extensions of a right to privacy with respect to one's sexual practices (such as the use of contraceptives) and a right to have an abortion (various privacy rights were held to emanate from the "penumbra of rights" guaranteed by the Bill of Rights).

Those aspects of privacy provide background to the subject of this book. They are related to confidentiality, but indirectly, spiritually, one might say. "Confidentiality is closely related to privacy, but not identical," one survey suggests. "It refers to the obligations of individuals and institutions to use information under their control appropriately once it has been disclosed to

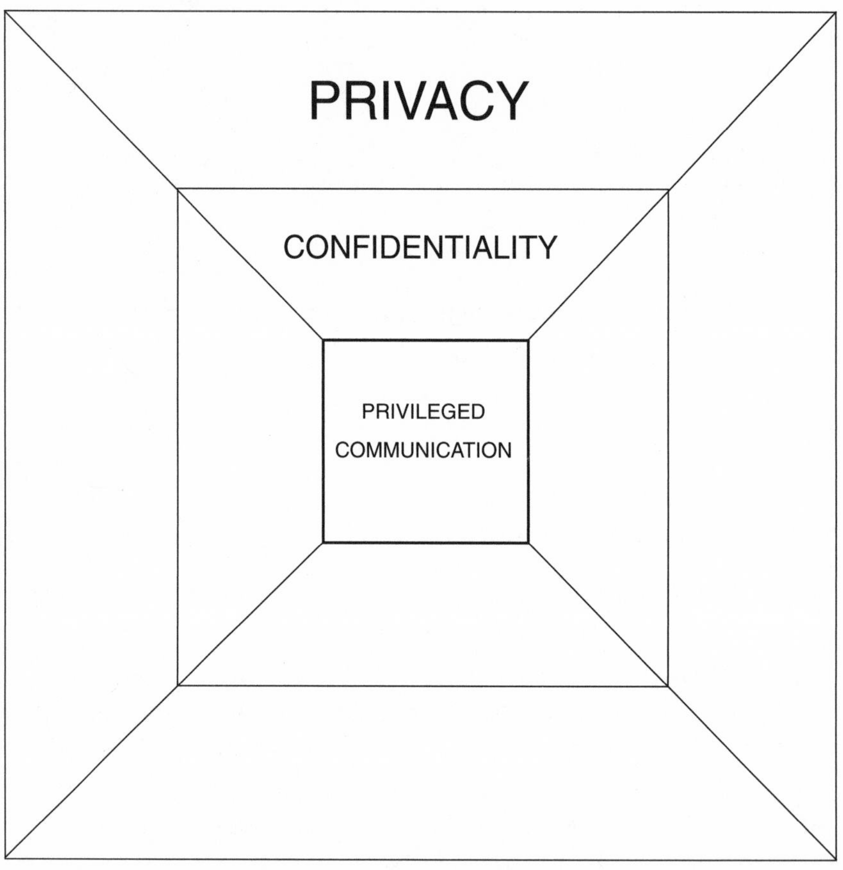

them. One observes rules of confidentiality out of respect for, and to protect and preserve, the privacy of others."[1]

A classic article written in 1890 by the scholars Samuel D. Warren and Louis D. Brandeis (later a Supreme Court justice) first explored the idea of a right of privacy. They discussed the notion that one's "thoughts, sentiments, and emotions" cannot be compelled to be expressed, and if they are expressed, one should retain the power to "fix the limits of the publicity which shall be given them." Individuals should have, the authors posited, the power "to decide whether that which is his shall be given to the public," and, for their own peace of mind, the power to prevent publication. The right would apply "to forestall profits" or to prevent mental pain and suffering from obnoxious publicity. "The facts relating to one's private life" may be kept private for the "exclusive use and enjoyment" of that person.[2]

These protected "thoughts, emotions, and sensations" compose an individual's "inviolate personality," their right to privacy, to be let alone. To violate these rights would amount to a "breach of confidence." People have the right "to keep from popular curiosity" such personal and private information. Warren and Brandeis ended their landmark article with the rhetorical question, If the law protects one's home, should it close the front door yet "open wide the back door to idle or prurient curiosity?"[3]

The authors' elegantly written and innovative thesis led to a century of continuing legal development of the emerging right of privacy. Though the present state of exposure of privileged thoughts and communications is likely to have been beyond the imagination of these brilliant scholars, their ideas provide an intellectual foundation for modern claims for confidentiality.

The right of privacy is not mentioned specifically in the Constitution. Various provisions in the Bill of Rights have been interpreted to protect different aspects of the now commonly mentioned right of privacy. The continuing expansion of privacy rights has touched on many personal features of modern life, some quite controversial.[4]

Analyzing the evolution of what he called "the evanescent concept of privacy" in the century following Brandeis and Warren's article, lawyer-scholar Ken Gormley concluded that it has been a "revolving map of jurisprudence."[5] Privacy touches on tort law, state law, and constitutional law, with no one overall definitive or coherent concept, no static conceptual rationale. In different periods during the last century, privacy law focused on unwarranted publicity, sexual intimacy, residential solitude (the sanctity of the home), and snooping on people and places and information (bank and phone records, cars), as well as the right to silence and anonymity. Some state constitutions—Florida's for example—explicitly include privacy rights, as does the Universal Declaration of Human Rights.

Today, the elastic word *privacy* pertains to different things: search and seizure, abortion, paparazzi behavior, Internet invasion—in a philosophical sense, the right to be left alone, personal repose, solitude, sanctuary, autonomy.

The evolving constitutional right of privacy remains "largely undefined," University of Chicago legal scholar Philip Kurland wrote in 1976. There are three partially revealed, though not fully ascertained, aspects of privacy, he reflected. "The first is the right of the individual to be free in his private affairs from governmental surveillance and intrusion. The second is the right of an individual not to have his private affairs made public by the government. The third is the right of an individual to be free in action, thought, experience, and belief from governmental compulsion."[6]

Kurland's three aspects of privacy cover some, but by no means all, areas of the broad subject of confidentiality. Though they embrace many other subjects, these aspects of privacy do not cover many confidentiality issues that have nothing to do with governmental activity.

By the end of the twentieth century, privacy meant many things to different people—Fourth Amendment immunity from strip searches and government agents barging into your home, liberty rights to your personal bodily freedom (contraception and abortion), organizational anonymity under the First Amendment's freedom of association (sometimes in conflict with the press's First Amendment freedom to portray you against your will), insulation from workplace testing and monitoring.[7]

One survey of U.S. privacy laws concluded that they are narrowly focused, in contrast to the "trans-sectional" approach in Europe and elsewhere. Privacy protections appear in many federal laws—the 1974 Privacy Act, the Fair Credit Reporting Act, the Freedom of Information Act, FOIA, the Family Educational Rights and Privacy Act, the Right to Financial Privacy Act, the Electronic Communications Privacy Act, and the Health Insurance Portability and Accountability Act, to name some of the better-known pieces of legislation.[8]

Confidentiality

This evolving right of privacy is distinct from confidentiality, though the terms are sometimes intermingled. The term *privacy* is used to describe general demands for anonymity, control over one's identity, self-determination, ownership of personal data, and the right to be left alone; *confidentiality* refers to keeping personal secrets and information private.

Evolving technology has raised new questions about the right of privacy and about confidentiality, as chapter 10 describes. In the mid-1960s, Columbia University law professor Alan Westin, in conjunction with the New York City Bar Association Committee on Science and Law, examined the alarming impact on individual privacy of what was then new scientific technology—electronic, optical, acoustic, and other sensing devices.[9] Professor Westin examined the extent to which individuals and institutions managed information that they communicated to others and at the same time sought to maintain anonymity and reserve. The problems noted then are all the more challenging today as a result of new and more sophisticated technologies that threaten confidentiality.

Privacy-rights experts and devotees are concerned about the erosion of personal freedom created by modern technology.[10] Many of their concerns about the loss of confidentiality are raised by the common enemy—advanced technology's capacity to appropriate, store, and disseminate confidential conversations, records, and information. Not all concerns about the modern surveillance society touch on issues of confidentiality, but some do. It is one thing to discover and disclose another person's shopping history or reading habits. It is quite another to invade that person's medical or legal records. The offenses are related, though the policy considerations are different.

General definitions of confidentiality pertain to personal intimacy and private secrets. One aspect of confidentiality pertains to legal policies that protect certain specific kinds of confidences from exposure—even from court orders. Rights of privileged communications raise intriguing questions of social policy. They are relational rights that have been protected because the law honors the sanctity of specific relationships: a physician's duty to maintain the confidentiality of a patient's medical records, a lawyer's duty not to reveal his client's confidences. Historically, these confidential relationships were preserved for the public good, unless extraordinary countervailing reasons existed for disclosure.[11]

Confidentiality comes in varying shapes and sizes, one court remarked in a case holding that scholars had a qualified First Amendment academic freedom that protected their confidential research interviews.[12] Other confidential matters may not be privileged under the law—for example, secrets between friends or family members or in business dealings. Those relationships may be—and should be—confidential, but they are not privileged.

Privileged Communications

The philosophical difference between confidentiality and privileged communications was noted in a 1776 English case. A witness in a bigamy trial, a lord no less, was asked if the lady in question told him that she was married. The gentleman stated that "as a man of honor . . . I cannot reveal it." To this, the presiding judge, Lord Camden, replied that it was not "befitting the dignity of this high Court of justice to be debating the etiquette of honor at the same time when we are trying lives and liberties."[13] A modern commentator remarked with comparable gentility that it would be "a monstrous thing to require that secrets . . . should be dragged into the garish light of litigation."[14]

Confidentiality is a principle of legal ethics that governs when communications may be disclosed and when, more commonly, they should remain confidential. Privilege—more absolute—protects against compelled disclosure in a deposition or trial proceeding. "Everything that is privileged is also protected by the confidentiality principle but the converse is not true."[15] The broader protection of confidentiality is governed by professional rules of ethics and contractual arrangements; the more limited concept of privilege is governed by statute and the common law.

Historically, state secrets involving national defense and international relations were protected. In addition, several classes of relationships have been considered so special that the law deemed it improper to intrude on their confidentiality: confidential relationships between clergy and their parishioners, between lawyers and their clients, between doctors and their patients, and between husbands and wives. The rationale for protecting the sanctity of communications within these privileged relationships was obvious and reasonable; there was deemed to be a social interest in protecting the confidentiality of these conversations so that these intimate relationships could thrive. In these limited situations, privacy was more exalted than the search for truth in civil and criminal cases. Under the common law and various statutes, Anglo-American law has traditionally honored the privileged confidentiality in these specific situations.

In modern times, new groups have claimed similar exceptions: news reporters and their sources, social workers and their clients, rape crisis centers (and other victim assistance centers) and crime victims. As a general rule, protecting confidentiality makes good sense. We all want to know that our private conversations will remain private. Whether they should be deemed privileged, as well as confidential, is another, more complex, question.

There is a fundamental distinction between confidentiality generally and privileged communications specifically. Communications between parties may be confidential, and that confidentiality may and should be honored in most situations. Privilege goes one step further, insulating the parties from sanctions for refusing to testify in a legal proceeding or produce documents requested by subpoena. In these instances, the reluctant party claims that there is a greater societal interest in preserving the confidentiality of their relationship than there is in revealing the requested information. The consideration, then, is the morality of disclosure in situations in which confidentiality is sought for good and socially sound reasons.

Conflicts with the Adversary System

The rule of testimonial compulsion—that witnesses properly subpoenaed to testify in a trial must do so unless a recognized specific exception applies—evolved in early English common law. It was articulated in 1612 by Sir Francis Bacon in the Countess of Shrewsbury's trial, according to a classic treatise on evidence. "All subjects, without distinction of degrees, owe to the king tribute and service . . . of their knowledge and discovery. . . . They ought themselves undemanded to impart it; much more if they be called and examined, whether it be of their own fact or of another's, they ought to make direct answer."[16] In 1742, Lord Chancellor Hardwicke enunciated the fundamental rule that the legal system is entitled "to every man's evidence."[17]

By the early twentieth century, the respected evidence scholar John Henry Wigmore reported that this duty to testify would be meaningless unless there is power to compel testimony; to punish such disobedience is part of the basic concept of the judicial power in the United States.[18] Trials seek, as everyone who has seen one will recall, "the truth and the whole truth."

In the world of legal writing and scholarship, perhaps no one person so dominated a field as did the late John Henry Wigmore, whose treatise on evidence was widely considered the Bible. The modern adapter of Dean Wigmore's classic treatise on evidence in the area of privilege, Professor Edward J. Imwinkelried, authored an exhaustive two-volume work dealing exclusively with evidentiary privileges.[19]

In his landmark treatise, Wigmore explained the rationale for making exceptions to the general rule requiring all people to give evidence in a court of law. In the case of certain relationships, communications may not be disclosed if four fundamental conditions are satisfied: (1) the communications were made in confidence; (2) the element of confidentiality is essential to maintain the parties' relationship; (3) there is a community need to "sedulously" foster the relationship; and (4) the harm to the relationship caused by disclosure would exceed any benefit from the disposal of the litigation.

An English judge in 1851 described the balancing test as one that considered not "the impropriety of violating the confidence reposed" but whether "the collateral inconvenience, which would ensue if no such confidentiality were reposed, would preponderate over the direct mischief produced by a chance of failure of justice resulting from the exclusion of evidence."[20]

Wigmore questioned the applicability of the fourth condition to the attorney-client privilege, the applicability of the first condition to the spousal privilege, the applicability of the second and fourth conditions to the physician-patient privilege, and the applicability of the third condition to the priest-penitent privilege. And he emphasized that "the mere fact that a communication was made in express confidence, or in the implied confidence of a confidential relation, does not create a privilege." Wigmore cited cases involving clerks, trustees, commercial agents, bankers, journalists, and others in which confidences were not considered privileged. The predominant value in the context of the legal system (different criteria might apply in other contexts) is the administration of justice. "No pledge of privacy, nor oath of secrecy, can avail against demand for the truth in a court of justice."[21] The law does not honor honor; it condones limited privileges.

Legal historians have traced the evolution of privileged communications to old evidentiary rules of competency and to the nature of the jury system.[22] Categories of people—spouses, for example—were deemed incompetent as witnesses for archaic and paternalistic reasons, as is described in chapter 7, on the spousal privilege. They were disqualified as being self-interested or likely to be untruthful.

With changes in the jury system—scholars place the evolution as occurring from the fourteenth to the sixteenth century in England—and the adoption of compulsory process, also a fifteenth- and sixteenth-century innovation, there was less need for incompetency rules. Since witnesses were required to testify before jurors who did not personally know the facts of cases, their motives were not challenged, and incompetency rules were largely replaced by the adoption of specific privileges for some witnesses not to testify in particular situations. It was thought that a greater social good derived from these witnesses not being required to testify. Privileges in derogation of laws requiring testimony were exceptions to the general rule and were based on unique rationales.

Wigmore advanced the pragmatic, albeit speculative, rationale that but for the absolute guarantee of privilege, patients or clients or penitents would not communicate information essential for their relationship to succeed. Thus, the privilege must be absolute and not subject to exceptions based on countervailing interests warranting disclosure in specific situations. Wigmore's was "a bright-line standard." It was "cost-free to the judicial system," Professor Imwinkelried suggests, because under this theory the privilege "suppresses only evidence that would not exist but for the privilege."[23]

Modern scholars—Professor Imwinkelried for one—have suggested that this is an unrealistic premise. A patient who is in severe pain will communicate with the doctor, however reluctantly, without regard to the question of confidentiality. If asked, no doubt the patient would prefer a commitment to confidentiality; but under extreme circumstances, confidentiality would not remain a condition precedent to a patient's seeking help.

A preferable rationale, in Professor Imwinkelried's and other experts' views, is one based on personal autonomy and decisional privacy. For citizens to make intelligent, critical choices, they need expert advice from doctors, lawyers, clergy, and others. To ensure that they get such expert advice, the argument goes, governments (courts, legislatures) should "promote autonomy in the sense of decisional privacy" by, in Professor Imwinkelried's words, "creating enclaves for intimate communication."[24]

Charles Alan Wright and Kenneth W. Graham, the authors of a well-known treatise on evidence, have defined the rationale for privileges not as empirical but as humanistic: "What kind of people are we who empower courts in our names to compel parents, friends, and lovers to become informants on those who have trusted them?"[25] But such an ethical standard leaves us with the question, In the search for truth in trials, when should courts intrude on confidential communications?

Early jurisprudential rationales for confidentiality rules based on humanistic theories (that confidentiality promotes decency by ensuring privacy) and instrumental theories (that confidentiality is needed to preserve certain relationships) prevailed at different times. They eventually fused, and ultimately became one rule that derives from both ideological sources. Some scholars use the broad and subjective term *personal autonomy* to rationalize the basis for confidentiality.

As reasonable as rules about confidentiality and privileged communications are, they nonetheless raise a dilemma. All confidentiality is questionable if the overriding goal is to get to the truth in an adversarial system. For this reason, the noted British utilitarian philosopher Jeremy Bentham argued that most privileged communications were "rubbish"; in his opinion, only rational inquiry relatively free of exclusionary rules could ensure "rectitude of decision." Exclusions lacked empirical verification, shielded antisocial conduct, and produced mischief by allowing guilty people to escape punishment, he theorized. "Exclude evidence, you exclude justice," he cautioned. Sounding very much like modern conservative critics of the claimed "gamesmanship" of the American criminal-justice system, Bentham argued that innocent clients should be willing to have their attorneys testify; only the guilty ones would want to insist on confidentiality—but for antisocial reasons. Similarly, offering spouses confidentiality permits "schemes of injustice" between married couples, making them accomplices in crime. Bentham did think that guaranteed confidentiality was required in two instances: in confessionals with priests and to protect state secrets.[26]

Protecting confidentiality is inconsistent with getting at the truth, the fundamental purpose of the trial system and the rules of evidence; it precludes critical evidence. And as a practical matter, there is no way to prove definitively that relationships would be chilled or would not exist if the parties to them were not guaranteed confidentiality. Wouldn't sick people still use their doctors even if there was no assurance of confidentiality? To what extent should the law endorse humanistic concerns underlying confidentiality? If guilty criminals lose personal succor and psychic relief by losing the confidentiality of their confessions—say, to their psychiatrist or social worker or priest—should we care? These questions and others are discussed in the chapters dealing with the specific privileged communications presently recognized by the law.

In her book *Secrets,* the philosopher Sissela Bok offers four moral rationales for confidentiality. First and foremost, she proposes, is the need for individual autonomy over personal information. People should be able to have secrets—for reasons of privacy and self-protection—especially where this does not conflict with the rights of others. However, that right must be conditional: if a person is infected with a contagious and dangerous disease, it would be morally wrong to hide that fact from innocent others. Second, Bok states, is the need people have for private relationships and loyalties with friends and family and organizations. Third, when a promise of silence is made, an obligation may exist for contractual reasons—in business, for example, parties may agree not to publicize trade secrets. The professional confidentiality of doctors, attorneys, priests, and other professionals is Bok's final category; it is premised on the value to society in protecting the privacy of these relationships. Since all these refuges of secrecy can cause problems, regardless of the value of their rationales, Bok judiciously suggests that their invocation should be considered prima facie, and should be subject to exceptions; for example, a doctor should not disclose a patient's secrets for gossip, but he might well do so to prevent a suicide.[27]

The protection of confidential communications creates a confounding conflict between competing societal interests, not between right and wrong. It involves the rare instances in which secrecy is deemed so important that it preempts the search for truth in the trial system. There are strong reasons to encourage confidentiality between the parties so that important values—treatment, professional and legal advice, public information—are encouraged by the law. Yet competing interests may be present—law enforcement particularly—and no legal system could exist if people could claim that they are beyond the reach of the law because some higher public purpose is served through preserving the secrecy of their relationships with their confederates. There is a cost-benefit calculus in striking the appropriate balance between the need for evidence and the protection of privacy. But there is no scientific logarithm for measuring the respective weight of these subjective values.

Unlike privilege, most rules of evidence are created and enforced to ensure the truth and reliability of evidence in a trial. For example, hearsay evidence is excluded because it is unreliable; it is not susceptible to cross-examination and verification. If A attempts to testify to what B told him, the adverse party cannot cross-examine B to disprove his remarks to A. Therefore, A's testimony about B's comments is deemed secondhand and unreliable. But if A is a professional (such as a doctor) and is called to testify about a privileged communication (for example, what B, a patient, told A in A's professional capacity), the exclusion on the basis of privilege keeps B's arguably highly reliable evidence (though there are exceptions, patients generally don't lie to their doctors, and clients generally don't lie to their lawyers) away from the trier of facts.

The rationale for the two rules is different; the hearsay rule seeks to ensure the truth by excluding unreliable evidence; the privilege rules seek to protect specific relationships at the risk of neglecting the truth. The hearsay rule protects the theoretical purity of the adversary process (it may or may not aid the search for truth); the privilege rules frustrate that process by keeping presumably reliable evidence from the trial. Behind both rules is the Sixth Amendment protection of the right to confront witnesses in criminal trials.

There is a difference between privilege rules and exclusionary rules under the First, Fourth, and Fifth Amendments. The constitutional exclusionary rules are designed to discourage government misconduct—breaking into someone's home is an illegal search; coercing a confession violates the self-incrimination clause—even at the cost of losing credible evidence.

The evidence seized or coerced may be probative (drugs found on the premises) or questionable (a confession made under duress may be inaccurate). Like the privilege rules, these exclusionary rules exist to promote a social policy. But unlike privileges, these constitutional exclusionary rules cannot be tampered with by courts and legislatures. Privileges are designed to encourage relationships; constitutional rights exist to discourage government misconduct. The former may be conditional; the latter are close to absolute.

Some claimed constitutional rights are similar to privileges in that they are rationalized on the basis of the same "instrumental reasoning" that Dean Wigmore claimed is given for protecting privileged communications. Without such a privilege, or "quasi-privilege" as Professor Imwinkelried labels it, it is argued that news sources would not provide reporters with tips and informants would not divulge information to law enforcement authorities. Hence the contentious claim that anonymous news sources should be protected by the First Amendment.

Extensions of Privilege

The classic professional ethical rules that apply to lawyers, doctors, and priests are parallel to but different from privileges. Professionals are monitored by their professional organizations. What and when they may and may not divulge is governed by bar and medical and church rules. Those professional rules bind professionals, but they are not evidentiary rules that determine what evidence is and is not admissible in court. The rules may differ in their application, enforcement, and extent.

The Judicial Conference of the United States and the Supreme Court proposed rules governing privileges to Congress, but Congress rejected such rules. Preferring to allow the federal courts to evolve rules for the federal system, Congress passed Rule 501 of the Federal Rules of Evidence, which permits courts to develop rules governing privileged communications on the basis of common-law principles as interpreted "in light of reason and experience." The states are free to adopt rules of their own, and all have, through either statute or case law.

Laws and professional codes that protect privileged communications are not unique to the United States. According to a recent report from the

European Union, the practice of protecting confidentiality is common abroad, especially in the legal profession.[28] Common-law countries (the United States and the United Kingdom predominantly) have different rules from civil-law countries (European countries), however, and these differences are reflected in their rules regarding privileged communications.[29]

Under the present approach in America, privileges are not favored and may be justified only if there is a transcendent public good that outweighs the search for truth. In determining whether there is such a public good, courts should consider whether there is an "imperative need for confidentiality"; whether "public ends" would be served; whether the evidentiary cost would be modest; and whether any federal rule would have a negative impact on state practices. This approach is reasonable, and is based on the historical ideal of the federal system that the states should be versatile jurisprudential engineers of social policies.

In considering the evolution of new privileges, the federal courts are conservative, as they should be, about condoning impediments to the judicial process. For example, federal courts have been reluctant to add peer review to the growing list of common-law privileges.[30] The Supreme Court unanimously denied the University of Pennsylvania's claim that it had a First Amendment–based right to refuse to disclose peer-review materials that were relevant to a claim of sex discrimination in the denial of tenure. To add another privilege, the Court ruled, would both frustrate a proper investigation and "lead to a wave of similar privilege claims by other employers . . . who play significant roles in furthering speech and learning in society."[31] As important as the peer-review and tenure process is in universities, and as ticklish as the disclosure of faculty deliberations and evaluations is, the Court would not create a new privilege claimed to be needed for academic freedom. Similarly, in a malpractice case, peer-review records of a surgeon were not deemed privileged. Under federal law, the court noted, "privileges are disfavored."[32]

An anthropologist has pleaded for a qualified privilege for social science researchers. Noting that there are no statutes or Supreme Court decisions or state laws protecting researchers, he argues that there are public-policy reasons for such a privilege. Drawing comparisons to attorneys and their work-product privilege, and journalists and their state shield-law protections (Delaware's shield law also covers scholars), he makes the case for a balanced privilege to protect scholarly researchers. Indeed, he notes several cases in which courts, on balance, decided that it would be a miscarriage of justice to burden scholars by forcing them to disclose confidential information they gathered in researching subjects in the public interest, when no violations of law are involved.[33]

The problem with limiting the expansion of privileges is that the rationale for all accepted privileges applies equally to others that may be claimed. The victims' rights movement of the twentieth century has generated valuable organizations dedicated to assisting in the treatment and protection of crime victims—battered wives and rape victims, for example. Advocates argue, understandably, that confidentiality is a critical feature of their work, an essential need of their clientele, and a socially valuable public purpose. But the unclear constitutional right to privacy that underlies these claims can conflict with the clearer constitutional requirement that defendants be given the opportunity to confront and examine their accusers. The law is unsettled whether crime victims have an absolute privilege, a qualified privilege, or any privilege at all.[34]

The relationship between parents and children is another compelling example. Ancient Jewish and Roman laws recognized, and modern laws in several countries now recognize, a parent-child privilege. But, except for federal courts in Nevada and Connecticut, and four states (Idaho, Minnesota, Massachusetts, and New York), the United States does not recognize this exception to the duty to testify.[35] Such a privilege would raise tricky issues: How old must a child be before asserting his or her privilege? How does a policy maker deny parents access to their children's school records when parents pay the tuition, or to a medical record of their daughter's abortion when the daughter is dependent in most other ways on her parents?

Recent cases and academic studies have questioned the American position. This issue (and many others) was brought to light in 1998 during the Monica Lewinsky scandal, when Lewinsky's mother was subpoenaed by the investigatory special grand jury. In the aftermath of the Kenneth Starr–Monica Lewinsky contretemps, Congress proposed a law (though it was not passed) that would have made family communications privileged.[36]

A recent survey reported other comparable instances: parents of an eighteen-year-old girl accused of killing her baby were called to testify; an elderly mother was subpoenaed to testify against her policeman son, who was accused of cheating on an exam; a ten-year-old boy was called before a grand jury to testify about charges that his father killed the boy's brother. Instances such as these appall most people. One wry commentator remarked: "John Gotti's parents were not subpoenaed."

The idea behind a parent-child privilege is very similar to, but perhaps more compelling than, the idea behind the spousal privilege (parents are forever; not all marriages are). Familial harmony and privacy underlie both relationships. The additional element of fragile dependency is stronger with children than with spouses. Of course, the proposed privilege raises policy questions: Should such a privilege be reciprocal? Should adverse testimony be excluded? Should adopted children, stepchildren, and foster children be covered? Extending privileges can be a slippery slope—once we acknowledge one new privilege, where does it end, and how do we deny another?

Is the very notion of privilege elitist? In a dissent in *Jaffee v. Redmond*, Justice Antonin Scalia noted that "the word 'privilege' . . . is . . . derived from the Latin words 'privus' and 'lex': private law."[37] In her book *Secrets*, Sissela Bok notes that confidentiality may be a code word to create a sense of self-evident legitimacy, one used to "deflect inquiry." Such a categorization may "confront the questioner with what seems like a premise fundamental to an entire profession and hint that anyone who ventures to question that premise will have to question, in turn, the justification for the entire professional edifice built upon this foundation."[38] In recent years, professional organizations—accountants, for example—have lobbied for legislative expansions of privilege to their constituents to enhance public perceptions of their profession and to add status to their members.[39] Journalists have argued that it is not a "reporter's privilege" that they require, but a public's right to know that they seek to protect.

One may question whether privileges are products as much of political power as of legal reasoning. Some modern legal theorists describe the development of privileges in terms of political power. "The real roots of privilege law lie in the power of those benefiting from it."[40] Unlike theories based on the protection of relationships or the sanctity of personal privacy, the power theory does not seek to justify privileges. Rather, the theory seeks to explain them. Power theorists contend that politically powerful groups have the ability to secure favored treatment from the authorities who grant evidentiary privileges. There does seem to be a correlation between the existence of a privilege and the degree of political influence of its beneficiaries. Fundamental privileges in American jurisprudence protect powerful groups—lawyers, doctors, religious leaders, and the state—from being forced to reveal information. As one study points out, "the vast majority of new privileges have been created by statute, a process that certainly requires the exercise of political power."[41]

The Proper Perspective

In this book I advocate that, as a matter of social policy, confidentiality should be encouraged and expanded and notions of privilege should be reconsidered and confined to clear and commanding situations. No absolute privileges make sense. As many laws now provide, heretofore privileged relationships may be confidential, but the law must allow for disclosure in exceptional circumstances. In this respect, Professor Imwinkelried's judgment should be heeded: "We should not view privilege doctrine from a narrow, legalistic perspective," because "privileges relate to broader issues of extrinsic social policy."[42]

I examine the rationale for, the wisdom of, and strains upon traditional privileged confidential communications. And I assess, in view of modern needs and realities, arguments for adding more categories and modifying existing categories of privileged communications. In doing so, I provide insights into the legal and moral justifications of human dealings among people and professions whose involvements are based on crucial social relationships. Modern rules should reflect important modern values. Privacy, the broader canvas on which all questions of confidentiality are displayed, is also discussed. But my focus is on confidential relationships generally, and particularly those that are considered so important that their protection and sanctity are privileged.

The trend in the United States and abroad is to define privileges by statute and for courts to interpret privileges conservatively to minimize the frustration of the search for truth and justice. All states have privilege statutes or court-fashioned rules; a few follow common-law rules. Most states create privileges through statutes, which vary in their coverage. The federal courts have created their own common-law rules, as Congress urged them to. Thus, the federal rules evolved in the last quarter of the twentieth century through federal court rulings rather than through legislative acts as in some states.[43] Legislative rules are more democratic but also more political; judge-made common-law rules are evolutionary and cultural, but they can be more controversial if they defy widespread cultural practices.

In the following chapters, I consider the broadest and most common privileged communications, as well as attempts to expand them, in light of the public interest. Customs, laws and regulations, and professional norms are considered, as are infringements on confidentiality posed by modern technologies.

2

GOVERNMENT SECRETS

> I can never express, in terms sufficiently strong, the detestation and abhorrence which every American should feel toward a system of State secrecy. It never can conduce to public utility, though it may furnish pretexts to men in power to shelter themselves and their friends and agents from the just animadversion of the law,—to direct their malignant plots to the destruction of other men while they are themselves secure from punishment. In a government of responsibility like ours, where all the agents of the public must be responsible for their conduct, there can be but few secrets. The people of the United States have a right to know every public act, every thing that is done in a public way by their public functionaries. They ought to know the particulars of public transactions in all their bearings and relations, so as to be able to distinguish whether and how far they are conducted with fidelity and ability; and with the exception of what relates to negotiations with foreign nations, or what is called the diplomatic department, there ought to be nothing suppressed or concealed.
>
> —Mr. Botts, arguing at Aaron Burr's trial, 1807

The most confounding of all conflicts between competing demands of confidentiality and openness is raised by the needs and practices of government secrecy. In his 1967 book *Privacy and Freedom,* law professor Alan Westin notes that as a practical matter, "internal policy making requires some secrecy even in a democracy." Clandestine police work, for example, is generally condoned and often applauded; but when it becomes overzealous, it can raise constitutional questions. The philosopher Sissela Bok describes the resulting conundrum in her book *Secrets:* "Every government has an interest in concealment; every public in greater access to information." All governments have what she called a "primordial sense" of the need for secrecy. But cynics fear, and Woodrow Wilson said, that "secrecy means impropriety."[1]

Few would dispute that some government work must be secret—ship movements in time of war is the classic example. Indeed, one federal court stated: "The importance of confidentiality to decision-making processes is recognized throughout the American institutional, administrative, and judicial processes."[2] The dicta of the late Supreme Court justices Robert Jackson and Arthur Goldberg that the Constitution is not a suicide pact[3] is often quoted to make the pertinent point that national-security interests must not be ignored, or else there will be no individual liberty to protect. Our own Constitutional Convention in 1787 was held in secret, and James Madison's notes on those proceedings were not released until a generation later.

The problem is that all governments prefer to operate in secret—it is efficient and self-protective. It hides mismanagement, bungling, and misconduct. Secrets are not necessarily protected because they are so valuable, one book about secrecy notes, but "because of their innate fragility and inability to withstand scrutiny."[4] The late Harvard Law School dean and U.S. solicitor general Erwin Griswold had argued in the government's Supreme Court brief in the *Pentagon Papers* case that disclosure would pose "grave and immediate danger to the security of the United States." He confessed later that he saw no "trace of a threat to the national security" but rather was concerned "with government embarrassment."[5]

Governments are inclined too often to use constitutional and national-security claims to justify overclassifying information or intragovernmental communications as secret. History has demonstrated too often how corrosive government in the dark can be.

What Is a State Secret, and Who Decides?

The general rule, one authoritative treatise concludes, is that the term *state secret* covers military, diplomatic, and international—inherently governmental—information.[6] There are few illustrative cases, and the assumption has been that the state-secrets privilege would cover private parties (contractors, spies) working for the government. The Freedom of Information Act describes a state secret as information that is specifically labeled so by executive order for national-defense or foreign-policy reasons; state governments may not classify information as a state secret. The state-secrets privilege is akin to, but different from, executive privilege.[7] The problem is that Congress has deferred to the federal courts on questions of privilege and the courts have deferred to the executive branch, essentially providing it with a free pass.

The state-secrets privilege evolved from common law, not the Constitution, but it has constitutional implications in protecting the executive power to preserve military and foreign-affairs information. In this area of governmental action, courts understandably defer to the executive. If the executive official properly claims the state-secrets privilege with respect to certain information and the court determines (even without seeing the information) that its use would be central to the case at hand, the evidence usually will be deemed privileged.[8]

The state-secrets doctrine has historical roots, deriving from the British Crown's practice of denying judicial requests for information.[9] Such requests were improper for "curious and impertinent eyes," one court in India stated.[10] Chief Judge Baron Pollock stated that "the production of state paper would be injurious to the public service" and that the public interest must prevail over individual interests of private suitors. That decision is not for judges but for departmental custodians.[11] The leading modern British case held that ministerial objections are conclusive.[12]

In the United States, Chief Justice John Marshall dealt with the state-secrets privilege in 1807 in a case involving Aaron Burr's attempt to subpoena President Jefferson. Burr sought documents required for his defense—letters purporting to destroy him, written to the president by a general, the chief witness against him. The court ruled that Burr was entitled to see the documents: they were essential to his defense, which he had a constitutional right to pursue, even against the president.[13] Only if it is demonstrated that disclosure of the evidence would endanger public safety should a court deny access to relevant evidence. The presumption is to favor legal processes against all citizens unless state secrets or national security is shown to be at risk.

In 1875, the issue arose again, in a contract claim for reimbursement for clandestine service rendered behind rebel lines during the Civil War at the request of President Lincoln. The Supreme Court ruled that the secret agent's claim could not be brought—both parties' lips were forever sealed—because disclosure of confidential government secret services is forbidden.[14] The matter involved clandestine action in time of war, the exception to the rule requiring access to evidence in legal proceedings.

That historic precedent was followed in 2005 when the CIA was sued by claimants alleging that they were not paid for their cold-war espionage services. Chief Justice William Rehnquist upheld the dismissal of the suit on state-secrets grounds, asserting that forcing the government to litigate such claims could lead to "graymail"—that is, lawsuits brought to induce the government to settle out of fear that litigation would reveal classified information.[15]

The state-secrets claim was infrequently raised before World War II. The *Reynolds* case in 1953 highlights the modern dangers in the excessive application of this rule. That case involved claims by widows of military pilots and crew who were killed while testing secret electronic equipment on a B-29. The secretary of the Air Force claimed that the pilots were on a secret mission and that disclosure of records of secret electronic equipment on their flight would hamper national security. The privilege, the court ruled, belongs to the government, and though it is "not to be lightly invoked," the government need not defeat the purpose of the privilege by being required to disclose the very facts deemed necessary to be kept secret.[16] The Court never reviewed the documents, but simply accepted the government's claim, abdicating its judicial role. As a result of the ruling, the claimants accepted less to settle the case. Years later, when documents were declassified, it was revealed that there were no state secrets, only evidence of government misconduct that would have been embarrassing to the government had it been disclosed. The court had been misled.[17]

Curious about her father's death, a daughter of one of the crew members killed in the crash discovered the declassified accident report. She found that the report contained no secret information about the event but described "a sad, very dark comedy of errors that led to the death of my father and eight other men." "How could the government lie," she asked? Is this how the government should act when it makes a mistake? Neither an expert nor a lawyer, she asserted before a conference of experts in 2008 that "judicial review must be the watchdog that guards against actions by the Executive that chip away at the moral character of this country."[18]

The perverse ruling in *Reynolds* is often the quoted authority for the modern state-secrets privilege.[19] The claim of privilege is raised in the overwhelming majority of cases involving torts and contracts, wrongful death claims, libel, patents, and Resource Conservation and Recovery Act claims. And the privilege has often been applied with the same unjust results as in the *Reynolds* case.

How the state-secrets privilege evolved in the *Reynolds* case from a rule of evidence to an immunity doctrine, from a historical common-law rule into a modern state-secrets defense, is a story that is explained in detail in *Claim of Privilege,* a book by Barry Siegel, who had access to the records of the three plaintiffs' families and attorneys.[20] The government initially did not claim the common-law privilege pertaining to military secrets but based its refusal on common-law evidentiary rules. The divided Supreme Court, in a time of cold-war pressures to elevate national-security interests, reversed the trial and appellate court decisions in favor of the plaintiffs and, in doing so, deferred proper judicial checks and balances to the exclusive determination of the executive.

In his classic treatise on evidence, Dean Wigmore presented the case for judicial review of state-secrets claims: "Shall every subordinate in the department have access to the secret, and not the presiding officer of justice? Cannot the constitutionally coordinate body of government share the confidence? . . . The truth cannot be escaped that a Court which abdicates its inherent function of determining the facts upon which the admissibility of evidence depends will furnish to designing officials too ample opportunities for abusing the privilege. . . . Both principle and policy demand that the determination of the privilege shall be for the judge." If a court of justice requires government material, there should be no privilege, he suggested, citing Patrick Henry's rhetorical comment that "the veil of secrecy . . . is an abomination" susceptible to partisan politics and personal self-interest. "The responsibility of officials to explain and to justify their acts," Dean Wigmore argued, "is the chief safeguard against oppression and corruption." Since officials are immune to suits for their legitimate acts, he added, "what remains of real and intrinsic secrecy?" Nothing, Wigmore urged, except "an obstruction to justice and a refuge for cowardly oppressors." Secrecy permits the power of public officials to say that "white is black, and that he must be believed," in the words of an 1863 English decision.[21]

Unfortunately, the courts have not followed Wigmore's wisdom and have upheld claims of state secrets, even when invocation of the privilege was questionable. A case dealing with damages claimed by the family of a summarily dismissed clandestine CIA officer was thrown out of court because the CIA claimed privilege. "Even the most compelling necessity cannot overcome the claim of privilege if the court is ultimately satisfied that . . . secrets are at stake," the CIA director claimed. The judge said that she had no choice except to accede, though the basis of the CIA's claim was redacted from the public record. In another case, a libel suit against *Penthouse* magazine was dismissed because the plaintiff's expert witnesses might have revealed military secrets.[22]

That kind of deference to executive arbitrariness leads to oppressive actions. In *El-Masri v. United States,* a German citizen of Lebanese descent sued the CIA and its corporate contractors for kidnapping and drugging him when he was vacationing in Macedonia, and torturing and imprisoning him under inhumane conditions in Afghanistan. He was blindfolded, stripped, tranquilized, and peremptorily flown away. Half a year later, when the CIA realized that it had the wrong man, he was released from the secret facility and abandoned on a hilltop in Albania. He found his way home, and sued the United States with assistance from the American Civil Liberties Union (ACLU). But when the government (the CIA) claimed that litigation would necessitate the divulgence of state secrets, his case was dismissed.[23]

The Fourth Circuit Court of Appeals upheld the lower court's dismissal of the case. Even explaining to a judge in chambers why the privilege should apply may itself "create an unacceptable danger of injurious disclosure," the court ruled, in an example of "Alice in Wonderland" thinking. The U.S. Supreme Court refused to hear the appeal, in effect providing the government with a grant of immunity for its outrageous conduct.

The Fourth Circuit acknowledged that invoking the state-secrets privilege "pits the judiciary's search for truth against the Executive's duty to maintain the national security." In such a dilemma, judicial control over trials "cannot be abdicated to the caprice of executive officers." In this country, the separation of powers is designed to prevent such wrongs. At the same time, however, the court asserted that the executive's need to preserve state secrets "cannot be placed entirely at the mercy of the courts."[24]

The ACLU attorney, who has litigated several state-secrets cases, including the *El-Masri* case, reported the worldwide repulsion over the U.S. government's actions in that case: "It has now been confirmed, by eyewitness testimony, by government and intergovernmental reports, by parliamentary investigations, German prosecutors have sought indictments against thirteen CIA agents and contractors for their role in this. The Council of Europe, which represents forty-nine European countries, has . . . concluded that the CIA was responsible for the kidnapping and abuse of Khaled El-Masri."[25]

Because few judges are likely to second-guess claims of state secrecy, government officials are often too ready to claim it. In times of emergency, we can be left with harsh results. Personal claims are subordinated to claims of national security because "a nation without sound intelligence is a nation at risk."[26] Critics have claimed that the state-secrets doctrine has been "unmoored" from its origin as a conditional evidentiary privilege.

Cases such as *Reynolds* and *El-Masri* have reached patently unfair results. In a 1998 case, Air Force workers (and their surviving family members) near Groom Lake, Nevada, who claimed that they were injured at a secret government facility by the government's violation of hazardous-waste storage and disposal practices were denied their day in court when the Air Force asserted that defending the case would expose state secrets. In a bizarre twist, the court applied a "mosaic theory," ruling that disclosing apparently innocuous information is covered by the state-secrets privilege if in the aggregate those innocent bits and pieces combine to suggest a state secret. "The business of foreign intelligence gathering in this age of computer technology is more akin to the construction of a mosaic than it is to the management of a cloak and dagger affair. Thousands of bits and pieces of seemingly innocuous information can be analyzed and fitted into place to reveal with a startling clarity how the unseen whole must operate."[27] The government cannot be forced to disentangle classified information.

Allowing critical evidence to be excluded from a case at the election of the defending party is to sidestep the judicial process at the caprice of executive officials who may be trying to cover up wrongdoing. Why couldn't a judge privately assess the claims and control the publicity about true state secrets? Judicial oversight is an appropriate and necessary check and balance on the other branches of government. The mosaic theory led to a punitive result in one case against the CIA,[28] prompting critics to conclude that "the mosaic theory turns many of the assumptions of liberal democracy inside out."[29]

Courts have admitted in these cases that the result may be concrete unfairness to specific litigants in the interest of protecting a theoretically greater public value. Judges on the Ninth Circuit Court of Appeals in San Francisco commented on the government's argument that the "utmost deference" must be paid to executive judgments about security needs. "Utmost deference" does not mean abdication or a rubber stamp, one of the judges commented during oral arguments in a pair of cases disputing the government's claim that post-9/11 government surveillance efforts cannot be challenged in court because of national-security concerns.[30]

The state-secrets defense has been raised more frequently in recent years, particularly since the 2001 terrorist attacks. In the late 1980s, a military intelligence employee was convicted of espionage for publicizing secret and confidential records of a U.S. naval intelligence agency. The purloined photographs were published by *Jane's Defence Weekly* and later by other news organizations. The defendant claimed that his acts were not "within the mold of classical spying," because he had provided the information to a news organization, not a foreign power. The U.S. courts did not agree. "In an ideal world, governments would not need to keep secrets from their own people, but in this world much hinges on events that take place outside of public view," the appellate court ruled. The First Amendment does not override the government's and the public's interest in "discharg[ing] those government duties upon the performance of which freedom of all, including the press, depends." The rights of the press are subject "to the restraints which separate right from wrong-doing," the court ruled.[31]

Although the rationale for protecting true state secrets is manifestly obvious, its abusive nature is clear as well. Government agencies may disagree about the proper balance between national security and personal privacy.

For example, a Homeland Security directive was challenged by NASA's Jet Propulsion Laboratory. NASA told Congress that a new standardized federal employee ID system may have enhanced security but that it unnecessarily intruded on employees' personal lives, collecting racial, financial, and medical information.[32]

Disquieting disclosures early in 2007 demonstrate the constant danger of state misconduct in security matters. An internal Justice Department report revealed that the FBI had acted improperly under the Patriot Act, improperly issuing national security letters (calling for e-mails and private records) to American telephone companies, Internet service providers, banks, credit companies, and other businesses without a court order. The Justice Department's inspector general discovered that tens of thousands of such letters had been issued, sometimes concerning the wrong people. One report stated that in a three-year period ending in 2005, fifty-two thousand people's private information was added to a database that was accessible to thousands of law-enforcement agencies and foreign governments. The inspector general uncovered "mistakes, carelessness, confusion, sloppiness, lack of training, lack of adequate guidance and lack of oversight."[33] That story is every civil libertarian's, true patriot's, and paranoid's fear come true.

In 2007, the Ninth Circuit Court of Appeals analyzed the current status of the state-secrets privilege in the context of concerns about terrorism.[34] The case involved warrantless electronic surveillance by the government. The government claimed that the state-secrets privilege warranted dismissal of the case or summary judgment in its favor.

The trial court carefully analyzed the state-secrets privilege, emphasizing the necessary role of courts in reviewing these claims and asserting that a court must strike a balance between appropriate respect for the government's concerns and due process for citizens challenging the government. The dismissal of a case based on the states-secrets privilege is a "drastic" and "draconian" remedy, and the court must prudently satisfy itself that there is in fact a danger to national security. Once it does, the privilege is absolute.

But the government's saying that something is a state secret doesn't make it so. The trial court denied the government's motion to dismiss the case. Although the Ninth Circuit upheld the government's state-secrets claim, the court did not dismiss the case and remanded the case to the district court to determine whether the Foreign Intelligence Surveillance Act (FISA) preempts the common-law state-secrets privilege. The appeals court expanded on the nature and importance of the state-secrets privilege, carefully protecting the secrecy of the government's filings in support of its claim of privilege by conducting an in camera review, but also recognizing Congress's dictates about the importance of disclosure noted in the Freedom of Information Act. The executive inevitably errs on the side of secrecy, but the judiciary appropriately balances competing interests. The court noted that the Constitution grants the government no such zone of unreviewable power over the nation's people.

Our allies in democratic countries all around the world—the United Kingdom, Canada, Australia, Ireland, Spain, and Israel—have empowered their courts to closely scrutinize executive invocations of secrecy. The independent judiciary should not "consign [the] fight against terrorism to the twilight shadows of the law," in the words of one Israeli opinion.[35]

Pending legislation would give judges the right to review such classified information to determine if its disclosure would compromise national security. In response to entreaties from the American Bar Association (ABA) and constitutional-rights organizations, the State Secrets Protection Act aims to foreclose the misuse of the state-secrets privilege claim in cases where it is a "cover-up," sponsors Senators Ted Kennedy and Arlen Specter announced. The bill provides authority for trial judges in civil cases to privately review state-secrets claims by the government, to ensure against the privilege's misuse.[36] In criminal cases, the Classified Information Procedures Act provides comparable procedures for trial judges to assess the validity of government state-secrets claims, as do FISA and the Freedom of Information Act.

If courts do not exercise their constitutional powers to review the classification of state secrets, privately and ex parte, there is no check on illegal executive action, which creates a constitutional imbalance in favor of executive power, and a challenge to the rule of law. "Liberty and security are mutually reinforcing," two experts recently reminded us.[37]

The Association of the Bar of the City of New York and the ABA proposed a wise, balanced approach to addressing government claims of state secrets in civil cases. The government would be required to explain to the presiding judge in camera the basis of its claim, offer discovery of nonprivileged material, and substitute nonprivileged evidence for evidence assessed by the judge as warranting secrecy.[38]

Classifying State Secrets

Inextricably related to the confidentiality of state secrets is the fundamental question of government classification of its records, the statutory scheme by which government documents and information are classified as secret and thus kept from public scrutiny. It is the most fundamental example of privileged communications and confidentiality. The problem, as one study reported, is that "the potential use of the privilege is coextensive with all the classified material in the possession of the United States."[39]

Sources speak to government investigators under promises of confidentiality. Law-enforcement agencies could not operate without access to reluctant witnesses. But although promises of secrecy may further important social goals such as crime prevention and whistle-blowing, secrecy also raises the potential for mischief and abuse. Many classified records do not have a redeeming protective purpose for their classification as confidential. But all bureaucrats in government agencies have the proclivity to hide behind claims of "classified confidential." If wrongdoing can be shielded by the very wrongdoers' shield of secrecy, citizens have no redress of their legitimate grievances.

The government-wide system of executive classification of sensitive records began during wartime under President Franklin D. Roosevelt and was expanded under later administrations during the cold war. The Clinton administration attempted to contain the classification of records, but since September 11, 2001, classification has expanded under President George W. Bush. Few would deny the justification for classifying some selective government information, but recent history has demonstrated that the process is far too extensive and has been abused.

Classified information falls into three categories: top secret, secret, and confidential, the latter defined as "information, the disclosure of which reasonably could be expected to cause damage to the national security."[40]

Several examinations of the classification system over the years have resulted in criticisms of the system's application, expansion, and costs. The

Coolidge Committee in 1956 reported that the classification system had "vague standards, failed to punish overclassification," which had reached "serious proportions," and had lost public confidence. The Wright Commission in 1957 also criticized overclassification and recommended abolishing the "confidential" category. The Moss subcommittee in 1958 again called for punishing overclassification. The Seitz Task Force in 1970 called for "major surgery" of the system that would eliminate 90 percent of classified technical and scientific information. The Stillwell Commission in 1985 criticized the "implementation" of existing policies. In 1994 the Joint Security Commission found "unacceptable levels of inefficiency, inequity and cost."[41]

Despite these critical analyses by prestigious independent experts, the classification system and its problems remain, and in the wise words of the 1997 commission headed by the late senator Daniel Patrick Moynihan, the system "simply will not let go." The commission concluded that the classification system has proliferated, is conducted by millions of self-interested people administering complex regulations so that "secrets in the federal government are whatever anyone with a stamp decides to stamp secret. . . . Such a system inevitably degrades."[42] We have become "a nation of secrets," a book from 2007 concludes.[43]

The secret mine of government information was addressed by the 1966 Freedom of Information Act (FOIA) (amended in 1974 and 1986), which provides procedures to make federal executive-agency records accessible to the public.[44] The goal of FOIA is to ensure transparency of government records. The Supreme Court stated that FOIA was designed "to ensure an informed citizenry," "check against corruption," and "hold the governors accountable to the governed."[45] FOIA was supposed to "open agency action to the light of public scrutiny."[46] Full disclosure is mandated unless clearly exempted by the statute.

The first exemption from disclosure under FOIA covers matters classified for national-security reasons. Originally, courts deferred to agency conclusions about national security; in recent decades they have scrutinized agency determinations somewhat more rigorously. Also exempted from release are documents that are "privileged," that invade one's privacy, or that would interfere with law enforcement.

The FOIA process is expensive and slow, and it can be daunting. It effectively puts the burden on citizens to pursue their interests in discovering information instead of on the government to justify its claim for confidentiality. A recent survey of FOIA practices in eighty-seven government agencies and departments disclosed that instead of responding to FOIA requests in the "timely manner" called for in the law, agencies took months and years to respond—in the extreme, fifteen to twenty years![47] The system is "plagued by delay and backlogs." In March 2008, Senators Patrick Leahy and John Cornyn introduced a bill to strengthen FOIA, a much-needed measure given that FOIA requests have fallen 20 percent, personnel have been cut 10 percent, backlogs have tripled, and denials have increased 10 percent.[48]

Neither FOIA nor the regulations designed to permit declassification by interested agencies and officials have succeeded in adequately opening government records to the public. We are thus left with a "disturbing new culture of government secrecy," as one editorial suggests.[49] A pending case involves claims for access to about 5 million missing e-mails from White House servers. FOIA requests were denied on the theory that the Office of Administration is not subject to FOIA, though it has been in the past, and challengers believe that the records are subject to document-preservation laws.[50]

The steady stream of studies of the classification system for government records has uniformly described both an increase in the volume of classified documents and a decrease in declassification (declassification was accelerated during the Clinton administration), both exacerbated dramatically since September 11, 2001. Indeed, there has been a rise in the reclassification of declassified documents in this recent period. During the first four years of the Bush administration (2001–2004), classifications rose from 8 million to 23 million; declassifications dropped from 100 million a year to 29 million a year.[51] Derivative classifications occur by the millions (over 14 million in 2005) as a result of a secret appearing in a document, which document then is derivatively classified and becomes a secondary market in secrets.

This secrecy machinery costs over $7 billion to run, at an incalculable cost to litigants, historians, common sense, and notions of democracy.

Recent press reports have disclosed that government agencies classify about ten thousand documents *every day* according to one report, seventeen thousand a day according to another. That amounts to millions of documents every year.[52] The *New York Times* reported that the federal government classified 15.6 million documents in 2005, almost double the number classified in 2001, when the Bush administration came to office.[53] During the first four years of the Bush administration, 64 million records were classified and the number of records declassified dropped by 174 million. At the same time, the Bush administration encouraged agencies to reject FOIA requests whenever possible. So many documents are now classified that the term has no meaning, former *Time* magazine editor Norman Pearlstine has noted, and "much of what is classified is of dubious value to anyone."[54]

Despite the evolution of sunshine laws aimed at opening the operations of government, and despite a consensus among experts that the classification system is too pervasive and expansive and that there is a major need to declassify documents, these critical findings have been ignored. In fact, the trend of controlling the secrecy of government information has expanded. As one newspaper editor remarked, "Labeling something 'classified' or important to 'national security' does not make it so. The government overclassifies with abandon. And the definition of 'national security' is elusive."[55] During the Bush administration, government concealment became a national issue and, along with journalists' claims that a source of leaked government documents is privileged information that need not be revealed, generated some well-known court cases. (The litigation involving journalists' claims of privilege is discussed in chapter 9.)

Overclassification has serious implications: it prevents the public from accessing information—information that rightly belongs to the public. The government is merely the temporary controller of public information. Classification can become the equivalent of censorship. Vice President Richard Cheney told the Secret Service that he would exercise "exclusive control" of logs listing who visited his home and office. Responding to complaints by a public-interest group, the White House said that releasing this information would "impinge on the ability of the [Office of the Vice President] to gather information in confidence."[56] Vice President Cheney's office even refused requests by the National Archives and Records Administration for confidential information that was being collected pursuant to federal law—just one example of the "penchant for secrecy" exhibited by the vice president.[57]

In 2006, the White House sought to prevent the publication of an op-ed article in the *New York Times* by two former executive officials on the need for diplomatic relations with Iran, claiming that they used classified documents of the National Security Council (NSC). A former NSC official and a former foreign service officer, the authors—who had secured CIA publication-review approval and had written often on security affairs—argued that they knew "the importance of protecting sensitive information" as well as "the importance of shared knowledge." They wrote in response to the government's redaction of their article: "National security must be above politics. In a democracy, transparency in government has to be honored and protected. To classify information for reasons other than the safety and security of the United States and its interests is a violation of these principles."[58]

Since the subject of this op-ed piece was a matter under public consideration at the time, the government's action raised an important question: When should information be made publicly available to allow the public to participate in the making of policy decisions? And when does the government legitimately require secrecy in order to effectively govern? As a practical matter, the attempt to suppress information usually results in that information receiving wider attention. Under such a system, no side wins.

The classification problem also arises in civil and criminal litigation. Whether or not the government is a party, it may intervene and object to the disclosure of evidence that it deems necessary to protect from public disclosure. Various court decisions have attempted to strike an appropriate balance between deference to the government and challenges to the caprice of executive officials.[59] Final responsibility lies with the courts to decide, in camera, the merits of government claims of secrecy. In criminal trials, defendants may claim access to government documents, frivolously or legitimately, to use in their defense. Cases have been dismissed on the rare occasions that the government has decided that it is more important to protect the secrecy of its records than to prosecute a defendant.

The line between justifiable governmental claims of confidentiality and overly autocratic claims is elusive. It is easy to agree that openness and sunlight are good disinfectants and that the pitiless light of public glare is salutary, as civil libertarians have argued. But all three branches of government, like all private organizations, have a legitimate need to protect the confidentiality of some of their work. Military secrets like those pertaining to troop movements—the classic example—are easy and obvious to defend. So too are diplomatic communiqués and sensitive national-security records. The problem, however, is to draw the line there and make it difficult to traverse—to balance self-preservation against appropriate public access.

The Deliberative-Process Privilege: When Government Deliberations Should Remain Secret

Access to intragovernmental advice, communications, and discussions is a different but related question. Lord Clarendon noted in 1640 that it would be horrible if government officials "find that they might be arraigned for every brash, every inconsiderate, every imperious express or word"; such a policy would impede their advice and weaken the king they served. In 1888, Justice Field expressed his fear that discovery of government documents would inhibit free communications by officials.[60]

Dean Wigmore referred to extensions of the state-secrets privilege to communications between officials of government as a "bastard communications privilege." He argued that "it is a mockery to reserve, against righteous claims, a privilege of testimonial secrecy."[61] He quoted prestigious early American law authorities in support of his view. Chief Justice Agnew of the Pennsylvania Supreme Court wrote, in 1877, "The rights of life and public safety are too sacred to be subordinated to any right to conceal the authority by which they are destroyed or jeopardized. . . . A contrary doctrine [to disclosure] strikes at the essential and fundamental principles of a free government." When matters should be deemed to be questionable acts of authorized officials and when they are state secrets are judicial questions. Government misdeeds are "in their very nature public and cannot be concealed from the inquiry of the law," Chief Justice Agnew concluded.[62]

For these reasons, claims of confidentiality concerning insider communications have been questioned. Yet there is a reasonable basis for the claim in limited situations. Recent Supreme Court nominees, for example, have understandably refused to discuss conversations they had with colleagues and superiors when they were government attorneys early in their careers. Give and take, brainstorming, drafts of positions, inside conversations, and ruminations ought to be private unless there are extraordinary countervailing reasons.[63]

The eloquent late Supreme Court justice Benjamin Cardozo explained the rationale for protecting organizational confidentiality in a case dealing with the need for the secrecy of grand-jury deliberations. Analyzing the rationale for grand-jury secrecy, he wrote: "Freedom of debate might be stifled and independence of thought checked if jurors were made to feel that their arguments and ballots were to be freely published to the world." He added, "A juror of integrity and reasonable firmness will not fear to speak his mind if the confidences of debate are barred to the ears of mere impertinence or malice."[64]

U.S. Supreme Court dictum in an 1803 case suggested that there is an executive privilege protecting the confidentiality of conversations between high-ranking executive officials.[65] Until the twentieth century, this question was raised infrequently. The Supreme Court unanimously confirmed and expanded on the privilege, and on Cardozo's rationale for it, in the celebrated Nixon tapes case. Noting that there is an executive privilege protecting the confidentiality of conversations between executive officials, the Court decided that such a privilege is qualified, conditional on a judicial balancing of competing needs.

The historic Watergate case involved the special prosecutor's demand for White House tapes of presidential conversations with aides and advisers who were indicted for conspiracy and obstruction of justice.[66] The president claimed that his executive privilege was absolute and stemmed from his constitutional executive powers. He argued that communications between government officials and their advisers must remain confidential if candor is to be encouraged and the decision-making process enhanced.

Communications protected by executive privilege (or the deliberative-process privilege) must be predecisional (that is, they must have taken place before the adoption of an agency policy) as well as deliberative (that is, they must have been part of the give-and-take consultative process).[67] The privilege protects recommendations, drafts, proposals, suggestions, and personal opinions, but not the policy of the agency.[68] Executive privilege is related to, but different from, the state-secrets privilege of confidentiality.

Executive privilege is a qualified privilege deriving from the constitutional separation of powers that insulates executive officials from improper meddling with their work. The state-secrets privilege is grounded in inherent necessity, but has only a remote constitutional source (the foreign-affairs power of the executive set forth in Article II). The Constitution specifically addresses secrecy only in connection with Congress's records. President Nixon attempted to raise what were illegal communications to the level of state secrets. The Supreme Court ruled that the deference courts must show the government's claim of state secrets does not apply to "a President's generalized interest in confidentiality."[69]

Chief Justice Warren Burger, writing for a unanimous Supreme Court, asserted that the executive privilege is presumptive but may be overcome, and that the judiciary is the final arbiter of the appropriate balance between conflicting constitutional powers. Although there is a public interest in the confidentiality of secret executive communications—particularly those pertaining to military, diplomatic, and national-security interests—upon in camera inspection courts may determine whether the presumptive privilege applies. In Nixon's case, there were neither secrets of state nor legitimate executive deliberations to protect, only criminal conversations.

There is a public interest in the integrity of the judicial system and its need to ascertain facts and search for the truth, which may transcend the executive privilege. Confidentiality itself is not mentioned in the Constitution, so courts must determine the appropriate balance between the general privilege of confidentiality and the specific need for evidence, especially in criminal trials. That delicate balance has always been a judicial responsibility. History has recorded the impact of this decision on the Nixon presidency. The decision is clear: the privilege of government secrets is not absolute.

But there is a proper need to protect some legitimate deliberations between government officials. The Supreme Court asserted in the *Nixon* case that the confidentiality of high-ranking government officials' communications was "too plain to require further discussion." The Court recognized that "human experience teaches that those who expect dissemination of their remarks may well temper candor with a concern for appearance and for their own interests to the detriment of the decision-making process."[70]

In subsequent cases, courts expanded on the rationale that advisers would be dissuaded from expressing unpopular opinions for fear of public disclosure. One opinion noted that "the critical role that confidentiality plays in ensuring an adequate exploration of alternatives cannot be gainsaid." Without the assurance of confidentiality, "they [advisers] will almost inevitably be inclined to avoid serious consideration of novel or controversial approaches."[71]

The same rationale applies to all government decision making. It was the basis for complaints about the disclosure of Supreme Court deliberations in books such as *The Brethren: Inside the Supreme Court.* One can favor the broadest broadcasting of Supreme Court public operations and nonetheless respect the Court's need for privacy in its unofficial "inside" deliberations.

The question of a judge's privilege arose in the impeachment of Florida federal district court judge Alcee Hastings, who is now a congressman. There, the question was the prosecutorial access to appointment diaries, guest sign-in sheets, and telephone logs maintained by the judge's secretary. They were deemed not to be covered by a claimed qualified privilege of confidentiality that protects judicial communications. The court "found no case in which a judicial privilege protecting the confidentiality of judicial communications has been applied," but noted the probability that one exists among judges, and between judges and their law clerks. The court presumed that there was so little express authority for the principle because "its existence and validity has been so universally recognized," and is an inevitable product of the tripartite separation of governmental powers. Judges, like presidents, the court wrote, require "open and candid discourse with their colleagues and staff to promote the effective discharge of their duties." For judges, such confidentiality protects independent reasoning free "from improper outside influences," and safeguards "legitimate, privacy interests of both judges and litigants."[72]

In a 1971 case, Chief Justice Warren Burger commented on the judicial privilege: "With respect to the question of inherent power of the Executive to classify papers, records, and documents as secret, or otherwise unavailable for public exposure, and to secure aid of the courts for enforcement, there may be an analogy with respect to this Court. No statute gives this Court express power to establish and enforce the utmost security measures for the secrecy of our deliberations and records. Yet I have little doubt as to the inherent power of the Court to protect the confidentiality of its internal operations by whatever judicial measures may be required."[73]

Having worked as a government attorney in the Air Force JAG and in the Department of Justice, I understand the policy that protects deliberative communications between officials, not only attorneys. However, that predecisional privilege should end when government policy is set and government action occurs. At this point, officials are held responsible for their acts.

The general executive deliberative-process privilege covers "all material reflecting the actual predecisional, mental, or deliberative process—inter- and intragovernmental evaluations, expressions of opinion, and recommendations on policy and decision-making matters."[74] The rationale is to promote the free flow of ideas among government officials in order to allow them to govern effectively, while safeguarding the integrity of governmental decisions. It is a qualified privilege; courts will not approve it if the claim for access is deemed relevant, necessary, and serious, and not likely to chill intra-agency discussions. Most states have adopted a conditional deliberative-process privilege.[75]

A 2005 Supreme Court decision addressed the question of when the judicial decisional process should be considered internal and confidential and when it should be considered part of the court's record and must be available to the parties. The case dealt with the Tax Court's two-tiered procedure in which a special trial judge conducts an initial hearing and prepares a draft report with factual findings to a judge of the Tax Court, which is generally adopted by the full court. The Tax Court did not make the report public. The Supreme Court held that such reports—magistrate reports are comparable—are not internal, collegial deliberative processes but are a part of the public record, which must be open, not confidential.[76]

Some government administrative records—unlike public documents and records, and more comparable to inside conversations—do require confidentiality, except in extraordinary circumstances. IRS tax records, personnel information, census forms, and other personal information required by government agencies should preserve the confidentiality of the information, absent strong reasons requiring its exposure. But hearings held by the House Ways and Means Committee in May 2007 revealed that the IRS was contracting out to private agencies the collection of taxpayers' debts. Tax records, like police records of unsubstantiated charges or informants' information, require particular care and confidentiality because reputations and lives may be at stake.

An interesting case was decided by the Court of Appeals for the D.C. Circuit in 2007. An illegally intercepted tape recording of a cell-phone conversation between members of Congress was given to Representative Jim McDermott, who provided it to the press and to the House ethics committee. The conversation pertained to Speaker Newt Gingrich. Representative John A. Boehner, one of the participants in the cell-phone conversation, sued McDermott and won. The court ruled that the First Amendment did not protect the defendant, who was bound by the confidentiality rules of the ethics committee not to disclose information before the committee. The integrity of the investigative process and the need for collegiality were a proper basis for such a rule which trumped the First Amendment claim in such a situation. "When Representative McDermott became a member of the Ethics Committee, he voluntarily accepted a duty of confidentiality that covered his receipt and handling of the Martins' illegal recording. He therefore had no First Amendment right to disclose the tape to the media." The court awarded $60,000 in damages, as well as attorneys' fees, to the plaintiff.[77]

Conclusion

In the last quarter century, and emphatically since 2000, the claims of secrecy in government have escalated dramatically—and frequently with unjust consequences—and have been unsatisfactorily monitored through judicial review. Government records are the public's records. If the public cannot scrutinize government policies by checking government records, democratic society is endangered. The balance between secrecy and transparency of government records is a defining question about the state of democratic society. Confidentiality should be the rare exception, not the general rule. In recent years the government has claimed more privacy for its actions but has provided the citizenry with less. That trend leads to a dictatorship.

The ultimate question of confidentiality and privilege must be a judicial one, whether it pertains to state secrets, classification, or the deliberative process. Unless the government demonstrates a real overriding public interest in confidentiality, information should be open to the public. That ultimate decision is within the province of what a wise common-law jurist called "the private perusal by the judge. . . . In the case of the judge, you have sacred guarantees; in that of the politician, you have none."[78]

There is no greater example of the power of judicial review than the ability of courts to review challenged demands for executive material and to determine if and when the exercise of privilege will be upheld or overruled. In the *Nixon* case, that determination led to the initiation of the impeachment process and ultimately to the president's resignation. The Bush administration was excessively secretive and was embroiled in scandals and controversies over its policies, proving again the famous remark of Baron Acton that secrecy degenerates "even the administration of Justice."[79] That which does not bear discussion, he admonished over a century ago, is not safe.

In cases of government secrecy and expanding claims of executive privilege, the clash between needs for confidentiality and secrecy on the one hand and conflicting needs for openness and transparency on the other hand is most dramatic. Here, the public interest in openness is most manifest. Government claims of secrecy, more so than private conflicts in which individuals claim confidentiality and the public merely has a derivative interest in the claim, can be—and often are—self-protective and not in the public's interest. Indeed, the public's interest is in the availability of what really are the *public's* records; the government is just the temporary guardian of the records. One federal judge commented: "Democracies die behind closed doors. . . . It [the government] selectively controls information rightfully belonging to the people. Selective information is misinformation."[80]

3

THE ATTORNEY-CLIENT PRIVILEGE

> The greatest trust between men . . . is the trust of giving counsel. For in other confidences men commit the parts of life; their lands, their goods, their children, their credit. Some particular affair; but to such as they make their counselors they commit the whole, by how much the more they are obliged to all faith and integrity. The lawyer must have the *whole* of his client's case . . . to give any useful advice. . . . That the whole will not be told to counsel unless the privilege is confidential, is perfectly clear.
>
> —Francis Bacon, *Of Counsel*

Democracy, Henry Adams's perceptive novel about the manners and politics of nineteenth-century Washington, D.C., explores the moral dilemma posed by a lawyer's disclosure of a scandal he knew about from his professional work for a client. John Carrington, a young attorney in Washington, is infatuated with a wealthy widow, the novel's chief character, Mrs. Lightfoot Lee. She is courted by, and courts, a clever and powerful senator, later a cabinet member, who is likely to run for president, Silas P. Ratcliffe. Worried that Mrs. Lee will marry Ratcliffe, the ardent Carrington sends her a letter disclosing confidential information (which he learned about while representing a client) that casts Ratcliffe in a bad light. His gamble works; Mrs. Lee is discouraged from accepting Ratcliffe's offer of marriage.

Carrington violated the rules of his profession to protect a woman he loved, not to right a political wrong and serve a possible public service—itself not a valid reason to disclose a professional confidence, but arguably a more selfless one. Carrington's professional "sin," if you will, allowed Ratcliffe to avoid public political damage, though it destroyed his private love interest. Arguably, everyone lost: a client's confidential information was disclosed improperly; a public wrongdoing remained undisclosed; a private mischief—albeit honorably intended—was perpetrated. Or did they? How was Carrington's deceased client hurt by this later private revelation? What is the rationale of the attorney-client privilege and the dilemmas created by it?

The History of the Privilege

Under early English common law, an attorney could not testify in his client's case. The theory was that favorable testimony would likely be biased, and unfavorable testimony was considered disreputable, unbelievable, and equivalent to self-incrimination.

In the era of Elizabeth I, when compulsory process evolved and oral proof by witnesses was permitted as evidence, the attorney-client privilege was deemed an exception to the right of litigants to compel testimony. Forcing an attorney to testify against his client would be dishonorable and ungentlemanly, it was thought. Historically, the privilege was based on the attorney's honor, not the client's privacy as it is today. Counsel was required to keep the client's secrets. The privilege was historically limited to litigation, not simple counseling; since the eighteenth century, however, both litigation and transactional communications have been covered.

In the eighteenth century, the doctrine changed. The search for truth was deemed the primary goal of the trial process. It could not be obstructed by an attorney's pledge of secrecy, no matter how honorable; but the nature of the attorney-client relationship was thought to require security for the client. "That new theory looked to the necessity of providing subjectively for the client's freedom of apprehension in consulting his legal adviser, and proposed to assure this by removing the risk of disclosure by the attorney even at the hands of the law."[1]

By the late eighteenth century, the old view disappeared and this new one prevailed—as it does to this day, when the privilege belongs to the client rather than the attorney and is based on the subjective notion that "the guiding hand of counsel" is required for the client's well-being and peace of mind, which in this context is in the public interest. A Massachusetts court in 1833 declared that the privilege was based on the notion that "so numerous and complex are the laws by which the rights and duties of citizens are governed, so important is it that they should be permitted to avail themselves of the superior skill and learning of those who are sanctioned by the law as its ministers and expounders . . . that the law has considered it the wisest policy to encourage and sanction this confidence, by requiring that on such facts the mouth of the attorney shall be for ever sealed."[2]

No negative inference may be drawn from a client's insistence on the secrecy of his confidential communications with counsel; there should be no suggestion that the information privileged would be unfavorable to the client. There are exceptions—in cases of prospective crime or fraud, for example—and they are noted in bar rules and codes of ethics. The privilege is qualified, not absolute.

The Supreme Court formally recognized the privilege in 1826,[3] and it has been followed rigorously since then. The privilege is "central to the legal system and the adversary process," Justice Anthony Kennedy wrote in a California case when he was a circuit court judge.[4]

The jurisprudential rationale for the attorney-client privilege has been challenged. The very basic concern about all privileges is that they violate "a fundamental maxim that the public . . . has a right to every man's evidence," said the dean of American evidence law, John Henry Wigmore. The nineteenth-century British philosopher Jeremy Bentham argued that privileges violated "the truth theory of adjudication." Professor Edward Cleary, an important academic in the fashioning of the modern American rules of evidence, called privileges "blockades to the quest for truth."[5] The essential rationale of the adversary system is challenged by rules that exclude evidence that would lead to the discovery of truth.

Bentham, along with some early common-law judges, complained about the immoral impact of the rule of privileged communications, in much the same language as modern conservatives who chide the criminal-justice system for being a game of chance more than a search for truth. If the guilty client is deterred from seeking legal advice (a false defense), the argument goes, there is no harm to justice; the innocent client has nothing to fear, so won't be deterred.

Is the system better "for affording to criminals a chance of escape," Bentham asked? The safety of the innocent is not jeopardized by eliminating the rule of privilege. The law should not be the enemy of the innocent, this argument proposes; why dread the truth? Attorneys do not—should not—hire themselves out to frustrate justice or delude juries through artifice. "The professional lawyer would be a minister of justice, not an abettor of crime," Bentham argued, were the attorney-client privilege eliminated.[6]

Why, critics ask, should disclosures of confidential communications between an attorney and client be deemed treacherous or immoral betrayals of trust? If discovering the truth and punishing misconduct are the goals of the justice system, what is the mischief in seeking evidence from attorneys, cynics ask? So what if a denial of this privilege would discourage clients from confessing their guilt? Why should the law encourage delinquents from escaping the consequences of their acts? Why make an attorney an accessory after the fact to a crime by allowing the attorney to assist the wrongdoer in concealing crime and escaping punishment?

If the privilege is denied, the charge continues, innocent clients will be aided and the guilty ones will not be able to frustrate the law and evade the truth. Is the trial system a pernicious game? Where does virtue lie in this jurisprudential conflict? Shouldn't the lawyer be the minister of justice and guardian of truth, rather than an abettor of crimes and suborner of mendacity? As Bentham asked: "Whence comes it that any one loves darkness better than light, except it be that his deeds are evil?"[7]

Despite these contentions, the privilege did evolve in the common law. Dean Wigmore reported eighteenth-century cases in which judges described the rationale for the client's privilege to demand that his communications with his attorney remain secret.[8] The legal system had become more complex and necessity required attorneys to act for clients. Thus, it would have been destructive of business relations if attorneys could disclose their clients' remarks; it would have been as if the clients had done so themselves.

Once business required the involvement of professionals trained in the administration of justice and jurisprudence, it became necessary that citizens be able to consult with their skilled representatives and feel safe that in doing so their private thoughts and remarks would be protected from disclosure. "The communication must be privileged to the utmost extent, or it will not be made," an 1837 case declared.[9] And the privilege covered not just communications in connection with court cases but general counseling as well, recognizing that professional advice was required to avoid litigation as well as to engage in litigation. Even the identification of a client can be privileged if it would be tantamount to revealing confidential information about that client.[10] The privilege is mutual and may be claimed by the client or by the attorney on behalf of the client, but it can be waived only by the client.[11] One modern court called the privilege "the most sacred of all legally recognized privileges."[12]

Modern American law expanded the privilege to cover corporations and their employees.[13] One legal scholar suggested grandly that this privilege "has survived historical scrutiny because a confidentiality shield is a necessary tool for effective operation of the American jurisprudential system."[14]

Attorneys must be able to deal with favorable and unfavorable information regarding their clients, on their own or using assistants, and must be free from invasions of their confidentiality by others in the course of litigation.

The privilege has been honored in Supreme Court opinions, bar rules, and state statutes. It is spelled out in the ABA's Model Rules of Professional Conduct as a "hallmark of the client-lawyer relationship," and in the *Restatement of the Law Governing Lawyers.*[15] It is even deemed by some to be integral to the Sixth Amendment's right to counsel, the Fifth Amendment's protection against self-incrimination, and the right to privacy. It is subject to few exceptions: to prevent a crime or fraud, to defend oneself, or if the client agrees.

The principle of confidentiality between attorneys and clients has two sources—the general law of evidence and the rules of professional ethics. The evidentiary privilege prevents attorneys only from testifying against a client; the professional code of ethics applies in all contexts and governs all types of information—not merely communications—from all sources if the information is garnered from the representation of a client.[16]

Supporters of the attorney-client privilege argue that there is no social cost to this privilege, because without it the client would not have provided the incriminating evidence in the first place. Morally, it would be as wrong for attorneys to be made into informers as it would be to force them to become "a cloak for criminal conspiracy," one commentator argued.[17] Drawing a distinction between advice about prior wrongdoing (privileged) and future wrongdoing (not privileged) strikes a reasonable balance.

The privilege does not apply if attorneys can prevent a crime or fraud, rather than defending one that has taken place, or when they are mandated to disclose otherwise confidential information for countervailing policy reasons. When statutes require reporting, the confidentiality rules must be trumped.[18]

The chief exception to the attorney-client privilege is the crime-fraud rule, which is designed to prevent abuses of the proper relationship between attorneys and clients. The rationale of the privilege is the importance of clients being able to discuss their past misconduct and future behavior without fear of disclosure. That protection "takes flight if the relation is abused," as when communications are made in order to commit future crimes or fraud. Then, "the seal of secrecy is broken."[19] Thus, if one has committed a bad act, he or she may consult with counsel and be protected. But the client may not abuse the privilege to further a fraudulent or criminal scheme. "Law and society consent to the attorney-client privilege on these preconditions" to both "safeguard the privilege itself and protect the integrity of the professional relation."[20]

A moral complexity has been noted by the philosophy professor Bruce Landesman: Does a requirement that lawyers disclose certain categories of client communications make them "agents of the state"? Of course, lawyers are agents of the courts, but that is different from being forced to be agents of the police or prosecution against their clients.[21]

In addition to the "instrumental" rationale, which argues that without the attorney-client privilege clients would not consult attorneys, is the "humanistic" rationale. Some scholars contend that personal autonomy or privacy, some basic sense of decency, is what is at stake in the attorney-client privilege. The inquiry should be made, one treatise suggests, about what kind of society would empower courts to compel intimates to betray their trusts.[22] As fiduciary agents of their clients, attorneys have a duty of loyalty to them, and society has an interest in this social investment in a just and moral system.

Professor Imwinkelried's exhaustive examination of the philosophical underpinnings of the attorney-client privilege concludes that the instrumental rationale, although the majoritarian view over time, was based on anecdotal, self-serving, and empirically unsupported proof. The relatively few recent (1960, 1980) studies on the causal relation between clients' disclosures to attorneys and the assurance of a later privilege are inadequate and exaggerated, and thus misplaced, Professor Imwinkelried concludes. That said, he does not question the overall wisdom of the rule, only the rationale for it. Others have questioned the rule's wisdom, noting that criminal defense attorneys invariably do not want clients to be totally open with them, fearing that if they (the attorneys) know about guilty conduct, they may be prevented from pursuing avenues of defense.[23]

To accept the notion of privilege, one must subscribe to the idea that there is a greater good to be attained by ensuring the inviolability of conversations between attorneys and their clients. Some ask whether a greater number of people in society would be better served when the goal of the justice system is truth rather than the protection of one client's self-protecting, self-serving interest, which may or may not lead to the truth.

A knowledgeable modern critic has questioned the rationale that confidentiality permits attorneys to assist their clients in following the law. "The net effect of confidentiality," this observer argues, "is probably to reduce compliance with the law."[24] Confidentiality, he claims, encourages attorneys to advise clients how to get around the law, exploiting loopholes and technicalities, and playing the odds of not getting caught. Someone aiming to conform to the law does not need confidentiality; only those seeking to circumvent the law do. That hostile view of legal counseling is severe, even if it is occasionally appropriate.

Theoretical and philosophical debates aside, the law historically has protected the legal counseling process. That protection provides attorneys with an advantage over other professionals, one that is not always in the public's interest. That judges, most legislators, and legal theorists are lawyers, and inclined to be empathetic, no doubt had something to do with reaching this result.

Modern Practice

Today, fresh issues concerning the attorney-client privilege arise because the relationship between attorneys and clients has changed so dramatically. The *Masterpiece Theatre* image of an anxious client sitting in the quiet chamber of an old-fashioned counselor seeking personal advice about his property or her inheritance or disclosing intimate personal facts required for the lawyer to provide advice is quaint. Of course, that type of intimate practice does still goes on, and I have particularly enjoyed that very private and personal part of representing clients. There is a unique faith between strangers, a sense that the lawyer is providing important advice that should and will remain private. The client relies on the private communion as a necessary feature of that relationship. A total stranger arrives in an attorney's office and, entering into a private pact with the attorney, shares very personal confidences about his or her life, plans, desires, problems. There is a certain sanctity to the relationship—not unlike the sanctity of relationships with pastoral or psychiatric advisers—that makes the attorney-client relationship more than just a mere business relationship. Of course, clients' concerns are private and should remain confidential.

The contemporary law practice—much, though not all, of it—is much more complex and public than it was in earlier times. Other people—assistants, secretaries, consulting experts, colleagues—are often part of the modern attorney-client meeting. The privilege extends to agents of the modern attorney: colleagues in very large firms, as well as assistants and experts whose work is indispensable to the attorney. Many law firms are so large and vast that lawyers have complicated procedures simply to determine if there is a conflict of interest because a colleague in a distant office has a competing matter or client. Documents are now routinely digitized and stored in less than perfectly private files. Nonlawyers routinely advise the public about "legal" matters (probate, real estate, taxes). Lawyers, and all their aides and colleagues, advise clients about arguably "nonlegal" matters (financial, media, and personal issues).

The attorney-client privilege applies in situations of externship teaching, a pedagogical part of the academic world. When law students perform clinical work in the course of their training, they owe clients a duty of confidentiality. Faculty supervisors are not privy to the confidential communications between their students and their clients and supervising attorneys. Whatever ethical dilemmas this may cause law professors, the bar's disciplinary rules do apply to the student's confidential communications.[25]

Facilitative colleagues are deemed part of the attorney-client privilege. Attorneys regularly use psychiatrists, polygraph experts, accountants, business (or marketing) consultants, and other independent contractors whose expertise is needed to render legal services. These consultants may or may not have the benefit of the attorney's privilege. For example, courts have deemed some accountants' communications privileged if they are acting like "translators" of complex tax law, but not when their advice is not integral to providing legal (as opposed to business or other) advice. Representing children poses special problems for lawyers, who must balance confidentiality rules with the need for outside social-service consultants and the clients' limited capacity.[26]

Law firms have begun outsourcing some of their work concerning administrative tasks such as travel, record storage, and accounting. The aim is to cut costs by moving some work to low-cost places like Delhi, India. The practice raises the concern "that confidential client documents or information could be leaked, stolen or simply lost."[27] When law firms try to reduce infrastructure costs by outsourcing "back-office" operations such as those relating to computer networks and billing records, they jeopardize old-fashioned confidentiality. When costs and efficiency compete with privacy, confidentiality can become an endangered species.

Extensions of the Privilege

Whether the attorney-client relationship exists, and thus whether the attorney-client privilege applies, is scrutinized conservatively by courts.[28] In order for the attorney-client privilege to apply, a professional legal adviser must provide legal advice. When, for example, union officials for the Patrolmen's Benevolent Association of New York City sought to claim the privilege with respect to the advice it provided to union members regarding a federal criminal investigation, the court ruled that no privilege attached to protect those communications; being akin to a legal adviser is not sufficient.[29]

New claims for exceptions to the attorney-client privilege have evolved as new situations have arisen. For example, with the American Psychiatric Association's recognition, in 1980, of post-traumatic stress disorder (PTSD) as a basis for personal-injury damages, some observers called for a limited waiver of the attorney-client privilege to allow inquiry into information provided to clients by their attorneys about PTSD symptoms. Forensic experts may want to know if a claimant's attorney coached the claimant about symptoms and encouraged false claims. That concern blurs the line between proper advice and improper coaching.[30]

PTSD is not the only medical-legal area where claims concern subjective symptoms, so there could be no end to such exceptions, especially among people who view personal-injury lawyers cynically. Proponents of the waiver argue that it would be akin to the exception to the doctor-patient privilege in cases where the patient puts his or her mental condition at issue. Because there are competing public-policy considerations on both sides of this debate, and no constitutional issue in civil cases, legislatures could go either way in determining the situations in which the privilege applies, or could leave it to judges to determine, on a case-by-case basis, whether the privilege applies.

For there to be a privilege, there must be a communication. An attorney was allowed to describe his client's appearance in a competency hearing. Only the substance of their conversations was deemed privileged, the court ruled, "not the fact that there have been conversations" or that the client appeared to understand them. Those facts were not "intended to be held in the breast of the lawyer," the court ruled, even though the attorney-client relation "provided the occasion for the lawyer's observation."[31]

Although courts have been chary about extending this privilege, they have also stretched to preserve attorney-client confidentiality. For example, the idea that the client's privilege survives the trial or matter involved has been interpreted to mean that the privilege continues to apply even after the client's death. This interpretation can cause unjust results. A 1976 Arizona Supreme Court case points up the perversity of too absolute a rule.

William Wayne Macumber was convicted of two counts of murder and given two concurrent life sentences. Before Macumber's trial, another person confessed to having committed these crimes to the two attorneys who defended him. After their client died, the state bar's ethics committee advised the lawyers that they could testify as to their client's confession so that an injustice could be avoided. During Macumber's trial, however, the court did not allow their testimony. The court allowed Macumber to be convicted without the jury hearing about the other person's confession—surely a fact that would have raised reasonable doubt. To make matters worse, it was the trial judge who raised the privilege (the confessor being dead), as the law permits. "The privilege does not terminate with death."[32]

One of the dissenting judges on the Arizona Supreme Court suggested that the defendant's right to present a defense should have prevailed over the deceased's "property" right because the deceased client could no longer be prosecuted. One commentator noted the perversity of the ruling: "The constitutional right of the accused to present his defense is rendered subservient to the reputational interest of a dead client in keeping his disclosures quiet."[33]

When Claus von Bulow's attorney wrote a novel after von Bulow's acquittal, von Bulow's children sued for damages and sought to use the attorney's disclosure of client confidences as a waiver of their father's privilege. The court held that the lawyer's book, *Reversal of Fortune,* waived the attorney-client privilege only with regard to communications noted in the book, not with regard to other confidential conversations between them. One not trained in the rigors of legal education might question such compartmentalization. This "novel" question, as the court described it, preserved the confidentiality of the attorney-client relationship on matters not in the publicly marketed book as a matter of fairness. The court recognized that its decision permitted the privilege to be used as "both a sword and a shield."[34]

The deceased-client privilege is an example of a wise rule that when extended too far can create an unjust result. An interesting case arose in the course of special prosecutor Kenneth Starr's investigation of the so-called travel-office scandal in 1993—"so called" because no prosecution resulted from the investigation. The White House counsel, Vincent Foster, committed suicide before the investigation concluded. But he had discussed the matter with his attorney, and his attorney's notes were subpoenaed by Starr, who claimed that the privilege did not apply. The trial court concluded that there was no exception to the privilege; the appellate court ruled that there was, and ordered production. The Supreme Court upheld (by a 6-to-3 vote) the posthumous application of the privilege, concluding that there was no appropriate balancing test to discern if exceptional circumstances warranted an exception to the attorney-client privilege.[35]

Lower courts had urged, wisely, that in limited cases—for example, where the evidence is critical to a just conclusion of a criminal case—the privilege be relaxed.[36] Many states have refused to make exceptions to the absolute privilege, on the ground that to do so might discourage clients from communicating with attorneys. A few states have allowed exceptions where compelling circumstances warranted.

Why courts cannot be trusted to balance competing interests and decide this question in ways that do not frustrate justice is puzzling. Given the facts of the case, the result in the Travelgate case seems wise. But the sweeping denial of exceptions in all cases, as in the Macumber case, is unwise; courts should not slavishly follow the rule when doing so leads to a miscarriage of justice.

A Virginia case illustrates the need for a judicial exception to the general rule of privilege.[37] The attorney for one of the defendants in a felony-murder case observed prosecutors coax and coach his client to modify his testimony so that his codefendant could be identified as the triggerman and thus eligible for capital punishment. After the trial, the attorney asked the state bar's ethics adviser if he could make this information public and save the life of the convicted murderer. He was told that he could not.

When, ten years later, the death-row convict appealed his death sentence (on other grounds), the attorney again sought permission to release the confidential information. The attorney stated that he would have maintained his exculpatory secret if the bar's ethics authorities had insisted that he do so. This time he was told that he could release his confidential information. As a result, a state judge commuted the convict's death sentence to life imprisonment. One can question why the law should permit such an extreme injustice to result from a rigid rule about confidentiality.

A North Carolina attorney faced a hostile judge when he testified, against the judge's admonition, about his dead client's remarks that might have freed an innocent man convicted for a double murder and sentenced to life imprisonment. The experienced lawyer argued that he had an ethical and moral imperative to disclose these confidential conversations. Lay observers are critical, understandably, of a rule that permits grave injustices. Some states permit exceptions to the confidentiality rule to prevent an execution; only Massachusetts allows the exception to prevent wrongful incarceration.[38]

A classic and dramatic example of the painful, if not unjust, implication of a rigid rule governing client confidentiality arose in 1973, in what became known as the *Lake Pleasant Bodies* case. Robert Garrow stabbed and killed an eighteen-year-old student who was camping in the Adirondacks. A statewide manhunt resulted in Garrow's arrest. Police suspected that Garrow also killed three other campers who were missing. Frank Armani, a local attorney with no criminal-law experience (and a former classmate of mine), was assigned to defend Garrow. Armani recruited a successful criminal defense attorney—Francis Belge—to work with him on the case.

Garrow told his attorneys that he killed all three of the other victims and raped the two who were young women. He told his lawyers where the bodies were hidden. They went to the sites and found the three remains, but left them there and told no one—neither the law-enforcement authorities nor the families of the deceased. Student hikers eventually found the bodies.

Armani and Belge put Garrow on the witness stand during his trial, and he confessed to the three other murders and two rapes—as part of his insanity defense. Garrow was convicted and sentenced to twenty-five years to life in prison. He escaped from prison, and was shot and killed.

The attorneys publicly admitted that they had known about these additional crimes for six months, but argued that they were constrained from taking any action—advising law-enforcement authorities or the families of the victims—because of the rules of confidentiality. They were harshly judged by the involved parties and vilified by the general public because they withheld information about the corpses and protected the murderer (they did offer the information as part of a plea bargain that was rejected).

Belge was indicted for violating public-health laws requiring a decent burial for dead bodies and obstructing justice. Attorney organizations pleaded in his defense, arguing that a judgment against him would destroy the attorney-client privilege and force attorneys into a Hobson's choice. Which social institution is owed an attorney's duties—the legal system or the public? Should the rules of evidence overwhelm rather than aid the search for truth and justice?

The New York court dismissed the charges against Belge, reasoning that "the effectiveness of counsel is only as great as the confidentiality of the attorney-client relationship." Belge had, the court decided, "conducted himself as an officer of the Court . . . to protect the constitutional rights of his client."[39]

Armani was torn by his ethical dilemma, understandably, and felt ashamed in his community, even though most of his professional colleagues supported him. He said in a television interview, "To me it was a question of which was the higher moral good . . . the question of the Constitution, the question of even a bastard like him having a proper defense, having adequate representation, being able to trust his lawyer. . . . It's a terrible thing to play God." Armani anguished over the agony of the victims' parents: "Your mind screaming one way. Relieve these parents! . . . One sense of morality wants you to relieve the grief."[40] His torment, as well as the families', must have been unbearable; any attorney would feel that way.

Legal theorists have debated the dilemma created by this case, and there is no totally acceptable answer. One expert even questioned whether a decent ethical person can ever be a lawyer. The law elevates, as it must, the adversary system, the presumption of innocence, the right to counsel, and rules of confidentiality. Is this a separate morality? If so, might there be exceptions? Who strikes a balance between common morality and professional or legal morality, and by what standards?[41]

Media Management

The expanding role of attorneys in the use of the media to try cases in the court of public opinion represents an example of the attempt to expand the attorney-client privilege. Lawyers often make public appearances to argue their clients' cases in the media, viewing that as part of their work—especially in cases involving celebrities and public figures. In the highly publicized Martha Stewart case in 2003, a public-relations firm, working in concert with the defendant's lawyers, claimed that its records were protected by the attorney work-product privilege (see the next section below for a discussion of this privilege) and thus could not be subpoenaed by the grand jury investigating the case. Its position was approved by the federal judge in the case, whose opinion "thrilled" public-relations firms, according to one legal analyst.[42] The judge accepted the attenuated argument that the public-relations firm was hired not to influence the general public but to influence the government, which was being influenced improperly by unfair media coverage pressing for an indictment.

That case was an exception to the general rule. In the few other cases addressing the question of public relations in the context of the attorney-client privilege, courts have ruled, appropriately, that media efforts by public-relations consultants are not equivalent to the legal performance by attorneys on behalf of the same clients, except in the rare instance where the public-relations consultant or advertising agency assists the attorney in rendering legal advice. The argument that a public-relations adviser is an agent of the client, and thus protected by the privilege, has not been adopted. That such advice is of incidental tactical use to the attorney is not a sufficient basis upon which to invoke the attorney-client privilege. The general rule is that when attorneys are performing nonlegal functions, those functions are not privileged. "A media campaign is not a litigation strategy," one judge admonished.[43] An attorney who is consulted but does not render a legal opinion is not a party to a confidential communication.

A Washington, D.C., lawyer who has represented many newsworthy clients (including the president of the United States) argues that modern lawyering has public-relations features that should be covered by the attorney-client privilege: "The legal advice includes advice on effective handling of the media in areas that might have legal impact on the client, such as mitigating potential liabilities, avoiding prejudicing the jury pool, increasing the chances of reasonable settlement, and especially, for a public company, correcting misstatements of fact that can have adverse effects on shareholder values. . . . That advice is part of the overall legal advice rendered to the client. . . . [The] media can have substantial impacts on legal issues, liabilities, and outcomes."[44]

The advent of cable television has exponentially expanded public discussion of high-visibility cases (making them highly visible in the process) by attorneys and others, and this question is likely to keep arising. But because privileges to avoid process are against the policy of seeking truth, the attempt to expand the attorney-client privilege is likely to be very strictly construed. Public relations by their very nature are meant to be public.

Bar rules forbidding lawyers from making public statements about pending cases have been modified to allow attorneys to make fair replies to public charges. But this does not directly answer the question whether participating in trial strategy should be a privileged situation.

Work Product

The attorney work-product privilege was not, as might be expected, an integral part of the historical attorney-client privilege. Centuries after the advent of the attorney-client privilege in English common law, and as a result of modern trial practice, the U.S. Supreme Court fashioned this aspect of the attorney-client privilege in 1947. Justice Frank Murphy articulated the rationale for the work-product rule: "It is essential that a lawyer work with a certain degree of privacy, free from unnecessary intrusion by opposing parties and their counsel. Proper preparation of a client's case demands that he assemble information, sift what he considers to be the relevant from the irrelevant facts, prepare his legal theories, and plan his strategy without undue and needless interference. . . . This work is reflected, of course, in interviews, statements, memoranda, correspondence, briefs, mental impressions, personal beliefs, and countless other tangible and intangible ways—aptly though roughly termed . . . the 'work product of the lawyer.' Were such materials open to opposing counsel on mere demand, much of what is now put down in writing would remain unwritten."[45]

The work-product privilege covers all the attorney's papers, correspondence, and notes related to the representation of a client in civil and criminal cases. It is a twentieth-century extension of a venerable privilege that evolved to perfect the adversary system by protecting the attorney's work beyond private conversations with a client.[46] It is designed to ensure that attorneys do not fail to gather information on their clients' behalf for fear that such information will be accessed by their opponents.

When counsel was asked by Justice Robert H. Jackson during the oral arguments in this case what the practical effect would be of his work product being produced into pretrial discovery, he responded, "Interviews will go unrecorded, unpleasant sources will not be pursued, and counsel will be tempted to keep files under his bed at home."[47] Justice Jackson noted in his concurring opinion that "discovery was hardly intended to enable a learned profession to perform its functions either without wits or on wits borrowed from the adversary." To allow this would be "demoralizing," he added.[48]

Especially in civil litigation, which is often expansive in its accumulation of documents, trial lawyers often battle over work-product claims. One side argues that the claim covers up relevant evidence, noting that everything an attorney touches is not work product. The reply is that clients need to be able to prevent the disclosure of an attorney's preparations to freeloading opponents.[49] These disputatious claims are costly, time consuming, and often vexatious. The essential question for judges now, as they assume central roles in determining discovery issues, is whether the demanded materials are overly protective compilations or true creative products of the attorney's work.

The U.S. Supreme Court has recognized the work-product extension of the attorney-client privilege as part of the federal common law. An attorney's work product cannot be made available to adversaries in litigation without undermining the privilege itself. The privilege applies to materials the attorney collects to prepare for trial as well as his or her analyses, ideas, notes, and related materials.[50] It protects corporations as well as individuals, protects communications with in-house and outside counsel,[51] and covers individual communications as well as internal corporate investigations.

The work-product rule is complicated by the evolution of modern technological advances that are now integral to law practice—the fax machine, cellular phones, e-mails. As one legal commentator noted, "Each modern technological advance has taken attorneys and their clients one step farther from the closed-door, personal interactions upon which the privilege was founded."[52] Courts assess questions arising from these new technologies on a case-by-case basis, questioning whether there is an expectation of privacy or whether privacy has been waived under the circumstances of different situations. Attorneys who do not take reasonable care to protect these communications may be found to have committed malpractice.

One commentator reminded lawyers that, like generals, old e-mails never die, "they just get deleted" and return to the "cyberspace graveyard."[53] A Justice Department scandal early in 2007 concerning politically motivated firings of U.S. attorneys was unearthed by the disclosure of extensive e-mail messages between Justice Department and White House officials documenting the questionable conduct.[54] Trial lawyers refer to e-mails as evidence mail, so common is it now to search litigants' computer records.

Although it is common for attorneys to use e-mail, there are steps worth taking to keep private communications confidential—use of disclaimers is commonly found on faxes, for example. The surest protection is not sending e-mail messages, which are often misdirected, may go through third-party Internet providers, and are susceptible to hackers.

Inside Counseling

A quasi privilege, akin to the attorney-client work-product privilege, has evolved. It pertains to internal "self-evaluative" reports that have been used by organizations and corporations seeking to reform their ways to avoid claims of misconduct. In situations involving product liability, securities fraud, environmental laws, affirmative action, and news and health-care organizations, claims were made that internal reform would be discouraged if organizations feared subsequent disclosure of their critical self-analysis. It is in the public interest, the argument goes, to promote voluntary, freewheeling exchanges within companies by protecting the confidentiality of these reports. The corporate structure raises tricky questions about this application of the attorney-client privilege. Shareholders own corporations; directors, officers, and attorneys manage corporations. In litigation over corporate affairs, should shareholders have access to the confidential communications of corporate employees whose misconduct they are challenging? How does such access influence corporate officers seeking advice in good faith for the conduct of the corporation's affairs?

A key case in 1970 involved a stockholder suit against the corporation and its executives.[55] The stockholders sought disclosure of legal advice provided to corporate management. The court adopted a balancing approach that weighed the parties' interests, considering the need to protect both management's right to seek legitimate advice and stockholders' ability to unearth misconduct. The corporate privilege is not absolute, the court ruled, and stockholders may demonstrate that corporate actions inimical to stockholders' interests warrant making an exception to the privilege. There has been extensive litigation on this point.[56]

In the case of corporations, there is confusion about who counsel's clients are. A breach-of-contract case dealing with questions of toxic-waste removal on property sold to the U.S. Postal Service by a private corporation sheds light on the distinctions between privileged and nonprivileged information accumulated by in-house corporate counsel. The trial judge ruled, after in camera inspection of disputed discovery documents, that the privilege did not apply to remedial environmental studies performed for counsel by outside scientific consultants, drafts of letters and documents by in-house counsel, documents exchanged between corporate employees and copied to counsel, correspondence between lobbyists and counsel, or even to communications with corporate officials on how to respond to a congressional inquiry regarding the transaction (the latter a claimed executive-deliberative-process privilege). In-house-counsel communications may be covered by the privilege, the court ruled, if they are within the scope of the employees' corporate duties as counsel.[57] Since in-house counsel performs nontraditional tasks, courts must determine if the claimed privileged communications were made in counsel's capacity as counsel or as business advisers, though the lines between the two roles can be close and blurred. Courts need to determine the dominant role played by counsel and whether communications were made with a justifiable expectation of confidentiality. Factual data cannot be privileged, because it is not deemed part of the lawyer's defense strategy, which is protected.[58] Since no client confidences or legal advice were part of these documents, there was no privilege.

Litigation inside corporations, or against corporations by outsiders, may require exceptions to the attorney-client privilege. For example, a qualified privilege would encourage intraorganizational reform. The privilege being qualified could be overcome if extraordinary circumstances warranting disclosure were demonstrated. Otherwise, organizations should be protected from having to provide to their antagonists road maps that would undermine their motives to reform their policies or address employee misconduct.[59] Where the privilege has been recognized, it has applied to analysis, not facts, and has not protected against disclosure to regulatory agencies or grand juries.

A related problem emerged at the start of the twenty-first century. The Justice Department and the SEC took an aggressive stance in criminal investigations of businesses in the post-Enron era. The Justice Department issued a memorandum noting factors it would consider in determining its actions against corporations.[60] The government suggested that if corporations waive the attorney-client privilege voluntarily (if the waiver is indeed voluntary and not coerced), such a waiver would affect the government's charging decisions and sentencing positions. The government's motive was to reduce the need to offer immunity to cooperative insiders and to toughen action against plundering companies, a goal the public applauded.

Lawyers, major bar groups, and the Chamber of Commerce complained that this policy was overreaching and chilling because it discouraged corporations from conducting in-house investigations and audits for fear that their records would be used against them and to punish them for their internal clean-up actions.[61] The policy was terminated. The verdict was that such rules sabotaged the attorney-client privilege and eroded the constitutional protections that underlie it.

That prosecutorial policy, along with federal sentencing guidelines that allowed judges to consider confidentiality waivers in determining sentences and statutes requiring corporate employees and others to report corporate misconduct,[62] created an unintended dilemma for corporate attorneys and their clients: either it undermined internal housekeeping or it provided their opponents with a bonanza of sensitive confidential information.

Such requirements—although well intended—subject some employees to "the cruel trilemma of self-accusation, obstruction of justice or discharge,"[63] and potentially lead to a proliferation of civil suits based on third parties' attempts to discover confidential records. The waiver policy's impact on organizational culture and ethical conduct is compromised by such laws, critics have complained. Internal policing could be inhibited out of corporate executives' fear of indictment and litigation, and malfeasance would go undetected—the opposite of what the government intended. The instinct is to fight, not to reveal, one experienced lawyer noted. "If you let regulators in, you lose control of everything. Suddenly, they start exposing problems you didn't know existed. Some say the safest route is to fight and hope regulators won't be able to make their case."[64]

Mediation

As law practice has evolved, so too has the application of the confidentiality privilege to the trial process. For example, in the final decades of the twentieth century, a judicial reform movement called alternative dispute resolution (ADR) evolved. The idea was to expedite and make the litigation experience less expensive and rancorous. Mediation, essentially a form of nonbinding arbitration, is its key model, and all states (except Delaware) now allow or require mediations as an early—and often final—step in the trial process and provide for some level of confidentiality to protect those negotiations. Clients may meet mediators with or without lawyers, and although mediators need not be lawyers, most are. So the attorney-client privilege underlies the mediation process.

Mediation has become a popular means of settling disputes. Disputants choose mediation to avoid the rigors of protracted litigation, saving the courts—state and federal—valuable time and effort. Indeed, some courts require litigants to participate in some form of ADR procedure before proceeding in formal litigation. As an ADR mechanism, mediation is more conducive to amicable settlement than is the adversarial litigation process, and it may allow parties to settle their differences without unnecessarily escalating the dispute.

However, parties seeking the benefits of mediation do so under the assumption that participation in the mediation process will not expose them to the very risks they seek to avoid in formal litigation. Mediation participants' behavior during the procedure is, in large part, dictated by the belief that what they communicate will be held in confidence. "Confidentiality, therefore, is at once itself a virtue of the mediation process and a protection against disclosure of information for other purposes including subsequent litigation."[65]

The recent growth of ADR generally and mediation specifically has been called "epic" by one commentator—but not without "serious ethical quandaries" about attorney-mediators' conflicts "between confidentiality and professional responsibility."[66] All states have laws and rules governing confidentiality—and exceptions—in the mediation process. Most states provide an exception for reporting future crimes or harm to third parties, but only Minnesota allows mediators to report professional misconduct under codes of ethics for lawyers. Since most mediators are attorneys—although they need not be—the possibility exists that attorney-mediators can run into conflicting ethical obligations for confidentiality and for reporting. Since all states have many explicit exceptions to their confidentiality rules, one governing mediation could easily be added.

In 1998, a federal district court in California carefully analyzed the policies underlying the evolution of federal privilege rules and their extension to mediation.[67] In ruling that a federal mediation privilege should be adopted as a matter of federal common law under Rule 501 of the Federal Rules of Evidence, the court noted that all states have a confidentiality privilege protecting testimony and documents developed during mediation proceedings. The general acceptance of such a privilege is based on the need to encourage conciliatory proceedings in disputes and to decrease trial dockets. One court described the reason for such a rule as encouraging attorneys not to "feel constrained to conduct themselves in a cautious, tight-lipped, non-committal manner more suitable to poker players in a high-stakes game than adversaries attempting to arrive at a just solution of a civil dispute."[68] Participants in mediation, now a national practice, would not be open to using the process if they were not able to rely on the confidentiality of negotiations.

The rationales for a mediation privilege of confidentiality are the same as those for the traditional privileges covering lawyers: to insulate parties from discovery by third parties; to foster a relationship for public-policy reasons; to facilitate communications between litigating parties without losing evidence (which would not exist but for the privilege); to replace adversarial excesses in the trial process with conciliatory procedures; to economize the judicial system by saving the risks and expenses of trials, except in limited cases; and to encourage compromise. A New Jersey court in 2006 concluded: "Underpinning the success of mediation in our court system is the assurance that what is said and done during the mediation process will remain confidential."[69]

Mediation policies can conflict with other interests—discovery practices, for example. In a controversial ruling, the California Supreme Court decided that the mediation privilege, although qualified and inapplicable when a greater public interest in disclosure is demonstrated, precluded discovery of prejudicial investigative interviews, data, and photographs from a prior mediation concerning the same defendant.[70] Critics claimed that the ruling allowed parties to keep evidence secret unfairly by including it in mediation; in effect, mediation created a "backdoor" exception to discovery rules.[71] The California Supreme Court ruled that without protecting mediation confidentiality, litigants would be discouraged from engaging in mediation, a practice that is in the public interest. This was not deemed to be a case in which the mediation privilege must yield to a greater public interest. Not mentioned, though it should have been, was the result of the ruling, which hid from tenants in an apartment complex health and building defects that also affected them (this subject is discussed in chapter 8).

Communications between corporate or organizational clients and their in-house and outside lawyers are protected.[72] The privilege covers agents and employees under the organization's control and in its decision-making group. Government organizations are covered too.

Lawyers working for the government or for large organizations—corporations, private institutions—have complicated, nontraditional legal roles that raise questions about the applicability of the privileged nature of their communications. High-visibility public events in recent years—investigations of the president of the United States and his wife and staff by an independent prosecutor, and confirmation hearings of two Supreme Court nominees—dealt with the applicability of the attorney-client privilege to government attorneys. There are about twenty-six thousand attorneys in the federal government alone—many more in state and local government agencies, along with thousands of corporate in-house attorneys—and their advice to their clients or to public officials has broad public impact. There is a greater and legitimate public interest in their work than in private counseling of private individuals.

The director of the Center for Ethics and Public Service at the University of Miami School of Law, professor Anthony Alfieri, has criticized the questionable changes in the role of lawyers and law firms in corporate practice. Writing in the *Miami Herald,* he says, "In the new era of corporate law practice, lawyers function more like entrepreneurs, and law firms operate very much like businesses."[73] Criticism and self-examination has led to some bar and regulatory-agency controls. But the morality of lawyers, especially in large organizations, where personal responsibility can be shifted and hidden, has been exposed in recent notorious trials such as Enron as in need of further scrutiny.

Confidentiality comes into play when the client, either a corporate client or a large firm's individual client, protects attorney misconduct by raising the protective curtain of confidentiality. A former federal prosecutor of environmental cases calls corporate privilege claims "the great citadel behind which corporate America hides its wrongdoing." By including corporate counsel in business dealings, he claims, "presto, ordinary corporate behavior unrelated to legal analysis is illegally designated privileged."[74]

Although the Sixth Amendment's guarantee that people accused in a criminal prosecution have a right to counsel is not the source of the attorney-client privilege, denial of the privilege is questionable and may be deemed to have constitutional implications. Coercing the privilege waiver, the ABA argues, interferes with effective counseling, client advocacy, access to justice, and proper functioning of the adversary system.[75] The fear is that a waiver of the privilege, intended as an incentive for high-minded corporate behavior, will have the opposite effect.

Corporations dealing with foreign-based counsel or doing business abroad "do not often enjoy the same protections of confidentiality," one professional report noted.[76] There is a danger that in-house counsel in Europe cannot claim the traditional lawyer's privilege for their internal communications with their corporate clients.[77] In-house counsel (and non-European outside lawyers) are treated differently from private attorneys (who are members of national bars and subject to bar ethics rules) for purposes of privilege protections and are thus hampered in their ability to police their corporate clients.

The attorney-client privilege in the European Union has been compromised by a recent E.U. ruling that permitted a government search of corporate in-house counsel records.[78] As one international general counsel warned, in-house lawyers' documents, correspondence, research, and written advice have become "a fertile hunting ground"; another commentator said that this ruling is "a trap for the unwary."[79] The problem arises in international arbitration, too.[80] As a result, sophisticated international lawyers may be tempted to put nothing in writing, and companies may be tempted to destroy written records and use external companies' record keeping when written communications are required.

And what about the unique problems of government attorneys? In an investigation of government misconduct, or when a government attorney's involvement in the government's business is questioned (as in recent

Supreme Court confirmation hearings when nominees were interrogated about their government service and refused to respond), is the attorney's client the public, or is the client the government agency itself? On one hand, it seems suspicious when a government attorney, past or present, refuses to answer legitimate public questions about his or her work. On the other, it is reasonable and important for government attorneys—all attorneys for that matter—to be able to brainstorm with colleagues and clients without the fear that those communications might become public. I would have been shocked if my conversations about investigations or pending cases while I was a federal prosecutor in the Department of Justice were later publicized. As noted in chapter 2, on government secrets, officials legitimately need to be able to assume that their private counseling and ruminations will remain confidential.

Post–September 11 civil-liberties curtailments by the federal government have impinged on the historical attorney-client privilege. The Patriot Act permits government eavesdropping (monitoring) on conversations between imprisoned defendants, detainees, and their lawyers. Intercepted communications are reviewed by a "privilege" team to determine if terrorism is imminent. The team is not neutral; nor is it accountable for its decisions. Traditional safeguards of the justice system were deemed contrary to the public interest in this time of emergency, Attorney General John Ashcroft announced.

Critics noted that the very existence of this power, even without its exercise, is a violation of the most vulnerable legal privilege because it inhibits the free flow of communications between attorneys and clients. One defense lawyer argued that the practice hurts the government because it inhibits attorneys from making inquiries of clients that might lead to cooperation with the government. Federal statutes already permit an exception to the privilege in extenuating circumstances with the intervention of a judge, arguably making this practice unnecessary.

Conclusion

Is the protection of attorney-client communications a modern form of professional protectionism toward which courts are especially solicitous? Historically, this privilege has benefited from judicial deference and understanding. As one court reported, "It is out of regard . . . to the administration of justice, which cannot go on without the aid of men skilled in jurisprudence, in the practice of the courts, and in those matters affecting rights and obligations which form the subject of all judicial proceedings. If the privilege did not exist at all, every one would be thrown upon his own legal resources. Deprived of all professional assistance, a man would not venture to consult any skillful person, or would only dare to tell his counselor half his case."[81] Yet in all other instances, courts have been amenable to exceptions to relational privileges because they are impediments to law enforcement and the search for truth.

It is not only economic or personal self-interest or self-aggrandizement that compels attorneys to claim privilege. Confidentiality rules permit them to practice with fewer problems extracting information from their reticent clients and thus enable them to manage their representation.

The public purposes behind the attorney-client privilege are wise and reasonable. Yet there are understandable, if self-serving, exceptions to the confidentiality rule that allow attorneys to reveal client communications in malpractice cases against them or in fee disputes. For example, the trial attorney for the terrorist Timothy McVeigh was allowed to disclose confidential communications when, in appealing his case, McVeigh accused him of providing an incompetent defense. Might there not be further, equally rational, exceptions?

One cynic concluded that this exception to the attorney-client privilege reveals a hypocrisy: "Confidentiality means everything in legal ethics unless lawyers lose money, in which case it means nothing."[82] Thus, confidentiality is not enforced in a fee dispute, or in a complaint against an attorney by his client, but it does prevent an attorney from exonerating an innocent defendant or finding a missing person.

Attorneys promote "needless secrecy," one critic argued, because confidentiality puts a premium on services they are uniquely qualified to provide. This inhumane instinct is "a marketing strategy, more than an ideology," in his critical judgment.[83]

The Supreme Court of Minnesota dealt with an attorney's conflict between his professional duty of client confidentiality and personal ethics. A trial judge had approved a settlement in a case involving a minor who was injured in an automobile accident. A potentially fatal aneurysm had been detected by a medical expert of the defendant's insurance company, but not by the young man's physician, parent, or attorney. The defendant's attorney did not disclose the potentially damaging evidence, on the ground that confidentiality rules precluded his doing so. The parties settled for $6,500.

Years later, applying for the army reserve, the young man who had been injured—now an adult—discovered the aneurysm and sought to vacate the prior settlement on the ground that defense counsel had concealed critical information and enriched its client as a result. The appellate court agreed and vacated the settlement. The state high court reasoned that although the lawyer had done the right thing at the time, the court would do the right thing at this later time, albeit a different "right thing." Although justified by professional-ethics rules of confidentiality, the attorney's concealment had created an "unconscionable advantage over plaintiff's ignorance or mistake," the court ruled. To condone that confidentiality, however, would be "to penalize innocence and incompetence and reward less than full performance of an officer of the court's duty to make full disclosure" in the nonadversarial settlement stage of the proceedings. "Equity will prevent one party from taking an unconscionable advantage of another's mistake for the purpose of enriching himself at the other's expense." The Minnesota Supreme Court noted in its opinion that "no canon of ethics or legal obligation" required the defense attorneys to inform the plaintiff;[84] but in their silence they ran the risk that the settlement could be set aside. In exercising this tortured thinking, the court was protective of the bar's confidentiality rules as well as its own power to bring about a just and conscientious result.

An episode of an old television series, *The Practice,* dealt with a more confounding version of this issue. There, a conscience-stricken defense attorney advised the plaintiff of a medical problem, acting against the interest of his insurance-company client. He was disciplined by the bar's ethics committee for doing so and taking the law into his own hands. That he saved a child's life, however laudable, was deemed to be no defense by the ethics committee. Most trial lawyers would agree with that professionally self-protective position, but most others would not. As in the Virginia case of the criminal who was sentenced to death when an attorney who had exculpatory testimony was told that he could not present it because of ethical rules of confidentiality, the equitable need for an exception based on exigencies of justice is clear.

Why not use a judicial balancing test in all cases where an issue is raised in good faith to determine if an attorney-client privilege should be enforced? That procedure is followed in cases dealing with accountants, doctors, journalists, and others. If a compelling competing social interest is established (such as the deceased-client exception mentioned earlier), courts could then permit an exception to the general rule of confidentiality. Professional rules of confidentiality would protect most interactions, unless a court ruled otherwise. As Mr. Carrington discovered in the novel *Democracy,* mentioned at the beginning of this chapter, there must be room for a rule that aims to encourage attorneys to follow the right rules and seek the moral result.

4

MEDICAL CONFIDENTIALITY

I swear by Apollo Physician and Asclepius and Hygieia and Panaceia and all the gods and goddesses, making them my witnesses, that I will fulfill according to my ability and judgment this oath and this covenant:

What I may see or hear in the course of the treatment or even outside of the treatment in regard to the life of men, which on no account one must spread abroad, I will keep to myself, holding such things shameful to be spoken about.

If I fulfill this oath and do not violate it, may it be granted to me to enjoy life and art, being honored with fame among all men for all time to come; if I transgress it and swear falsely, may the opposite of all this be my lot.

—The Hippocratic oath

The History of Medical Confidentiality

The Hippocratic oath has governed medical practice since 460 B.C. By the oath's terms, patient information provided to doctors is sacred, "not to be noised abroad," but rather to be treated as "holy secrets." It would be shameful for this information to be spoken about, physicians are admonished. The fundamental principle of patient confidentiality is founded on rational notions about the privacy of treatment. However rational, the principle has been weakened by the clanging nature of modern medical practice and the invasions of new technologies.

The English common law did not recognize medical confidentiality as a privilege not to testify.[1] In the Duchess of Kingston's trial in 1776, the distinction was drawn between medical ethics and legal duties. A surgeon who claimed that information he knew about a patient on a confidential basis could not be disclosed to an inquiring court as a matter of "professional honor" was admonished: "If a surgeon was voluntarily to reveal these secrets, to be sure, he would be guilty of a breach of honor and of great indiscretion; but to give that information in a court of justice, which by the law of the land he is bound to do, will never be imputed to him as any indiscretion whatever."[2] Law and medicine had different priorities.

Although under historical common law there was no doctor-patient privilege, in the nineteenth century some American state legislatures codified a physician-patient privilege to encourage people to seek medical care when needed, even for embarrassing or socially unacceptable diseases. After New York passed the first doctor-patient statute in 1828, other states followed with comparable laws of their own. Their common rationale was that the utmost confidence between doctors and patients was necessary to ensure correct diagnoses. As one treatise stated, "The saga of American jurisprudence has recorded many trying triumphs over the inadequacy of the English common law, and the seal placed over the physician's lips, when tempted to discuss his patient's affairs in private conversation, is one of these proud achievements."[3]

The policies of the various state laws were the same, but the substance differed. Some covered civil cases, some criminal, some both. The scope of what was covered varied; some referred only to specific diseases such as venereal or "loathsome" diseases. The privilege was not absolute; it was subject to generally accepted exceptions. Court rulings about these state privilege laws also included diverse interpretations about who and what was covered, when and how the privilege came into play, and when the privilege did not apply.[4] State laws also varied as to when the medical privilege might or should be waived, as in situations involving communicable diseases. Some state legislatures made exceptions to the medical privilege in cases of insurance fraud, personal injury, and will contests, leading observers to remark that there were so many exceptions that there was "little left but the smile."[5] As a result, today physicians may be more aware of the provisions of their medical codes than the pertinent legal requirements, and unaware that they may not be consistent.

Today, as a general rule, most physicians are required by state law to respect patient confidences unless the patient waives the privilege or the doctor is ordered to disclose information under the law in order to protect the community. It is deemed to be a matter of public welfare to make exceptions to the general rule of confidentiality if there are "overriding social considerations." Without such exceptions, doctors would be subject to a tort action for disclosing confidential information.

Most states (forty-three of fifty) provide a patient privilege, unless the patient puts his or her mental condition at issue in a trial—by claiming the insanity defense in a criminal case, for example, or suing civilly over an injury. Patients may rely on a "warranty of silence" when they confer with their physicians, unless a court orders otherwise.[6] There is even a de facto privilege in England, where it is reported that few judges compel doctors to betray professional confidences.

Physician-patient secrecy is also prescribed by medical ethics. The first code of medical ethics, published at the start of the nineteenth century (1803), required confidentiality. Confidentiality was required by the American Medical Association's (AMA's) Principles of Medical Ethics, which was adopted in 1847 and which is still in effect today. The American College of Physicians *Ethics Manual* describes confidentiality as a fundamental tenet of medical care. The World Medical Association has adopted similar ethics rules of patient confidentiality. So have the American Health Information Management Association and specialist professional associations such as the International Chiropractors Association and others.

Legal and medical literature describes the rationale for protecting the sanctity of doctor-patient communications as one of trust and confidence. Confidentiality rules are for the benefit of patients so that they may rely on the skill of the physician to find a cure or enhance recovery. Toward that end, patients must be able to speak frankly with their doctors, and with full candor. Thus, "only they themselves may unlock the doctor's silence in regard to these private disclosures." Patients should not have to fear that their disclosures to their doctors will become "public property." The health of one's mind and body is so intimate, so required for the road to recovery, that patients "must disclose all information in [their] consultations with [their] doctors—even that which is embarrassing, disgraceful or incriminating. . . . There can be no reticence, no reservation, no reluctance when patients discuss their problems with their doctors."[7]

The preservation of the patient's confidentiality is no mere ethical duty on the part of the doctor; there is a legal duty as well. The unauthorized revelation of medical secrets, or of any confidential communication given in the course of treatment, is tortious conduct that may be the basis for a legal claim for damages. Dean Wigmore confines the medical privilege to "professional physicians"; he does not apply it to pharmacists, nurses, or auxiliary practitioners.

The causal rationale, that patients would be deterred from confiding in their doctors if they feared disclosure of their communications at a later date, was questioned as highly speculative by Dean Wigmore and more recently has been questioned by Professor Imwinkelried and other scholars. There is no shame in seeing a doctor (with few exceptions such as in case of venereal disease), Dean Wigmore remarked; nor will sick or dying patients in extremis hesitate to seek medical care for fear of their malady becoming known. Other evidence scholars have noted that a patient can be compelled to reveal, during discovery or on the witness stand, any information that the patient revealed to a physician.

That may be so, but more so than in their dealings with other professionals, in their dealings with doctors patients do rely on confidentiality. People are embarrassed about their physical problems and prefer that their doctors treat them in confidence. An optometrist told me of a patient whose family and the patient herself had been in his care for many years. He examined her, and then referred her to an ophthalmologist to consider a symptom he discovered and whose treatment was beyond the scope of his practice. The specialist subsequently advised the patient that her diagnosis was a virulent sexually transmitted disease. The embarrassed patient asked her doctor not to tell the referring optometrist of the diagnosis, despite the specialist's explanation that it was a customary practice and important for the optometrist to know in order to continue with her contact-lens care. The embarrassed patient never went back to her optometrist.

However appropriate and balanced a confidentiality rule, confounding questions can arise. For example, when a patient sues a doctor for misconduct and seeks medical records of other patients to discover if there are patterns of misbehavior, a judge might on balance allow a limited exemption to confidentiality.

Confidentiality may be claimed from the world generally, but there should be no privilege from proper disclosures in court, experts have argued. It has been pointed out that medical practice flourished and expanded without any privilege. Much medical treatment is not embarrassing or intimate (for example, a broken arm or a cold) and need not require privileged status. And much medical diagnosis now is done by machines and tests that, although confidential, are more accessible than personal communications between doctors and patients.

Modern Medical Practice

Old-fashioned medical practice, where a patient visited a kindly, omniscient physician, they conversed privately, and others were not made part of the encounter, is a relic of a bygone era. One-on-one intimacy between physician and patient is disappearing. Indeed, the rationale for confidentiality—that the physician needs to know all in order to advise well—has changed. The insight of others often is required in order for the physician to adequately assess the patient's problem. Faraway strangers in our globalized world are hired to review reports and advise the doctor. We all have experienced this group approach to treatment.

Today, commonly, patients visiting a doctor's office are greeted by nonprofessional assistants who require the patients to fill out forms full of personal information about themselves and their families. Then, they are ushered into an inner waiting room where paraprofessionals ask more questions and note more personal information in the patients' files, sometimes also conducting tests or drawing body fluids. Eventually, the doctor arrives, reads the assistant's notes, converses with the patient, does what is to be done, and prescribes treatment.

Patients may be referred elsewhere for tests, or their blood or urine or other samples may be sent elsewhere to subcontractors who perform a finite service—analyzing a biopsy or reading an X-ray, for example. Some functions are now outsourced to invisible lay employees in distant foreign countries. After the examination or conference, the physician may transmit his notes via an electronic medical record by calling a local phone number that will send the patient's records to India, or some faraway place, with the doctor's and the patient's identification number. There, the records will be transcribed and sent back to the doctor or hospital, electronically. The doctor will approve the transcription as his or her official notes of that visit. Eventually these records are sent to the insurance company that covers the patient, and more strangers review and evaluate the patient's records to determine coverage or reimbursement.

These contacts are expanded when a patient is in a hospital. The bedridden, sometimes unconscious, patient is visited and his or her records are scrutinized by nurses, dieticians, therapists, residents, and countless others. A study estimates that "50 to 75 people need access to a patient's chart during a typical hospital visit." Another report states that 150 people (doctors, nurses, technicians, billing personnel) have access to a hospital patient's records and that millions of provider employees also have access.[8]

The evolution of employer-created medical centers has also altered doctor-patient relationships. Designed for the convenience of employees and to save employers money, the employee clinic raises new questions about the reality of confidentiality. Since the doctors are employees of the corporation, their allegiance to their patients is compromised.

Hundreds of large American corporations offer their employees on-site primary care for checkups, prescriptions, routine blood tests, and routine illness monitoring, either for free or for a modest co-payment. The clinics are run by part-time or full-time doctors, nurses, or physician assistants, or the clinics' operations are outsourced to independent treatment vendors. Companies that have such programs include Toyota, Qualcomm, Pepsi Bottling Group, and Credit Suisse.

If the doctors work for the employers, how can the employees be assured of the confidentiality of their medical records? Cigna, an insurance company that runs clinics for its employees and provides clinics for other companies, was quoted as saying that it views its role as a "partner with both the employer and the clinic's provider" to ensure that doctors are aware of their patients' medical history and needs. Aetna sees this as an opportunity to steer patients to treatment places, providers, and drug prescription options.[9] But what about the confidentiality of the employees' medical records if their employer seeks access, or if the provider markets their information?

Some legal experts have concluded that modern laws protect the confidentiality of employees' health records. But the wisdom and voluntariness of these expanding employer health programs and the interposition of independent administrative contractors of the employers aside, skeptics may question this conclusion. Urging employees to exercise and not to smoke and sensitizing them to wise health practices certainly are benign practices, and can contain costs as well. But employee medical report cards and questionnaires and health coaches inevitably lead to the availability of personal health records to outside vendors and the prejudicial scrutiny of unethical employers. These programs are extensive (for example, BB&T Corporation covers twenty-four thousand workers, Textron thirty thousand) and are becoming more common (Carlson Companies' hotel chain is about to start its national program). Enforcement of privacy-protection laws will determine the success of the trade-off between confidentiality and health planning.

MIB Group, a membership corporation formerly known as the Medical Information Bureau, maintains a database of medical data on about 15 million Americans, which it makes available to the approximately 470 insurance companies that are member-owners of MIB. Unidentified patient data also may be sent to its research subsidiary MIB Solutions with or without the patient's knowledge and approval. If approval is possible, clearly it should be sought. But what if a stroke patient is not in a condition to give approval and his representatives are not available? Compiling statistical data for research purposes serves a public interest—but personal information and identifying data must be protected.

The problem is that once data is gathered, its dissemination cannot always be controlled. The American Health Information Management Association reported that this collected information becomes a grab bag for "employers, government agencies, credit bureaus, insurers, education institutions, and the media," as well as "unauthorized data gatherers." U.S. health records are "commodities," *New York Times* science expert Gina Kolata reported.[10]

People are required to sign waivers before receiving medical treatment. Most waivers can hardly be called voluntary. One signs, or doesn't see the doctor. In addition, release forms sometimes authorize disclosure of patients' records, theirs and their dependents', to the insurer, hospital, medical facility, insurance company, "or other organization, institution, or person" having records or knowledge of them! These are excerpts from an actual release.

This new reality prompted a Chicago physician to conclude that the traditional doctor-patient privilege "no longer exists." This fundamental principle of medical practice, he wrote, "has become old, worn-out, and useless; it is a decrepit conceit." In one operation he described, the patient's records were accessed by almost a hundred health professionals and administrative personnel—attending physicians, consultants, nurses, nutritionists, pharmacists, students, secretaries, financial officers, chart reviewers, and insurance auditors. This global access to medical records, a product of team medical care, complementary high-tech additions to primary caregivers, and the vast and impersonal third-party payment process, "necessarily modifies our traditional understanding of medical confidentiality," was this doctor's understated conclusion.[11] The diverse diagnostic treatment model and the distant payment processes of modern medical care mean that it "takes a village" to serve a patient.

The Need for Access to Medical Records

There is an inherent conflict of interest in the confidentiality of medical records. Physicians need thorough medical records to treat patients appropriately. If parts of a patient's medical history are missing, the doctor might mistreat the patient—and might even be sued for malpractice for prescribing an inappropriate medicine or failing to prescribe an appropriate one. Several physicians have told me that they were frustrated and disadvantaged by their inability to get access to a patient's records held by another physician, records that they needed to attend to the patient properly—in an emergency surgery, for example.

On the other hand, if patients' medical histories are disclosed widely, they might be denied insurance or employment because of their medical histories. Their children might be denied insurance if there is a hereditary family disposition to a disease.[12] One physician remarked that a woman swiped her medical records from her physician so that her children wouldn't be prejudiced by the family's history of Huntington's disease. "The information belongs to me," she stated. In this era of genetic records—and antidiscrimination laws protecting them—people may be denied insurance or have high premiums because of their family medical histories.

The advent of genetic testing, which can lead to early diagnosis and preventive medical treatments, has created dilemmas for some patients. The fear of discrimination in employment and in insurance coverage has led some patients to avoid genetic testing for fear of the economic consequences if negative information is disclosed.[13] Some patients are handling their DNA tests privately so that they can control the disclosure of negative results.

In 2008, the Genetic Information Nondiscrimination Act was signed into law.[14] It prohibits health insurers and employers from discriminating against individuals on the basis of genetic information. The act prohibits insurance companies from denying coverage or adjusting premiums on the basis of genetic screening, counseling, or testing, or the use of new genetic therapies. Employers are prohibited from discriminating against employees on the basis of predictive genetic information. The act also strictly controls the use and disclosure of genetic test information.

The appropriate balance between patient privacy rights and employer or insurance-company requirements for information about those people they will be responsible for is elusive and fraught with competing legitimate needs. Employers who provide insurance and time off for their employees, for example, believe that they have a legitimate interest in a prospective employee's health condition—whether a potential employee has AIDS or is pregnant. A study in Illinois disclosed that "50% of the companies surveyed use employee medical records in making employment decisions."[15]

Employees and their physicians view information required for their employment as confidential. Is it fraudulent, or unfair, to conceal relevant medical information in bargaining for employment? Is it wrong to use medical information for purposes other than treatment?

Modern changes may have improved medical care, but what is left of confidentiality?—and should we care? The leading legal scholar of the rules of evidence, Dean Wigmore, reported that four conditions must be met for any communication to be deemed privileged: the communication must have been made in confidence; confidentiality must be required to maintain the relationship; the community must require that confidentiality be "sedulously fostered"; and it must be clear that the damage to the relationship caused by disclosure would exceed any benefit from the "correct disposal of litigation." Wigmore opined that the second condition is not generally present in the case of the doctor-patient privilege. Wigmore wrote after the old common-law era when there was no such privilege and before the modern era when the doctor-patient relationship has been so strained and stretched.

The addition of hierarchal institutions such as HMOs and insurance companies can cause conflicting loyalties to the organization-employer and the individual patient. One commentator remarked that with all the rules and exceptions designed by courts and legislatures regarding whether a physician should or should not maintain patient confidences, doctors will need lawyers to keep abreast of their professional responsibilities.

The patient privilege is rendered near meaningless because health-insurance providers have access to medical records. This incongruity leaves the doctor in a fiduciary relationship with patients and their records, while the insurance-company managers (not necessarily physicians) have access to them. Privacy laws have been passed to protect patient records, but once the records are outside the orbit of physician and patient, one wonders how private they remain.

Government agencies have access to patient records under Medicare, Social Security, and workers' compensation laws. Some employers have access to their employees' health records. Aggressive marketers can gain access to medical information from pharmacies, hospital employees, and motor vehicle departments. Private investigators have bribed hospital employees to obtain access to medical records in adversarial litigation, or when celebrities are involved. As a result of modern practices, the physician-patient privilege is more often breached than observed.

The radio host Rush Limbaugh found this out when investigators, suspecting that Limbaugh had engaged in illegal "doctor shopping," seized, pursuant to a search warrant, Limbaugh's prescriptions from pharmacists who provided Limbaugh with large amounts of two controlled substances prescribed by four doctors in a five-month period. Limbaugh learned of the seizure only when it was reported on cable television. Limbaugh argued that the seizure violated his medical privacy and the right to be let alone and to be free from governmental intrusions. In an odd coupling, the ACLU supported his position. The Florida courts disagreed. There was a search warrant. The records were sealed. Limbaugh had his opportunity to make his claim. The court ruled that Limbaugh's right to maintain the confidentiality of his medical records was trumped by the state's warrant in a criminal investigation. Limbaugh eventually conceded and agreed to submit to treatment and to pay the costs of the investigation ($30,000) and his supervision ($30 a month).[16]

Even the remnant of the doctor-patient privilege that still exists is not absolute. And for good reason. Doctors are required in most states to unilaterally disclose otherwise confidential information about their patients in certain situations, including when child abuse is suspected, when a patient has expressed an intent to harm others, when there is a risk that a patient will commit suicide or other self-destructive acts, when gunshot wounds are involved, and when certain communicable diseases are involved. There are sound reasons for more exceptions. Physicians have an affirmative duty to breach patient confidentiality by warning third parties of a patient's dangerous condition. The duty to protect privacy is replaced by a duty to warn the public.

In a child-neglect case, the D.C. trial court allowed into evidence medical records of a mother's mental illness and drug abuse because of their direct effect on her child's safety and welfare.[17] Courts must determine in these cases what is in the best interests of a child and must be flexible in applying technical rules of evidence. In another case, the court authorized the public-interest exception to the medical privilege, as well as to the husband-wife privilege, in a juvenile court in a case involving child neglect.[18] Indeed, doctors, nurses, law-enforcement officials, school officials, social workers, and mental-health officials are mandated to report child abuse. Privileges granted by the legislature may be withdrawn by it, the court wisely concluded.

When a mother attempted to retrieve her infant from a sheltered-care facility despite her history of drunkenness and mental disorders, the court permitted two of her doctors to testify about her mental condition.[19] Her claim that her constitutional right of privacy was violated was rejected by the court. That right must yield, the court ruled, to the well-being of the child, as the court balances—case by case—the probative value of the evidence in dispute with the harm disclosure would cause to the doctor-patient privilege.

Reasonable rules making exceptions to medical confidentiality for overriding social reasons are controversial and confounding. Social workers have told me that their work in hospitals and correctional institutions can be effective only when their clients can count on the confidentiality of their communications. "Trust" is the key, they understandably claim. Yet morally and legally, how can they withhold information about a client's medical condition—that a client has AIDS or is HIV positive, for example—when they learn that the client is having unprotected sex? Social workers are reluctant to become agents of the state, but how can they not be? Because of the unique public-health problem created by HIV, the trend is to exempt this situation from general confidentiality requirements and mandate reporting.

In some states, it is a crime to have sex if a party has HIV or AIDS. Even if there is no such law, shouldn't a doctor inform innocent parties who might be affected? In one case, a medical school denied a doctor with a sexually transmitted disease the right to return to the faculty after he was convicted of having unprotected sex. Did the school's denial constitute double punishment? How should society balance people's privacy interests against their community obligations?

What is the appropriate ethical pretext for divulging a confidence in the medical context? Possible harm to a large public? Or to one individual? One philosophical author raised the question in the context of a physician's duty to the girlfriend of an HIV-positive patient who, fearing that she would leave him, had not told her of his condition. What is the physician's obligation to her? To the general public? Is the patient's right so predominant that it may not be breached for a greater public purpose?[20]

A physician who treats an epileptic does not have the right to advise the state motor vehicle department that this person ought not to drive a car. In a less controversial setting, an optometrist objected to being required by state law to report certain communicable diseases to authorities. "In Pennsylvania, and other states, eye doctors are required by law to report drivers who fail to meet certain vision requirements to the state motor vehicle department. I felt the state was making me the enforcer. What the state should have done is require everyone to have their eyes examined and bring in the results; they would make determinations, based upon my report . . . not have me 'turn them in.' What the new law did was keep elderly drivers from having their eyes examined and therefore lose the protection of early detection of progressive eye diseases."[21]

The classic premise of doctor-patient confidentiality has been a matter of serious and passionate debate in the context of abortion. Some states have sought to require doctors to inform parents when a minor seeks an abortion. In one case, the Department of Justice claimed the right to access Planned Parenthood records of underage girls seeking abortion advice, arguing that the organization was not acting as a physician and that the records would provide evidence of statutory rape.[22] If the patient is an adult, there is no question that the doctor should not inform the parents unless the patient agrees. But why not advise responsible parents of a minor?

Critics of proposed laws that would require the doctor to inform the parents of an underage pregnant patient argue that breaching the patient's confidentiality could lead to problems when the father of the patient is also the father of the child, or is otherwise abusive. But what is the appropriate and moral practice in most situations when that is not the case? How about the father of the child? If there are legal obligations imposed on a father (married or not) under paternity laws, or if the father asks for information because he is a caring person, should the doctor inform him if the pregnant mother-to-be does not want him informed?

Genetic research raises new confidentiality questions, as the example involving Dr. Watson mentioned in the introduction demonstrates. Should researchers have access to people's medical histories in order to study the propagation of diseases? Though a person's genetic information cannot be totally protected, it can be hidden or disguised to some degree. Is genetic information owned by the individual patient? What about genetic relatives who are affected by it? If it is considered public-health information, may a doctor choose to advise relatives about relevant problems based on a patient's medical history? There have been cases in which courts have ruled that doctors have the duty to advise affected family members about their relatives' (parents') genetic disposition to disease.

The reason for the confidentiality of medical records is complicated by these equally rational rules requiring doctors to report medical information in specific situations—situations involving communicable diseases, gunshot wounds, battered spouses or children, patients who pose a danger to themselves or to others.[23] Conflicts can arise when the private interest of the patient conflicts with the welfare of the community. These conflicts—perplexing by their nature—are made more complicated by the questionable nature of some public policies advanced as justification for disclosure.

Shaken-baby syndrome provides an example in which a benign motive may create occasional injustices when the concerns of law and medicine clash. Over a thousand times a year, hospitals report possible infant assaults, as required by law. Often, there is no abuse. A neurosurgeon who has often testified as an expert witness in shaken-baby cases says that prosecutors have used hysteria to supplant science.[24] The law requires hospitals to report *all* injuries to babies to police and prosecutors, on the assumption that such injuries suggest abuse by the baby's parents. Mandated reporting to reveal suspected child abuse, noble in its motives but nightmarish in its implications to innocent parents, has ruined lives, not of injured children but of innocent parents. When emergency-room doctors report infant injuries such as shaken-baby syndrome to criminal-justice officials, as required by law, the child (albeit infant) patient's privilege (usually controlled by the parent) is violated, incidentally, by rule of law.

There can be confounding concerns about the confidentiality of AIDS patients' records. For example, for many years I represented an organization for ex-offenders, which did remarkable work in the community. Among other things, the organization ran a halfway house where former prisoners resided while they sought employment and eased their way back into the community. At one of the board meetings, the director of the halfway house asked for my legal opinion about a dilemma he faced. One of the men at the house had AIDS. He was about to start a job in the kitchen at a fast-food restaurant, preparing food. Could the director—should he—advise the prospective employer of this condition as a precaution? The director wanted to respect the resident's privacy and be helpful to him in his job search. But the director also wanted to be candid to the prospective employer, who employed other residents of the halfway house and whose goodwill he relied on. As a legal matter, the resident's medical history was confidential, but might the halfway house be vulnerable to a lawsuit by the prospective employer or a customer if the employee transmitted his disease by some foreseeable negligence—a cut finger, for example?

The difficulty of weighing the direct harm to a patient likely to result from disclosing his or her medical records against the countervailing public purpose to be served by that disclosure was dramatically illustrated in the 1972 presidential campaign. Days after the announcement that Missouri senator Thomas Eagleton would be Senator George McGovern's running mate, news was leaked that Senator Eagleton had a history of psychiatric treatment. He resigned from the ticket, though there was no evidence that his past problem was disabling or that it was a current problem. In 2006, tasteless press reports about the hospitalization of New York's governor seemed to cross the line between appropriate medical confidentiality and the public's right to know, by reporting his postoperative bowel difficulties.

The Impact of Technology

New technology has created additional controversies over medical confidentiality. Public-health professionals claim that databases of patient records—with controls to protect patients' identities—are useful in dealing with epidemics, monitoring drug sales, and expediting emergency diagnoses and medical care. Doctors have told me that to provide appropriate care, they need information from their patients' medical records held by other doctors, but are often hampered by well-intended restrictions. Others have been disturbed to find that in treating a patient for one problem, the patient's medical history—not required for the matter at hand—is made available to attending professionals.

Cancer research has been hampered because some information sources refuse to report patient data. Researchers have complained that total deference to patient confidentiality severely hinders cancer research.[25]

Recent exposés of lapses in military health care have noted that digital records designed for tracking wounded soldiers were not used in many cases. As a result, mistakes in treatment were made, delays in care ensued, and unnecessary and costly tests were repeated.[26] New technologies can aid medical care, but they may create new problems in the process if confidentiality requirements impose restrictions.

The Supreme Court considered the medical confidentiality question in 1977. The Court decided that a New York statute requiring that prescriptions for certain categories of drugs be filed with the state did not violate patients' constitutional privacy rights. The complainants argued that the state's collection of such information would stigmatize patients, and would make them reluctant to use certain drugs and doctors reluctant to prescribe drugs—all on the speculative assumption that the requirement would serve a public purpose. The Supreme Court ruled that states have the power to regulate the administration of drugs so long as they take reasonable steps to protect against the disclosure of patient information for improper purposes.[27]

Techniques for controlling access to medical records must be perfected to ensure confidentiality at the same time that these social policies are enhanced. One company is developing a radio frequency identification (RFID) chip that could be implanted under the skin of an individual's arm, providing a secure method for controlling and carrying medical information.[28] A recent study reported that one out of four doctors now uses some form of electronic medical records, and the number is rising. In other countries, the use of electronic records is much more common (89 percent of British doctors and 98 percent of Dutch doctors use electronic records).[29] Proponents argue that the use of electronic records improves patient care, reduces errors, requires fewer tests, and cuts paperwork. But critics fear that patient confidentiality is endangered by the potential for unauthorized access by companies, the government, and hackers, and they fear misuse by "thieves, rascals, rogues, and unauthorized users," in one influential congressman's words.[30]

In his book *The Limits of Privacy,* Professor Amitai Etzioni describes worrisome unauthorized and authorized abuses of medical records.[31] Stealthily selling medical records for profit or prurient purposes or leaking such information to the press (as in the case of the disclosure of the tennis star Arthur Ashe's HIV status or a politician's mental-health condition) are obviously deplorable, if not criminal. Of more systemic concern, Professor Etzioni suggests, are modern shifts in the administration of medical practice—HMOs' demand for more detailed information about patients and the computerization and linkages of medical records to vast institutional organizations (marketers, employers, researchers, credit agencies).

Professor Etzioni deplores authorized abuses, such as disclosures of employees' medical records by insurance companies to employers, as more pernicious than rogue acts of unauthorized disclosure that are covered by laws. He describes a vast marketplace in which medical records are sold by state governments, medical clinics, and drugstore chains, and kept in an international clearinghouse, MIB. Thus, products can, coincidentally, be pitched to ailing patients. A national commission of health specialists complained that the "United States is in the midst of a health privacy crisis."[32] Quality and cost control, along with the needs of medical research, provide the rationale for collecting medical information. Are there ways to collect data for the benefit of the public while protecting patient privacy?

One answer is informed consent. If patients knowingly and freely agree to specific uses of their medical records, there is no breach of confidentiality. However, when patients are required as a condition of receiving medical treatment to waive confidentiality, as is the case nowadays, their "consent" cannot be said to be freely given. And if they are not apprised of all the possible uses of the information that they have released, their approval cannot be said to be "informed." The realities of modern medical practice suggest that informed consent is a charade.

Professor Etzioni and others suggest techniques to control the loss of patient confidentiality—access and audit trails that track uses of collected information, smart cards with patient information that the patient controls, interface procedures that convert personal records into non-identifiable information, and layering access to hospital records so that only those intermediaries (for example, a nurse) acting in the stead of the attending physician have access to the patients' records. Strong penalties are needed to punish those who breach the firewalls of confidentiality that preventative technology provides.

Another student of privacy, Judith Wagner DeCew, has sounded the alarm about the loss of patient confidentiality in the modern technological state. Improper access, exploitation, unauthorized disclosure, and errors are products of our information age that harm citizens. She writes: "The possibilities of exploiting, aggregating, or misusing this information, including genetic testing results, drug test data, mental health records, information on pregnancy, and results from tests for sexually transmitted diseases and HIV status, to name just a few, make it obvious how important it is to preserve the protection that privacy affords individuals."[33]

Vast databases in which medical and other patient information is collected exponentially increase the potential for the loss of patient confidentiality. The information collected includes examination results, medications prescribed, test results, genetic blueprints, and behavioral data (for example, information regarding exercise, smoking and drinking, sex practices). In 2008, it was revealed that the medical records of twenty-five hundred patients participating in a clinical trial conducted by the National Institutes of Health's National Heart, Lung, and Blood Institute were compromised. A researcher's laptop computer containing unencrypted medical records was stolen from his car. "Patients are likely to be reluctant to participate in clinical trials if their privacy is not respected," the *New York Times* editorialized.[34]

DeCew notes that in Europe, Germany, Sweden, and the Netherlands have developed policies regarding the access, use, and control of medical records. In the United States, government and business have resisted regulation on the grounds that their use of medical records improves medical care, aids in the detection of fraud, and serves public-health goals (for example, the prevention of diseases and other research). But dangers to personal privacy through access by "secondary users of health information" remain, and we must find practical and enforceable ways of controlling access to information before all patient confidentiality is lost to the new and growing technology.

HIPAA

The Health Insurance Portability and Accountability Act of 1996 (HIPAA) was a major attempt by the Clinton administration to set national standards to protect the confidentiality of medical records and personal health information. HIPAA covers health plans, health-care providers, and health-care clearinghouses—the major original sources of health information, collection, and transmittal.

Under HIPAA, an individual is entitled to access his or her medical records. Information that does not identify individuals is not covered by the act's disclosure restrictions. The HIPAA Privacy Rule provides twelve exceptions to the confidentiality requirements, including exceptions for disclosures for public-health or law-enforcement purposes, regarding abuse victims, required in connection with judicial proceedings, for research purposes, required for essential governmental functions, and in connection with workers' compensation. Written authorization by the patient is required for all unauthorized uses, such as marketing. There are civil monetary penalties for violations.

However well intended HIPAA may have been, in some respects HIPAA has created the worst of both worlds. Professionals committed to following HIPAA regulations initially reported being frustrated in their daily duties by absolutist rules and burdensome paperwork requirements that they consider counterproductive, faculty members of a university medical school told me. At the same time, abuses are compounded by outsiders who have exploited confidential patient records for their private profit and have avoided penalties.

Enforcement is vital for HIPAA to be meaningful. A medical journal reported that "multitudes of organizations received information about patients' health records often without their knowledge or consent. These include care providers, insurers, pharmacists, employee life insurance companies and marketing firms." These computerized medical records can be accessed, copied, distributed "with the click of a hacker's mouse."[35]

HIPAA is double-edged, noted one experienced observer. "It is the holy grail of medicine: the medical records, an intimate snapshot of past, present, and future, imbued with the potential to inform or destroy, a document that can provide a road map to a cure—or a blueprint for a firing or demotion."[36]

One decade after the passage of HIPAA, the medical establishment has been educated to monitor the confidentiality of patient records. Press reports noted that twenty-two thousand grievances have been lodged complaining of wrongful revelations of medical records; fourteen thousand of them were closed or corrected voluntarily, but no fines have been imposed for any violations and only two criminal cases have been prosecuted.[37] When information about the injuries suffered by the actor George Clooney and his girlfriend as a result of a motorcycle accident in New Jersey was leaked to the press, twenty-seven hospital employees were suspended for one month for violating patient confidentiality. The local union complained that the suspensions were an overreaction.[38] In 2008, California's health department and the UCLA Medical Center revealed that in "a pattern of repeated violations," sixty-one patients' medical records were improperly viewed by hospital employees and may have been leaked to the press.[39] Many of the patients were politicians or celebrities, including the actress Farrah Fawcett; California's First Lady, Maria Shriver; and the entertainer Britney Spears.

HIPAA has raised consciousness about the importance of confidentiality in a complex modern medical-care system and has set standards for maintaining confidentiality. Enforcement will be the key to its success.

Medical Confidentiality in the Twenty-first Century

The goal of medical confidentiality has not been reached. A report from the Privacy Rights Clearinghouse warns about the various holes in the wall of privacy of medical records.[40] After asking, "How privileged is my medical information?" the organization lists the various ways that one's medical records may fall into unauthorized hands, in and out of the health-care industry. MIB, which maintains a database of 15 million Americans, collects data required of health- and life-insurance applicants. Employers may ask for medical information as a condition of employment. Government agencies collect medical information (for example, regarding Medicare, Social Security, workers' compensation). Direct marketers who provide medical screenings in nonmedical settings collect information. The Internet captures private disclosures when, for example, someone accesses information from a Web site about a particular disease, as is common nowadays as people educate themselves about their maladies.

The Government Accountability Office warned that the confidentiality of patients' accumulated health records is inadequately protected from "evil, nefarious purposes." Thus, while the private sector races ahead, creating vast databases of health records, people's privacy is left at risk. One expert, Mark Rothstein, reported that Wal-Mart, Intel, and others were creating a database of over 2.5 million employees.[41]

A recent book concludes that medical records today serve an expanded role, beyond use in primary health care. They are used "by employers and insurance companies to decide who should be hired and insured," "by hospitals and religious organizations to solicit donations," by marketers who buy them "in search of sales leads."[42] In view of the access of employers, marketers, businesses, researchers, and the expanded community of health-care providers, confidentiality of medical information is endangered.

One European expert has concluded that as more and more of what she refers to as third- and fourth-party entities have become involved in medical practice, "it would be better speaking of the patient's right to control sources and flow of information. . . . The question we should address is not: 'who, when, and what is entitled to breach confidentiality?' but 'How can the patient control the information flow concerning his/her self?'"[43] The answer is blunt: patients cannot completely control their medical information. The solutions—imperfect as they are—must come from policies of supervision and enforcement of confidentiality rules.

The late scholar Zechariah Chafee Jr. remarked that "while the law has been so solicitous about the doctor's duty to keep silent on the witness-stand, it has done little to protect the patient's medical secrets from disclosure to the world in general."[44] The ideal of Hippocrates remains, thousands of years after it was articulated; but for medical confidentiality to prevail in modern times, consciousness and enforcement standards must be raised.

5

PSYCHOTHERAPISTS

> Certain patients want their treatment to be kept secret, often because they have kept their neurosis secret; and I put no obstacle in their way. That in consequence the world hears nothing of some of the most successful cures is of course a consideration that cannot be taken into account. It is obvious that the patient's decision in favor of secrecy already reveals a feature of his secret history.
>
> —Sigmund Freud, *On Beginning the Treatment*

Although the general doctor-patient privilege is not recognized in some states or in the federal courts, has been deemed by many leading scholars to have a questionable rationale, and has been threatened by the changing nature of modern practice and technology, a relatively modern privilege has been created for psychotherapists. This privilege covers physicians, along with psychologists and related mental-health and social workers who are not physicians.

In psychoanalysis, patients are encouraged to keep no secrets from their analysts, no matter how embarrassing or unpleasant or compromising their disclosures may be. Therefore, it is deemed crucial for psychotherapy, more so than for other forms of medical treatment, that patients have the assurance of confidentiality. Psychoanalysts "have spicier facts to relate than physicians," a leading scholar noted.[1] The *Ethics Case Book* of the American Psychoanalytic Association states, "Confidentiality is a cornerstone of psychoanalysis."[2]

Whereas medical practice has historical roots but at best has had inconsistent and incomplete privilege protections, psychiatry is relatively new but its protections are solicitous and embracive. A respected scholarly treatise in the field of evidence has called this hostility to the doctor-patient privilege and uncritical enthusiasm over the psychiatric privilege a "remarkable bit of ideological schizophrenia."[3]

Evolving notions about the duality of the mind, the conscious and the unconscious, the inner world of the human psyche, were refined by Sigmund Freud early in the twentieth century. Dynamic psychiatry based on scientific methods became a widely accepted practice. One chief ingredient of Freud's treatment modality was the intensely private patient-therapist relationship. Patients are urged to reveal their innermost uninhibited thoughts, no matter how absurd, offensive, or embarrassing. In Freud's words, "Say whatever goes through your mind. . . . Never forget that you have promised to be absolutely honest, and never leave anything out because . . . it is unpleasant to tell it."[4]

Analysis involves an intimate partnership, one in which the patient becomes aware of the underlying sources of his or her difficulties by reexperiencing them with the analyst. Psychoanalytic treatment traces patients' problems back to their historical origins, helping them deal better with the effect of those problems in their lives.[5] One federal court noted that a "psychotherapy patient's most intimate thoughts and emotions are exposed. . . . The psychiatric patient confides in his therapist more utterly than anyone else in the world. . . . He lays bare his entire self, his dreams, his fantasies, his sin, and his shame." Confidentiality is critical.[6]

Patients expose their dreams, fantasies, sins, and shame under their therapist's commitment of confidentiality. They are assured that their therapist will maintain the secrecy of their conversations. All therapists who now follow Freud's approach—physicians and others—seek protection of their communications during treatment. Some psychotherapists keep sparse notes of their patients' conversations (psychotherapists' notes are excluded from HIPAA's patient-access requirement). The identity of patients and records of their treatment may be disguised or avoided to protect their confidentiality. So serious do some therapists consider the anonymity of patients that many took umbrage over the portrayal of an analyst identifying another analyst's patient at a dinner party of therapists in an episode of

The Sopranos. "A very egregious ethical violation," one real-life state psychiatric ethics official complained.[7]

As a result of the wide resort to psychotherapy in the twentieth century, powerful cultural forces were brought to bear on courts for the protection of this expanding form of treatment.[8] By the second half of the twentieth century, these cultural changes had led to the broad social acceptance of psychotherapy. After World War II, more patients sought therapy, and psychotherapy evolved from being practiced only by psychiatrists and psychoanalysts to being practiced by psychologists, social workers, nontraditional mental-health professionals, counselors, and nonlicensed therapists as well. Economic factors such as coverage of some mental-health treatment by health-insurance companies expanded access to large segments of society.[9]

Professional organizations and commentators were making the case at that time that the intimate free association and utter trust that is required in classic Freudian psychoanalytical treatment demanded confidentiality. Patients had to expose their dreams, the darkest recesses of their minds, to their analysts for the process to work. For this intimacy to happen, there was a critical need for strict confidentiality.[10] Although the physician privilege was imperfect or absent, psychiatrists lobbied for a privilege of their own.

In 1952, an Illinois case held—for the first time—that the very nature of psychiatric practice requires confidentiality, more than does general medical practice.[11] Illinois (like a dozen other states at that time) had no doctor-patient privilege. But the Illinois court—comparing the relationship between psychiatrist and patient to the priest-penitent relationship—permitted an analyst to claim a privilege against testifying about his patient. It was "the first significant judicial recognition of a need for different standards of confidentiality for 'psychotherapy'," one study concludes.[12]

During this evolutionary period, not everyone saw the psychiatric privilege as unquestionable. A leading academic writer in the field of evidence offered a wry and cynical analysis of the psychiatric privilege, questioning why "no one seems to have found it odd that the law should exclude evidence to ease the minds of persons who are by hypothesis mentally disturbed." The unverifiability of the success of psychiatric treatment, along with some of its documented imperfections, led some insider-critics to warn that "if psychotherapy were a drug, the FDA would ban it."[13]

Although most psychiatric professionals believe confidentiality is essential on utilitarian grounds (no confidentiality, no communication), empirical tests of this thesis, a sympathetic study admits, "have yielded weak or inconclusive or mixed results."[14] Reports indicate that psychiatric practices have not been inhibited in places where no privilege exists.

A study in the late 1990s raised questions about the fundamental need for confidentiality. The study reported that there was "a substantial disparity between Freud's recommendations (about confidentiality) and his actual methods." In twenty-three of Freud's cases, confidentiality was breached 53 percent of the time. Freud talked about his analysands—who were identified—with others, including his colleague Sándor Ferenczi, with whom he discussed his love affair with a patient that Ferenczi had referred to him, and another colleague with whom he discussed his daughter Anna (whom he was analyzing). From 1907 to 1939, "Freud consistently deviated from his published recommendations on psychoanalytic technique."[15]

In fact, the confidentiality of analysis in Freud's era was not an ethical or legal consideration. It was no more than a recommendation to physicians that they might follow or ignore. The daughter of Wilhelm Reich wrote about the betrayal of her father by his analyst, who ignored "all modern rules of confidentiality regarding talking about one's patients."[16] In her 2007 book *Freud's Wizard,* Brenda Maddox describes the close relations between leading practitioners in the emerging analytic movement, noting instances in which analysts "placed professional fraternity over a patient's request for confidence." Leading figures in the movement shared patients' stories, and Maddox reports that "Freud was breaking the rules of psychoanalysis at the same time as making them."[17]

Historical hypocrisy aside, the privilege is also justified on humanistic and privacy grounds—it is morally repugnant to force a betrayal of trust in such a context. The privilege has not been accepted as a constitutionally based right of privacy, though this form of intimate personal treatment is viewed by advocates as a cultural or social right of privacy—if not a legally recognized one.

Nonetheless, experts Charles Alan Wright and Kenneth W. Graham Jr. suggest that there should be an inclusive but qualified "patient's privilege covering all therapeutic professionals who treat people's physical and mental well-being." They argue that psychiatry is less a science than general medicine: "The existence of a broken heart is less subject to verification than a broken leg"; if we decide to protect one kind of treatment, why not all?[18]

Confidentiality is considered to be the patient's right and the analyst's obligation. Infringement by courts, the insurance industry, managed-care bureaucrats, peer review, and educational and professional development require more attention within the profession, one recent study remarks.[19] Breaches of confidentiality are "ever-present" in the analyst's professional experiences and professional conferences. The analyst's information, another study notes, can be prejudicial or misleading in another context outside of professional treatment. There may be more danger from disclosure of psychiatric evidence than nondisclosure—unsubstantiated claims of recovered memory, for example—suggesting that balancing the public interest in otherwise privileged information can be a "slippery slope." Although some professionals think that there may be a greater danger to the public from disclosure than from nondisclosure, others believe that confidentiality in this setting should be viewed as a "skin rather than a lock," something that is flexible and able to stretch for therapeutic purposes.[20]

In 1975 Congress refused to pass proposed privilege statutes for the federal system and instead passed Federal Rule of Evidence 501, which covers civil and criminal cases. It confined to the courts the power to evolve appropriate rules of evidence "in light of reason and experience." The courts have been conservative in creating new privileges, denying claims by accountants and journalists and other groups. But all fifty states passed laws recognizing the psychotherapist-patient privilege. The scene was set for the U.S. Supreme Court to rule on this subject, and it did so near the end of the century.

In 1996 the Supreme Court dealt with extending the general state-recognized psychotherapist-patient privilege to licensed social workers performing comparable professional psychotherapy. The reasons offered for extending the privilege as an evolutionary process of federal common law permitted by the federal rules of procedure were persuasive, despite critics' complaints that extending the privilege would prevent access to critical facts in the search for justice in trials.

The case, *Jaffee v. Redmond*, arose in a civil suit against a former police officer who shot and killed a man while on duty and the Village of Hoffman Estates, Illinois, which employed her when she was on the police force. The victim was brandishing a butcher knife and attacking another man. He disregarded the police officer's order to drop his weapon. The victim's family sued, claiming that the police officer used excessive force in the tense encounter.

After the shooting, the officer participated in fifty counseling sessions with a licensed social worker employed by the Village of Hoffman Estates. During the trial, the judge ruled that there was no legal justification for refusing to allow discovery of the treatment records, and thus the presumption was that the withheld information would have been unfavorable. The Seventh Circuit reversed, holding that the prevailing psychotherapist privilege should apply to social workers. Other circuits had disagreed about the extension of the psychotherapist privilege, so the Supreme Court took the case to resolve the issue.

The Supreme Court agreed with the Seventh Circuit that the officer-patient's "ability, through counseling, to work out the pain and anguish . . . depended to a great deal upon her trust and confidence in her counselor." The majority (7–2) opinion written by Justice John Paul Stevens acknowledged the centuries-old maxim that the public has the right to everyone's evidence, and conceded that exceptions must be based on a greater public good, one that transcends the search for truth. The privilege in the present situation, the Court ruled, was based on the same idea underlying other protected communications—the need to be able to disclose sensitive "facts, emotions, memories, and fears" without fear of embarrassment or disgrace.[21]

The Court relied on the representation of the American Psychiatric Association, an amicus in the case, that "confidentially is a sine qua non for successful psychiatric treatment." Even though most treatment today is not performed by psychoanalysts or even by medical doctors, by its nature the communications are intimate and warrant privacy protections.

Justice Stevens wrote that "the mental health of our citizenry, no less than its physical health, is a public good of transcendent importance."[22] Ensuring such professional assistance to police officers who operate in particularly stressful situations is in the public interest. In psychiatry, more so than in other fields of medicine, it is widely understood that the success of the process depends on the patient's freedom to speak freely, without being concerned that his or her innermost private feelings will be disclosed. There is a stigma, too, about the need for psychiatric care, which underscores these patients' need for privacy.

Justice Stevens cited the fact that over the past quarter century all states had passed laws protecting social workers' private consultations with patients as a further reason to adopt a consistent federal common-law rule. As a practical matter, the Court noted that licensed psychologists and clinical social workers provide essentially the same psychotherapy for clients who cannot afford treatment by a psychiatrist. Logically, the same privilege should be available to clients of psychologists and social workers. Several years later, a cynical commentator noted that geographically, psychiatrists—like investment bankers—are found disproportionately (one out of three) in New York and California, suggesting that psychiatry is a "privilege of the rich."[23]

As a result of the *Jaffee* decision, what began as a quasi-medical privilege—and one whose application to physicians themselves has been questioned—has been recognized and made available to lay practitioners of mental-health services.

The Supreme Court noted studies offered by professional associations in favor of extending the medical privilege to therapists, but that data has been questioned as illusory, self-promotional, and based on scanty empirical evidence. As Professor Imwinkelried has noted, "available studies . . . do not bear out the assumption that . . . the evidentiary privilege has a major influence" on the typical patient.[24] Patients are more concerned with their imminent health problems and less aware of later litigation possibilities. And they are more mindful of personal privacy such as confidentiality with employers or in other personal situations than potential later litigation.

Justice Antonin Scalia and Chief Justice William Rehnquist dissented in the *Jaffee* case. The cost of excluding reliable and probative evidence, they reminded us, is "occasional injustice." In such cases, the justices complained, courts do "not merely . . . let stand a wrong," but they may themselves become "instruments of wrong" by erecting a barrier to the truth.[25]

When do the extensions of privileged communications end, the justices asked. Why not a parent-child privilege (as some European countries recognize), or one between a teacher and student? How about bartenders, they facetiously suggested. Their remark is reminiscent of one congressman's fear that, if the legislature was to create a new privilege, a Pandora's box of exceptions would result from lobbying pressures—even "social workers and . . . piano tuners" will be claiming privileges, he quipped.[26] In another "where will it ever end" aside in a case denying a privilege claimed by a university for its peer-review process, Justice Harry Blackmun noted his fear that comparable claims could be made by employment associations, writers, publishers, even musicians.[27]

Like Bentham centuries earlier, the *Jaffee* dissenters admonished that the Court's ruling ignored a "traditional judicial preference for the truth." They noted that in ten states the psychiatrist-patient privilege does not apply to social workers; that state definitions of social workers vary; that social workers are not professionals in the same way as lawyers, doctors, and clergy; and that states that do cover social workers have various exceptions to the privilege. They noted that fourteen organizations offered amicus briefs supporting the extension of the privilege to social workers, but they—the judges—stood alone "in pursuit of the truth in the federal courts."[28]

The two dissenters' view of professionals seems narrow (social workers are licensed), but their sense of humor shone through when they wondered, facetiously, where the trend would end. Don't people turn for mental-health advice, the dissenters asked, to "parents, siblings, best friends, and bartenders?"[29] Why is there not a mother-child privilege? How about a cab driver–passenger privilege, another gibing commentator remarked. The answer, of course, is that people may seek confidentiality in all quarters, but courts should be chary about extending privileges as liberally.

There is a need to draw lines in situations where the privilege does exist. Social workers often work in groups of collaborating professionals. They frequently work with medical officials on cases involving sexually transmitted diseases, for example, HIV. Social workers may be notified about cases by the attending physician and asked to assist in screening for applicable programs, working with families, and doing community outreach. At that point, the confidentiality of the relationship between patient and physician is lost, as others become privy to confidential information that will not be privileged. "The priority is that they trust us," one Miami social worker told me, describing her quandary over protecting the confidentiality of her patients, and recognizing that confidentiality is lost when others in the community are made aware of a client's medical problem. Also prejudicial is the access of government agents who are notified of the client's problem through the collection of data about socially embarrassing diseases.

Sometimes it is the law itself that creates dilemmas for social workers. My daughter, a social worker, counseled a young girl whose father was abusive. New York law required that she (my daughter) report the abuse to a government agency. If he was reported, the father would lose his temporary citizenship and work status, which would be a serious blow to the whole family, her young ward pleaded. My daughter feared that disclosure would be more harmful than consulting with the family and attempting to cure the problem. But she had no choice in the matter; the law was clear and she followed it—against her professional judgment. Other social workers have complained about their difficulty balancing their need to preserve the confidentiality of their patients' comments with laws mandating the reporting of such problems as suicide, homicide, and abuse.

As social workers perform an expanding array of professional services, confounding questions about confidentiality arise. A case in the District of Columbia dealt with two interesting questions: Who is covered by the social-worker privilege? And when is an exception to that privilege warranted?

The defendant in the case, Graham, sexually abused the child of his sometime girlfriend. When he went to a homeless shelter, he was required as a condition of admission to be interviewed by the shelter's social worker. He confessed the incident, was reported, and was indicted. At his trial, he attempted to keep out his confession to the social worker under the psychotherapist-patient privilege and under the Fifth Amendment, claiming that he was compelled to confess as a condition of entering the shelter.

The D.C. Court of Appeals ruled that the social worker, though unlicensed, was a health professional under the local statute.[30] The court also upheld a D.C. law that permitted disclosure of privileged communications "in the interest of public justice."[31] The court cited an Indiana case that noted that there is a "tension . . . between the privilege and the duty to report." Most states have privilege statutes but also mandate the reporting of acts of serious violence. The D.C. exception "in the interest of public justice" is a wise way to strike a balance between two competing laws. Since Graham was not compelled to go to the shelter, the court decided that disclosure of his confession to the social worker would not violate the self-incrimination clause of the Fifth Amendment.

What about group therapy sessions? There, no one-on-one relationship exists between patient and therapist. Other nonprofessionals are present.

In the notorious murder trial of Michael Skakel for clubbing to death Martha Moxley, a young woman who was his neighbor, controversial testimony was offered regarding his remarks at a group therapy session at a substance-abuse rehabilitation center. There, when questioned by other residents, Skakel made arguably incriminating admissions that he did not know if he killed her. One resident testified that Skakel told him that he (Skakel) did murder Moxley. "Michael was sobbing and crying. It was a really emotional thing," a prosecution witness, a former resident at Skakel's treatment center, testified.[32] His comments to the group were allowed as evidence.

The *Jaffee* ruling notwithstanding, not every claim of privilege by nonmedical therapists has been accepted by the courts.[33] In two homicide trials, one in Bangor, Maine, and the other in Larchmont, New York, state courts refused to extend the social-worker privilege to Alcoholics Anonymous (AA) members who claimed that the organization's twelve-step self-help program should qualify them as akin to protected mental-health practitioners.[34] Admissions to fellow AA members by suspects, however therapeutic, were not considered equivalent to the protected communications between patients and more traditional nonmedical, licensed mental-health providers or between clergy and penitents. Arguments that AA members offered assistance that is based on similar social values were not accepted.

There is a prevailing notion among participants in group therapy that all comments at such therapy sessions are confidential. *Confidential*, yes, but not *privileged*.

And even one-on-one therapy sessions by lay therapists raise questions. "We have no criteria when to breach confidentiality," one conflicted social worker pleaded to me. "When should I call a spouse or parent or health or legal authority because I *think,* but I don't *know,* that there is a danger to my patient that requires more than my therapeutic assistance?"

A spin-off of the *Jaffee* privilege is the privilege accorded to communications between crime victims and victims' counselors (including rape crisis counselors). Conversations between rape victims or battered spouses and victims' counselors are privileged by statute in over half the states. Communications by injured women, in pain and in danger, are obviously sensitive, embarrassing, and very personal. No one would deny the need for confidentiality in such a setting. The question of privilege is more perplexing, as illustrated by the case of the military cadet charged with raping a classmate, described in the introduction. These counselors may become adjuncts to attorneys and physicians of the victims, and come under the protection of their privileges. But the defendant in a criminal trial has a constitutional right to confront his accuser, to defend himself, and to present exculpatory or damaging evidence about the complaining victim. How should these conflicting claims be balanced? In one case, a military court judge ordered the arrest of a rape counselor who refused to release records of therapy sessions with two cadets who had been raped. She said that she was prepared to go to jail rather than release counseling records, which would intimidate victims. The defendant argued that his right to a fair trial outweighed the claimed privacy rights. The counselor was forced to choose between "justice and healing," she claimed.[35] One must distinguish carefully between confidentiality (which certainly is warranted) and privilege (which may not protect otherwise confidential communications from being admitted as evidence in trials).

The extensive use of group therapy for mental-health treatment is not the only phenomenon that undercuts the rationale for the privilege—namely, that without privacy patients won't open up about their mental problems. "Psycho-mikers," public talk shows on radio and television in which people's problems are aired before a wide audience, suggest that some troubled souls are open about their problems. Psychiatrists themselves sometimes write or lecture about their patients in ways that may or may not be transparent. The common tendency to explore all problems publicly—in memoirs, cable-television talk shows, advice columns—runs counter to the arguable need for complete confidentiality in these personal situations.

* * *

Confidentiality in the psychiatric context is a complicated issue, as was dramatically demonstrated in what a California court called "the tragedy of Tatiana Tarasoff."[36] A voluntary outpatient being treated by therapists at the University of California told them that he was going to kill Tatiana. The examining psychologist and two supervising psychiatrists thought that he should be committed for observation at a mental hospital. Their boss, the chief of the department of psychiatry, overruled them, and the man was released to the campus police. Satisfied that he was rational, the campus police released the young man after he promised to stay away from Tatiana. The troubled patient then went to Tatiana's apartment and killed her. No one warned her or her family of the threat—a fatal error of judgment, it turned out.

When the family sued, a divided state supreme court ruled that "when a therapist determines, or . . . should determine that his patient presents a serious danger of violence to another, he incurs an obligation to use reasonable care to protect the intended victim against such danger."[37] The result to Tatiana, the court decided, was a foreseeable danger, and the doctors had a duty to warn the likely victim of the risk she faced, and might have avoided.

It was not always so. At a meeting of a Chicago psychoanalytic organization before the *Tarasoff* decision, one analyst reported his treatment of a recidivist pedophile patient. Few of his colleagues questioned whether he had any obligation to report his patient's antisocial behavior to law-enforcement authorities. Most of his colleagues who were present focused on his treatment techniques. When one participant questioned why he did not deal with his patient's recidivism, the presenting analyst replied: "What can I do?" The profession's general view at that time was that the patient's comments during treatment were confidential and sacrosanct.

That a psychiatrist has a duty not only to patients but also to threatened third parties was a controversial ruling, but it is now followed generally, despite expert reports that therapists cannot reliably predict violent acts. The American Psychiatric Association advised the Supreme Court in one case that "psychiatric prediction of dangerousness is less accurate than chance" and that two out of three predictions are wrong.[38] The late justice Byron White noted that the association's opinion was disputed by many of its members and that its suggestion that psychiatrists should not be asked to make such a prediction was like asking one "to disinvent the wheel."[39] Predictions like this are made at various times in judicial proceedings and must be weighed, even if such predictions are not invariably correct.

There is now a settled public interest in protecting people from violence, even if that involves breaching the patient's confidentiality. The same thinking has been applied to other confidential relationships and ought to be applied to still others.

The *Tarasoff* court ruled that "by entering into a doctor-patient relationship the therapist becomes sufficiently involved to assume some responsibility for the safety, not only of the patient himself, but also of any third person whom the doctor knows to be threatened by the patient."[40]

A thoughtful dissenting opinion in that case noted that there is impressive professional literature that "psychiatric predictions of violence are inherently unreliable." As this jurist reminded us, "however desirable an infallible crystal ball might be, it is not among the tools of their profession." In his judgment, the ruling—now general practice—will cripple psychiatric practice because patients requiring psychotherapeutic dialogue will fail to communicate. If that occurs, the public will be more endangered than ever. To be safe from being second-guessed, the jurist feared, doctors will overpredict violence and will be more likely to commit patients. If there is to be a sacrificing of treatment of the mentally ill to a system of warning, that should come from the legislature, he suggested.[41] Indeed, state statutes now mandate that psychotherapists warn people who are endangered by their patients.

Fears that the *Tarasoff* ruling would hamper psychiatric treatment generally have proved to be baseless. There is no duty to disclose, an Iowa court ruled, if the potential victim knows of the danger.[42] If a patient is found to be a danger to himself or others, a privilege should not get in the way of taking discrete, prudent, professional action. As the California Supreme Court concluded: "The protective privilege ends where the public peril begins."[43] There is a societal interest in not concealing lethal information.

In 1980, a federal court in Nebraska followed the *Tarasoff* ruling that psychiatrists have a duty to warn others of their patients' dangerous proclivities.[44] In that case, an outpatient being treated at a Veterans Administration mental-health clinic bought a shotgun at Sears, entered an Omaha nightclub, and shot two people, killing one. The Nebraska court, like the California court, ruled that a special relationship exists between doctors and patients, creating a duty to warn third parties or to take precautionary steps to forestall foreseeable violence. A New Jersey court had ruled similarly in a comparable case a year earlier.[45]

A close friend and former colleague of mine, a well-known journalist and former government official, endured such an experience. A deranged young man did not know him personally but became fixated on him. My friend was warned first by local police and later by the man's psychiatrist, who advised him that her patient had a homicidal fixation on him. After repeated personal encounters, the patient's pursuit ended. But the experience was terrible, and the rationale for the exception to the rule of confidentiality was manifest.

Reasonable as the *Tarasoff* warning rule may be, it does raise potential problems for physicians generally, as well as for psychiatrists and other mental-health professionals. Doctors face daunting questions about foreseeability and their duty to warn third parties of their patients' confidential medical situations. Two cases, with opposing conclusions, suggest that doctors may need lawyers on call to advise them about their nonmedical duties.

A troubling spin-off of this privilege arose in a case in Maryland.[46] A psychiatrist testified in a bitter, contested divorce proceeding that the mother, his patient, was a fit custodian of her two children, also his patients. The husband complained to the medical board that the psychiatrist overmedicated his patients. The board demanded the patient's records. The doctor objected, claiming that the information was privileged. The stressful and expensive complaint dragged on for five years, with many hearings in which professional organizations supported the doctor's claim of confidentiality.

Awkward situations occasionally are created by the fact that only the patient can waive confidentiality. Patients, for example, may criticize a therapist—sometimes these criticisms are quite prejudicial to the therapists' reputations and careers. I defended a renowned analyst against charges of misconduct by an analysand and discovered that his colleagues had varied and conflicting views about the governing rules of confidentiality. Managing his defense was exacting and perplexing for this reason, among others.

Sometimes, the therapist and the patient's lawyer are at odds over what is in the patient's best interest. In a case in which I represented a rape victim in a civil suit against her landlord, her therapist refused to cooperate because she thought that putting her patient through the rigors of a trial would exacerbate her already fragile condition. Yet not pursuing litigation deprived the victim of necessary monetary reparations. I could not discuss her psychological injuries with anyone except her therapist, who refused to testify. The applications of these rules in practice are tricky—in that case, prejudicial—however clear the reason for the rules may be.

Refusing to expand the *Tarasoff* thinking to nonpsychiatric physicians, in 1995 a Florida court held that a doctor had no obligation to warn his patient's daughter that her mother's cancer was hereditary. The daughter claimed that he should have told her that she was at risk and should take preventive steps. The court considered such a duty to be too heavy a burden.[47] However, in 1996 a New Jersey court held that a doctor did have a duty to warn his patient's daughter that her father had colon cancer. When she sued her father's doctor's estate twenty-six years later, the court ruled that the doctor should have breached his patient's confidentiality and told his daughter of the medical danger so that she could have monitored her condition and detected and treated her condition early.[48]

Given the state of advancing genetic knowledge, what new duties do physicians have to report their patients' conditions to others, and with what damage to their patients' confidentiality? What is the precedential impact of *Tarasoff* in other medical contexts—for example, the optometrist and neurologist mentioned in chapter 4 who were conflicted about the need to report patients to public authorities when they foresee public dangers in their patients' conditions?

To this strained status of confidentiality in the treatment of mental-health patients must be added the caveat about the impact of new technology on patient privacy. Whatever the rules of evidence may be about forcing disclosure of mental-health records, the fact of modern life is that these records of people's most private and intimate personal problems are available to insurance providers and to intrepid, if illegal, hackers. Furthermore, confessions and discussions of people's eccentricities are common in the media, shocking proof that many patients (or "should-be" patients) do not respect their own confidentiality.

Reviewing a book on psychotherapy and confidentiality in the *New England Journal of Medicine,* a lawyer-doctor noted the many nontherapeutic purposes for which the diagnostic and predictive judgments of health professionals may be required by law to be revealed. In situations as diverse as "criminal responsibility, tort liability, insurability, career advancement . . . litigants, insurers, employers, and public officials" commonly require medical and mental health officials to reveal intimate patient information. Thus, he asserted, any suggestion that these privileged communications are confidential is "largely illusory." In conflicts between the law and the therapeutic perspective, he concluded, "reflexive deference to the law" is the general rule.[49] This sentiment prompted a psychoanalyst to wonder aloud to me, "Are there any secrets anymore?"

Other critics have suggested that "confidentiality in psychoanalysis and psychotherapy is a shambles," as a result of "the demands of managed care for detailed reports" and "broad computerization of confidential information" and the "American culture of disclosure."[50] Others have criticized the practice of disguised clinical accounts of patients as sacrificing patient anonymity for the furtherance of scientific study.[51]

Today, secrets, even those intimate ones communicated between patients and professional or lay mental-health therapists, may be shared in some situations. If it is appropriate to breach confidentiality in limited cases involving other privileged communications, why exalt the therapeutic relationship by considering it sacrosanct? To do so would underscore and stigmatize the negative image of this one kind of sickness over others. The conclusion that one is led to is that in all the situations mentioned—formal psychoanalytical sessions, discussions with social workers, group therapy sessions—confidentiality should be a governing principle, but privilege is not an absolute concept. As one court warned, the privilege should not be "frozen into the rigidity of absolutism."[52]

6

THE PASTORAL PRIVILEGE

> From whom did you receive that watch?
> WITNESS: I received it in connection with the confessional.
> HILL, J: You are not asked at present to disclose anything stated to you in the confessional; you are asked a simple fact—from whom did you receive that watch you gave to the policeman?
> WITNESS: The reply . . . would implicate the person. . . . Therefore I cannot answer it. . . . My suspension for life would be above a necessary consequence. I should be violating the laws of the Church, as well as the natural laws.
> HILL, J: . . . You are bound to answer. . . . You are not asked to disclose anything that a penitent may have said to you in the confessional. Do you answer it, or do you not?
> WITNESS: I really cannot, my lord.
> HILL, J: . . . Take him into custody.
> The witness was accordingly removed in custody.
>
> —*Regina v. Hay* (1860)

The rationale behind claims for a pastoral privilege covering confessions to clergy, although akin to the psychotherapeutic need for confidentiality, has a unique history. Psychotherapy in the secular world seeks to restore mental health to people by discovering the source of and assuaging their psychological torment and estrangement. In the religious world, there is a comparable search for forgiveness to expiate guilt and anxiety. That process is augmented by confession to representatives of God who, in his name, may forgive. One religious scholar, commenting on the function of religious counseling, used language reminiscent of mental-health terminology—"to help people handle their anxieties, guilts, fears, rages, doubts, and despairs."[1] The clever aphorist Oscar Wilde noted that "it is the confession, not the priest, that gives us absolution."[2]

Both forms of assistance—psychoanalytic and religious—require confidentiality to protect and encourage the acknowledgment of sickness in one case and of sin in the other. Psychoanalytic treatment is available to those who can afford it; religious confession to all who practice religion. In each case, the confessor has a need to confess and a hope for absolution.

One federal court in California considered, but rejected, the claim that the state's conditional privilege for psychoanalysts was unconstitutionally discriminatory because the state's clergy privilege was absolute. The appellate court ruled that the distinction did not impermissibly discriminate between those who sought counseling from clergy and those who consulted therapists.[3] Similarly, a California Supreme Court case held that a legislatively created absolute privilege for clergy did not render a lesser privilege for psychotherapists a denial of equal protection of the law, even though both clergy and psychotherapists provide a "sanctuary for the disclosure of emotional distress," and perform similar functions to serve similar needs.[4]

Whether a disorder is an illness requiring psychotherapeutic treatment or a moral infirmity requiring religious absolution, whether an individual's mind or soul is in need of repair, whether psychoanalysis or auricular confession is the answer, confidentiality is claimed by both professions if either process is to work.[5]

There are, of course, fundamental differences between pastoral and therapeutic practices. Under state laws, both clergy and therapists have a duty to warn third parties of their patients' proclivities to harm others, as the *Tarasoff* rule made clear (see chapter 5). But that exception to the pastoral privilege is treated differently by different churches. Although clergy and mental-health practitioners often act in similar situations—providing matrimonial advice and succor, and confessional assistance to criminals in and out of prisons, for example—their social responsibilities in these contexts vary depending on church rules. However comparable some of their features may be, their very different histories and roles fundamentally separate the two professions and their practices.

The first admonition of the Catholic Church about confession was in the fifth century, according to a study of religious confession. Pope Leo I decreed that confessions made to God via the priest for penance were "not to be revealed." By the ninth century, the church first legislated on the subject. Priests would be dishonored for violating the confession. They could be "made to do penance in perpetual pilgrimage, deprived of all honor." By the fifteenth century, "canonists and theologians [were] unanimous in emphasizing the strict obligation of the seal of confession."[6] Since the Middle Ages, "the seal [has bound] the lips of every priest." By the twentieth century, canon law decreed that "the sacramental seal is inviolable," and excommunication would be the price for its breach.[7]

Although all clergy offer private counseling, it is an article of faith in the Catholic religion that confessions are sacrosanct requirements for the confessor's salvation. Priests would be subject to excommunication and disgrace, to eternal damnation, if they were to reveal confessions. The clergy privilege covers members of the clergy who have a religious duty to keep confessions secret.

The clergy privilege recognizes the sanctity of confession and is based on the notion that confession soothes "the torments of a wounded conscience" and that it would be iniquitous to fail to protect the confidentiality of the confessional. The assistance to justice that might be lost by protecting confidentiality would be minimal, whereas the conflicts caused by violating this trust would be harmful to practitioners of their faith. Confessions may prevent mischief rather than hide it, advocates of privilege point out. Even the prominent opponent of privileges, the influential legal philosopher Jeremy Bentham, argued that it would be an unjust persecution to punish Catholics for following their religion's essential dictates.[8]

According to Catholic dogma, what a priest knows from confession he knows as a "representative of God, and not through human knowledge"; thus he is detached from it "as if he knows nothing." In the view of the Catholic Church, that information is beyond the control of the temporal courts.[9] An authoritative study reported that "no matter what a court may require, no matter what personal inconvenience or incarceration may result, unless he has the permission of the penitent the priest cannot reveal the contents of the confessional. To do so would violate divine, natural, and ecclesiastical law and subject him to permanent excommunication."[10]

One high-ranking Catholic Church official remarked that "the good of religion prevails over the good of justice."[11] Priests are subject to an inviolable sacramental seal of silence. They are to have no mortal remembrance of confessions; they hold information from confessions for God's ears. If a priest violates this rule, he commits a crime against the church and a sin against God, and he could be excommunicated. Failing to confess mortal sins can result in eternal damnation, according to Catholic Church law. Confessors themselves are required to confess, or suffer loss of salvation. There is no room for exceptions.

When Pope John Paul II visited the man who had attempted to assassinate him in 1981, he told reporters, "What we talked about will have to remain a secret between him and me."[12] If the pope himself abides by the sanctity of the confessional, it is unlikely that a local priest would not.

But man's law is not necessarily the same as God's law. The law of the state differs from the law of the Catholic Church. There was no clergy-penitent privilege in the early English common law. The privilege was first recognized as a result of the religious influences of the Catholic Church on the English courts after the Norman conquest in the early eleventh century. The Catholic Church was the national church then. Its laws prevailed and were observed by the king and the people, and enforced by ecclesiastical judges.

That certain laws are greater than those of the state, that mortal authorities may not override those heavenly statutes, are ancient and parochial views, not endorsed by the majority of people in the United States today.

The ancient rule of privileged communications between priest and penitent lasted until the Reformation in the sixteenth century. With the rise and influence of the Anglican Church, in which confession was voluntary, English common law denied the existence of a priest-penitent privilege that exempted clergy from the obligation to disclose the truth in legal proceedings.[13] By the mid-seventeenth century, the privilege had vanished from English law. Blackstone's classic treatise does not mention a confessional privilege. Many countries provide no privilege for religious confessions. The Catholic Church prospered through the post-Reformation centuries and to the present time without it.

Following the prevailing English practices, American common law originally denied the privilege. A privilege was first recognized in a New York case in 1813 as a necessary part of the freedom of religion of Catholic worshippers. In that case, a priest returned stolen goods to the owner but refused to reveal who gave him the items. The New York court protected the priest's privilege as a First Amendment freedom-of-religion right.[14] Four years later, the privilege was denied to a Protestant minister because confession was not a required part of that clergyman's religion.[15] Later, to avoid the appearance of partiality to one religion, New York passed a statute making the privilege available to all denominations.

Courts have followed the Wigmorean approach in judging when confidential communications between clergy and their parishioners is privileged. Wigmore's four criteria for permitting the privilege are (1) that the communication originated in confidence; (2) that confidentiality is essential to the relation; (3) that the community fosters that relation; and (4) that, on balance, the injury to the relationship caused by disclosure would be greater than any benefit to the litigation. It is this fourth criterion that raises a question about the appropriateness of an absolute privilege to protect all priestly confessions.

Most states now have statutes sanctioning the privilege for confessions of sins to religious ministers (of all faiths), but these statutes generally do not cover other pastoral communications. The U.S. Supreme Court has not ruled directly on the availability of this privilege, though it has said, in dicta, that this privilege "recognizes the human need to disclose to a spiritual counselor, in total and absolute confidence . . . flawed acts or thoughts and to receive priestly consolation and guidance in return."[16] The Supreme Court has approved Federal Rule of Evidence 506, and the *Model Code of Evidence* acknowledges the protection of confessional confidences.

The rationale, one court noted, is that "the rules of evidence have always been concerned not only with truth but with the manner of its ascertainment."[17] By the twenty-first century, the number of confessions had decreased, according to informed observers. The privilege, however, has become widely accepted, perhaps suggesting that the one is not predicated on the availability of the other.

The prevailing pastoral privilege is not an absolute privilege. Most laws exclude from the privilege communications regarding certain kinds of conduct and mandate that clergy report this conduct to appropriate authorities. Since most churches do not consider confessions a sacred sacrament to be absolutely protected, ministers, rabbis, and others have operated under a qualified privilege. Along with the Catholic Church, the

Episcopal Church also has a rubric declaring that "the secrecy of a confession is morally absolute for the confessor and must under no circumstances be broken." Thus, Episcopal clergy too are bound to absolute secrecy of penitential disclosures and "the obligation rises above the demands of the civil legal system."[18]

But the privilege claimed by these churches is not a part of general secular law in America today. Courts have ruled that even if clergy lose some of their esteem in their parochial communities and may be hampered in providing their professional services, they are not legally justified in violating laws requiring disclosure. Victims of crimes by priests, crimes that have only recently come to light, see the church's claim of privilege as a cover-up.

The privilege has it perversities as well as its benign compassion, especially for Catholics living in a secular society. In the 1953 Alfred Hitchcock film *I Confess,* a priest refused to disclose that his parishioner confessed to a murder that he, the priest, was suspected of committing. His priestly obligation to preserve his penitent's privacy was so profound that it prevailed over his personal need for self-defense. He would not divulge information that could have cleared him of the murder. This conundrum arises in real life as well—and not only in situations involving noble conduct.

Late one night in September 1987, Jose Antonio Rivera and his girlfriend were drinking in a Bronx public park when they were attacked and chased by a group of young men. Rivera was stabbed and beaten to death with a baseball bat and sticks. A few days later, his girlfriend—the sole witness—identified Jose Morales and Ruben Montalvo from a lineup as the attackers. The defendants claimed that they were innocent and refused a plea bargain that would have sent them to prison for one and a half to three years on a reduced charge. They were tried for murder, convicted, and sentenced to fifteen years in prison.

Twelve years later, a local priest, Father Joseph Towle, publicly disclosed that after the trial but before sentencing, Jesus Fornes, a teenager in his parish, had told him, at the boy's home, that he was guilt-ridden because he had committed the murder and the two others were about to be punished for it. At the time, the priest advised the youngster to admit his crime to the authorities, and gave him absolution for his sin. Fornes then went to a legal-aid lawyer, who told him that he could "conceivably be throwing away his life" if he confessed. Fornes had earlier told the two defendants' lawyers of his involvement, and they told the judge. But the judge would not accept the "second hand" report of the confession by the defense lawyers (by this time Fornes had invoked the Fifth Amendment and refused to testify).

Ten years later, while Morales and Montalvo were still in prison, Fornes was killed, and Father Towle agonized over whether he could then publicly disclose the information he knew from Fornes's confession. Officials at his diocese advised that the conversation was not a confession but a "heart-to-heart" talk, so the priest would not be excommunicated for violating the Catholic sacramental seal of silence. One wonders why that conclusion was not reached when it could have avoided a miscarriage of justice. The prosecutors refused to agree to Morales's and Montalvo's attorneys' request for release. An appeal was made to a federal court, and that judge ruled that Morales and Montalvo should be released, concluding that the confession raised at least a reasonable doubt as to their guilt. Before they were released, they had served thirteen years in prison.[19] Two "confidential" conversations—one with a priest, another with a lawyer—were considered more sacred than ensuring justice at a trial and avoiding tragically improper imprisonments.

In another case, an Episcopal priest, faced with a similar dilemma, followed a different course. According to a press report, an Episcopal chaplain at a detention center reported that an inmate confessed to a double murder. The confessor believed that the conversation was confidential, but since it was not a sacramental confession, the priest did not think that it was confidential. The priest told the Associated Press, "There was a young man here, suicidal, torn apart by what had happened. There were two young men—one of them just a boy—lying dead in a field somewhere. Their families were grieving; a decision had to be made."[20]

The military chaplain's response to his divided responsibilities was more sympathetic than that of the New York priest. Of course, as experts on the subject have warned, the chaplain's behavior "does serious harm to the principle of confidential communications with chaplains. If every minister, priest, or rabbi took this course in resolving the personal tensions and the ethical or spiritual problems presented in the confidential relationships . . . there would be little left of the principle—and much less reason for troubled persons to seek the counsel of spiritual advisors . . . trusted with the secrets of troubled souls."[21]

Catholic priests are not the only clergymen who abide by the absolute sanctity of the confessional. An Arizona man reportedly molested thirty-three young girls, including his daughter, in a twenty-year period. Church of Jesus Christ of Latter-Day Saints officials knew of the predator's problem because he had sought their help. He was referred to lay clergymen, who eventually excommunicated him but did not report his misconduct.[22] Texas now has a law requiring disclosure in cases like this, but it is what one commentator called a "lame duck" law because no prosecutions of clergy have been brought under it.[23]

Deferring justice and social well-being to the inviolability of the Catholic confessional led to a horrible result in Langenberg, Germany. A young butcher's apprentice confessed to committing a ghastly murder to his priest, who maintained the confidentiality of the information. Like Father Towle, he urged the young man to surrender to the police. The confessor later sexually tortured and murdered three eleven-year-old boys before he was caught four years later. He then confessed to seventy other attempted crimes.[24]

The Catholic Church is not only protective of its members, but also self-protective. When the Catholic Church set up a panel to look into its far-flung and historic sexual-abuse scandal, bishops refused to provide requested information. The panel chairman resigned, stating that the clergy "turned to their lawyers when they should have looked into their hearts."[25] Cynics and victims have challenged the church's interests, asserting that its policy protected repeated criminal acts.

In recent years the Catholic Church in the United States has been sued successfully and repeatedly by parishioners, most of whom had been abused, as children, by priests. The plaintiffs claimed that church officials were aware of the priests' dispositions to commit abuses but did nothing to stop them, in part because church officials deemed their evidence to be encumbered by the rules of the confessional. Prototypical were the cases investigated and reported by the State of New Hampshire in 2003. The investigators discovered that the diocese, with knowledge of the misconduct, took no action to punish or stop eight priests who committed multiple and repeated sexual assaults against underage boys. Indictments against the diocese were dropped when church officials agreed to safeguard children in the future, to report abuses, and to allow their efforts to be audited.[26]

The Catholic Church has settled 3,000 civil cases around the country regarding similar known patterns of abuse, usually settling the complaints confidentially. (The subject of confidential settlements is discussed in chapter 8.) The problem is most serious when clergy are themselves the abusers of children. Over 13,000 youngsters were known to be abused by priests; 300 priests were convicted of crimes, and 1,000 were severed from the ministry.[27] Litigation years later revealed that the church's sins had been concealed.

In recent decades the Roman Catholic Church in the United States has paid over $2.6 billion to thousands of victims of predatory priests, causing some archdioceses to go bankrupt and sell their property. The Boston archdiocese paid $85 million to settle over 550 claims; the Los Angeles archdiocese paid $650 million to settle over 500 claims. In San Diego, the diocese paid 144 people nearly $200 million for sexual molestations of youngsters occurring between 1938 and 1993.[28]

Historically, the church had covered up complaints about priests' misconduct, allowing them to continue their misconduct. One complainant asked, "Where can you take that check and cash it that will make you ten years old again?"[29] A law professor, expert in church-state cases, also noted that "these cases really are about the secrets . . . not about money."[30]

Not all the abuses by Catholic clergy involved the failure to disclose confidential communications and thus the decision to allow crimes to continue or go undetected. Nor were they based on church officials hiding behind confidential resolutions of complaints against clergy. Indeed, many offenses involved clergy using their confidential settings to engage in misconduct, a 2008 book reports. One investigation revealed that a brother had been guilty of a "violation of the seal of the confession, the illegitimate use against the penitent of confidential information revealed during the confession," among other sins. In this author's conclusion, the scandals were the result of "a clericalist mentality" that defended clergy rather than protecting the wards of the church.[31] The problems of confidentiality played a major part in this pathetic episode of church history.

Noting an unprecedented crisis in the church in the United States, the Conference of Catholic Bishops acknowledged that "secrecy has created an atmosphere that has inhibited the healing process and, in some cases, enabled sexually abusive behavior to be repeated." Protecting children, the bishops' report stated, is the mission of the church and its creator. Among its promises was "not [to] enter into confidentiality agreements except for grave and substantial reasons" and to commit to "transparency and openness." The report calls on church authorities to report an allegation of sexual abuse of a minor to public authorities and to comply with all civil laws.[32]

Although the general pastoral privilege has its origins in the Roman Catholic sacrament of penance, every state now has some version of a pastoral privilege in its statutes. The privilege protects all clergy, ministers, rabbis, and priests, generically, including leaders of nontheistic systems such as Ethical Culture, as long as they have religious roots. The federal government recognizes the privilege as well through the common law and Supreme Court dicta. The privilege is based on a recognition of the human need to disclose flawed acts and thoughts to spiritual counselors in order to receive consolation and guidance. One jurist wrote, in florid prose, that regardless of one's religion, a person whose "conscience is shrunken and whose soul is puny, enters the clergyman's door in despair and gloom" to find consolation and hope and resuscitation. "The clergymen practice the thought that the finest of all altars is the soul of any unhappy man who is consoled and thanks God."[33]

State laws vary, though most cover all religious officials, confine the privilege to the penitent, and have expanded their coverage of clergy and the scope of the communications covered.[34] There is one confusing element: When is a pastoral conference advisory, and when is it "religious"?

In the Father Towle case, years after the fact, the church permitted the priest to disclose confidential communications, deeming the conversation to have been not "confessional" but simply advisory. The Texas Supreme Court unanimously (9–0) ruled that it would be unconstitutional to interfere in church matters and dismissed a civil suit against a pastor who told his church elders, who in turn advised the congregation, about a parishioner's adultery, which resulted in her being shunned. She sued, claiming that the pastor knew about her affair from the confidential marriage counseling he provided. The court disagreed with her claim that the pastor was acting in his confessional role, agreeing with his claim that he was the couple's marital counselor. The court could not separate the two roles (how could one?) and decided that to interfere in church affairs would violate the First Amendment.[35]

The clergyman's lawyer called the decision "a great victory for pastors";[36] one wonders if it is a victory for congregations, who may not realize that their "confidential" conversations are with religious advisers who wear two not readily distinguishable hats. Religious officials regularly visit needy parishioners in hospitals, prisons, and other nonreligious institutions. They are there in their dual roles as providers of religious advice and personal solace. No doubt, their attendees communicate with them with that in mind. They may be surprised to find out subsequently that their confessions are not privileged.

The clergy privilege is interdenominational and applies to all clergy, rabbis, imams, and established Christian ministries. Even lay associates of religious clergy—a Muslim brother acting as a spiritual adviser, nuns, jailhouse "reverends" in some cases—occasionally have been covered by the privilege if they are acting for recognized religious officials and offering sacramental guidance.[37]

Others in comparable situations—church administration officials, unordained church deacons and elders, psychics—have not been considered to be in the protected class, though they may claim to be offering penitential counseling to their wards.[38] Courts have ruled differently in cases involving Alcoholics Anonymous counselors. The twelve-step program has been deemed by some as akin to a religious communication because participants are seeking spiritual guidance.

Religious needs may be met by other than clergymen. Contested cases have reached varied results when nonestablished—one might call them quasi-religious—representatives or laypeople exercising religious roles have claimed the protection of the privilege. For example, a Bible-society representative, alcohol-abuse and drug counselors, youth-facility officials, and a police officer who was also a religious counselor were not considered clergy for purposes of privileged communications, though they were acting in clergy-like roles in specific situations.[39]

The communications must involve spiritual matters to be privileged; they must be in a confidential and confessional setting, they must be private, and they must be for a religious or spiritual purpose. A New York court ruled that an Orthodox rabbi's disclosure of details of the contentious married life of a woman who sought his advice did not violate his obligation of confidentiality. She had come with her mother and a friend, who were offering her their help and assistance. The rabbi thought her conduct violated religious law and that her husband's lawyer needed to know that, and urged—successfully—that the court stay out of the dispute and not interpret religious rules. The trial court had ruled that the rabbi (one tabloid referred to him as "the Gabby Rabbi") had not violated the secular command "Thou shalt not tell," because the woman waived the privilege by including others in the meeting.[40]

Torah law is stricter than secular law in prohibiting the disclosure of confidential communications. Rabbis all have counseling duties as part of their pastoral work. And generally their counseling sessions are confidential. "Reveal not the secret of another," states Proverbs 25:9. "Do not go as a tale-bearer among your people," Leviticus 19:16 states. But because damage may occur if certain information is not disclosed, Jewish law and codes of ethics also instruct that confidences must *not* be kept if doing so would harm someone. In such cases, obligations to protect confidentiality are outweighed. American secular law mandates disclosure of confidential pastoral communications in specific instances and is more protective of secular public interests than Catholic rules.

Rabbis have told me that they would not hesitate to report an injustice such as the one in the Father Towle case, because in shielding misconduct they would be participating in an injustice, which is more morally reprehensible than disclosing a confession. On a related question, a rabbi told me that he had been rejected as a chaplain by the U.S. Air Force because he would not waive his privilege to identify antiwar protestors during the Vietnam War. He considered himself the sole arbiter of what information he would reveal; he was told that the military was the sole arbiter. Left out of the consideration was the choice of the communicant.[41] Jews may communicate directly with God, one rabbi explained to me; they do not need an intermediary, such as a Catholic priest, in such situations.

Although all professions that operate under protections of privilege for confidential communications also exempt some exceptional situations—domestic abuse, the planning of future crimes, child abuse, for example—a special dilemma is created for some Catholics. Child-abuse laws are a prime example. All states have statutory privileges protecting clergy, but many state laws also mandate the reporting of child abuse.[42] Various states deal with the problem in different ways. Most exempt clergy from the reporting requirement of suspected child abuse; some deny the pastoral privilege in child-abuse cases; others ignore the issue, leaving an embarrassing ambiguity.[43] About half the states mandate that known or suspected instances of child abuse be reported; about a third seem to include clergy under the grouping "all citizens" or "any person." In about ten states, ambiguity exists.[44] A recent survey of state laws governing the clergy privilege and the duty to report child abuse concludes that "in many states the clergy privilege trumps the obligation to report; in others, a fewer number to be sure, the obligation to report trumps the privilege; and in a third group, the question of the relationship is not answered in the statute."[45]

In a California case, a pastor and his assistant were convicted for not reporting the sexual abuse of a teenage girl by her stepfather. She had complained of her stepfather's repeated molestations to her private-school principal, who was also her family's pastor. The South Bay United Pentecostal Church ran the South Bay Christian Academy. The pastor-principal chose to handle the problem as an intrachurch matter and did not report it. He required the offender to apologize and attend a retreat. Later, the girl went to the police.

The California court ruled that the state's child-abuse reporting law clearly mandated the reporting of child abuse, even when doing so interfered with a claimed religious practice of handling matters within the church.[46]

A twist on the conflict between religious and professional obligations arose in 1988 when the official magazine of Jehovah's Witnesses, the *Watchtower,* ordered all 3.3 million Witnesses worldwide (750,000 in the United States) to inform church officials of any information regarding congregants' sins. The mandate applied even to attorneys and others whose professional codes require them to preserve client confidentiality.[47] Affected professionals faced violating church doctrine on the one hand or statutes and professional codes that conflicted with church doctrine on the other hand.

The California Court of Appeal promulgated a secular rule governing clergy, in a 2005 case involving the sexual abuse of three minors by a probationary Methodist clergyman at church-group events.[48] Four churches were sued by three young victims who were abused at youth-fellowship events in Walnut Creek, Pasadena, and Long Beach, California. The complainants argued that the church knew of the claimed molestations and did not take steps to cure them; rather, the church moved the clergyman to other areas where his misconduct—against twelve- and thirteen-year-olds—was repeated.

A church official reached out to the victims and sought to offer religious and spiritual healing at a weekend retreat. Two dozen attendees participated, and the pastor claimed that their conversations and correspondence were confessional and should not be made available through pretrial interrogatories or as evidence later at the trial. The trial court denied the church's claim of confidentiality.

The appellate court, following Wigmore's criteria, asserted that for a communication to be penitential it must be intended to be so and must be made in the course of a clergyman's duties that his or her church requires be secret. If third parties are present, the disclosures are not protected. Nor are they if the penitent does not intend them to be confidential.

The confessor need not be a member of the church, nor need the communication be about "a flawed act" for the privilege to apply, though the communication must be "confessional in nature." Statements by a fleeing suspect to a clergy member encountered by chance would not be considered confessional; nor would communications to an auditor of a church, courts have ruled. The privilege applies only when there is a "human need to disclose to a spiritual counselor, in total and absolute confidence, what are believed to be flawed acts or thoughts and to receive priestly consolation and guidance in return."[49]

Another California case, this one involving a large number of Catholic priests who were charged with sexually molesting children, dealt with the permissibility of disclosing church investigations into the treatment of the priests and admissions by the archdiocese.[50] In this case, the evidence was protected from disclosure because it evolved from a mediation hearing, which by its nature is required to be confidential.

Mandatory child-abuse reporting laws evolved in the second half of the twentieth century, sharing a similar history as the "duty to warn" exception to the psychotherapist privilege in civil litigation. In 1976, doctors were held to be civilly liable for failing to report child abuse.[51] A major review of the clergy privilege attributes child-abuse reporting laws to a landmark article by Dr. Henry Kempe describing the need for the detection of child abuse and intervention into abuse cases. There are over 3 million incidents of child abuse reported annually (many are not reported).[52] States and the federal government enacted statutes, but physicians were reluctant to report suspicions until the hammer of liability raised their consciousness.[53] Attorneys are exempted from mandatory disclosure laws. Is this because the law gives greater respect to its own? Or is there, as one commentator suggested, "a trendy disdain for deep religious conviction"?[54]

Given that there are several million reported cases of child abuse in the United States annually, and given that clergy are regularly confided in for advice and absolution, Catholic clergy face a dilemma.[55]

Children are particularly vulnerable and unable to seek redress. Those who are abused require champions to protect them. The venerable doctrine of *parens patriae* historically recognized the state interest in protecting children. The collision of interests arises because clergy—along with doctors, social workers, and child-care providers—are logical advocates for children. Clergy argue that they can deter child abuse effectively only if the confidentiality of their communications is honored.

In addition to the edicts of their respective churches, religious practitioners are governed by the laws of their states. The rules of their respective churches are usually consistent with their states' statutes. There is no canon or doctrine in most Protestant denominations or in Judaism that forbids disclosure of confidences.[56] Violating confidentiality is frowned on and discouraged, but it is not forbidden, except in the Catholic Church.

Neither Jehovah's Witnesses, Baptists, Mennonites, Moravians, nor others in the Anabaptist movement practice auricular confession. Pentecostal confession is to the congregation. "The shepherd . . . had no power or authority over the soul or conscience of any person."[57] Confessions to church members are not privileged under state law. Recipients of these confessions have a moral obligation not to disclose them but no legal privilege not to reveal them in legal proceedings.

A group of pastoral advisers at a seminar I conducted all said that they would have acted differently from Father Towle in the case noted earlier. Baptists have church bylaws; Presbyterians follow their *Book of Church Or-*

der and the advice of church leaders; Pentecostals follow state laws and church rules; evangelicals follow state laws; in administering spiritual assistance and counseling, rabbis follow Talmudic laws, codes of laws, and commentaries, along with applicable state laws. Muslim law (the Koran) states the prophet Muhammad's view that trust and confidence are qualities that will allow disciples to enter paradise. But an imam who withheld information about a murder would be considered guilty of committing a greater injustice to society. Imams derive spiritual authority from their community, not from a central authority in Islam. Thus, Muslims are directed to abide by the secular laws of their residence.[58]

The Catholic Church's position that priests may never disclose confidential communications with penitents is understandable as a matter of church dogma. But it raises secular constitutional questions. All states provide qualified statutory privileges, not absolute privileges. If laws attempted to single out one religion, they could be questioned on constitutional grounds. None do, but the application of a reporting rule in this context would cause conflicts only for the Catholic Church.

The First Amendment's free-exercise clause would seem to protect Catholic priests from the prejudicial impact of child-abuse reporting laws. But the establishment clause cuts the opposite way, prohibiting special treatment for any one religion. There is constitutional authority for the proposition that valid, neutral laws of general applicability (child-abuse laws would qualify) must be followed by Catholic priests, despite their free-exercise argument that their reticence is based on religious requirements.

One literary commentator has remarked that the establishment clause is the rock on which the pastoral privilege could shatter, but that "opposite the shoals of the Establishment Clause, the undertow of the Free Exercise Clause is equally powerful and may provide the privilege's constitutional basis." The privilege is, in this commentator's words, "a stark reminder of Western history's longest running conflict—that between the church and the state."[59]

In a case involving a Pentecostal church, the California courts drew the distinction between belief and action interestingly. The free-exercise clause's freedom to believe may be absolute, but the freedom to act is not.

A facially neutral law may have an incidental impact on religious practices and not be deemed unconstitutional.[60]

In a case dealing with two states' (Pennsylvania's and Rhode Island's) laws permitting state financial aid to church-related schools, the U.S. Supreme Court found the laws unconstitutional. The Court articulated a three-part test to determine whether exemptions for religions are valid: (1) Is there a secular legislative purpose? (2) Does the primary effect advance or inhibit a religion? (3) Does the law foster excessive governmental intrusion with a religion?[61]

In the United States, a strict wall has been deemed to separate church and state.[62] This view has been followed consistently, as have the consequential rulings that special privileges or dispensations for one religion are inappropriate and unconstitutional in the secular world. To permit them might be considered an establishment of religion.

Under a line of Supreme Court decisions, Catholics—priests and penitents—could be committing acts of civil disobedience by refusing to testify, or could be abetting a crime, if they were deemed to have violated laws of general applicability requiring their testimony. Justice Felix Frankfurter articulated the governing law in 1940: "Conscientious scruples have not, in the course of the long struggle for religious toleration, relieved the individual from obedience to a general law not aimed at the promotion or restriction of religious beliefs. The mere possession of religious convictions which contradict the relevant concerns of a political society does not relieve the citizen from the discharge of political responsibilities."[63]

Under this rationale, consistently followed in various Supreme Court decisions in the last half century, laws such as those against polygamy were upheld in the face of claims that they violated religious beliefs—in that case, those of the Mormon Church. Laws may not interfere with religious beliefs, the Court held, but "they may [interfere] with practices" if those practices are neutrally enforced.[64]

The Supreme Court held that an Oregon law criminalizing the use of peyote did not unconstitutionally prejudice members of the Native American Church who claimed the right to use the drug for ceremonial and sacramental purposes.[65] The state has a right to regulate the use of peyote, just as it regulates marijuana use by the Ethiopian Zion Coptic Church, even though it doesn't regulate the sacramental use of wine by the Roman

Catholic Church, courts have ruled. Congress later exempted Indian tribes from the prejudicial impact of this antidrug law.

Other Supreme Court decisions have upheld general regulatory laws that prejudiced certain religions as long as the laws were written in neutral terms, were secular in purpose, and were evenhanded in operation. The Supreme Court has upheld laws covering such disparate subjects as conscription for military service, child labor, Sunday-closing laws, the payment of Social Security, and the payment of taxes, all of which were claimed, unsuccessfully, to have violated individuals' religious beliefs. Such laws are different, Justice Scalia wrote, from laws that punish worship or, he wrote facetiously, that prohibit "bowing down before a golden calf." He added that it is not the Court's role to evaluate "the plausibility of a religious claim"; nor is it "within the judicial ken to question the centrality of particular beliefs or practices to a faith."[66] General laws of neutral coverage are not unconstitutional simply because there is a negative impact on a particular religious practice.

Judges have agonized over cases involving claims by Christian Scientists that their practices of spiritual healing deserve respect and not indictment, particularly when the health of children is involved. Courts have taken children from their parents when they (the courts) thought the children's lives were endangered, despite the parents' claims that their religious beliefs were inequitably judged.[67] Cases like these can generate debates over the wisdom of prosecuting parents for causing their children's death,[68] but not over the legality and constitutionality of doing so.

Under prevailing First Amendment jurisprudence, the freedom to act, unlike the freedom to believe, is not absolute. That such a view may cause "unavoidable consequences" to a minority religion has not been deemed reason enough to make exceptions.

In 1993, Congress passed (by a 97-to-0 vote in the Senate) the Religious Freedom Restoration Act.[69] The act prohibits the government from "substantially burdening a person's exercise of religion unless the government demonstrates that application of the burden to the person represents the least restrictive means of advancing a compelling interest."[70]

A case in Florida upheld a requirement that a full-face photo be included on driver's licenses.[71] A Muslim woman claimed that this requirement violated her free exercise of religion and equal protection of the law. She wore a veil as required by the Koran, the sacred book of Islam, and the Sunnah, the religion's rules. She argued that the law forced her either to violate her religion's rules or to lose her license. The Florida appellate court applied the Religious Freedom Restoration Act, which provides that neutral, generally applicable laws may impinge on religious practices if the state demonstrates a compelling governmental interest, the law is the least restrictive way of furthering that interest, and the burden on the complainant is not substantial. The court concluded its opinion by citing a 1961 U.S. Supreme Court case that stated, "We are a cosmopolitan nation made up of people of almost every conceivable religious preference. . . . Consequently it cannot be expected, much less required, that legislators enact no laws regulating conduct that may in some way result in . . . disadvantage to some religious sects."[72]

How current constitutional law would affect a challenged priestly privilege is unclear. The local, state, or federal government's position in cases like these—use of confessional evidence in a prosecution, for example—likely would be that the integrity and efficiency of the trial process compellingly requires confessional testimony and that there is no less restrictive means of getting such confessional evidence. Whether invading the sanctity of the confessional is the least restrictive means of achieving a compelling state interest raises a classic confrontation of church-state issues, one that would be politically unpopular, but upon which matters of life and death might hinge. Wigmore's fourth factor to consider in applying a privilege—the balance between the values of disclosure versus that of protection—ties into the "least restrictive means" rule and suggests a balancing rule rather than an absolute one.

The general public right to everyone's evidence aiding in the ascertainment of truth is inconsistent with the notion of any privileged communications. Nonetheless, the pastoral privilege has been honored for utilitarian reasons (to preserve this important societal relationship), for practical reasons (ensuring public faith in the understanding and reasonableness of its government), and for reasons of privacy (spiritual discipline requires the encouragement of confession). Ours is a religious society that encourages repentance and spiritual salvation as necessary for civil and moral reasons.[73]

Courts evaluate claims of privilege with the overriding notion that deference to religious activities must yield to the requirement that full disclosure is required for the trial process. The pastoral privilege is rooted in the need for spiritual rehabilitation and solace. That rule may be rational and reasonable by church standards, but it may be illegal and imprudent under state law and by secular standards.

Although prosecutors, legislators, and courts will be understandably tolerant of priests who follow absolute church rules about confidentiality, and although challenging that practice is not the proper role of secular authorities, the priests' accountability in serious and extreme criminal situations like those noted in this chapter is also clear. Civil disobedience may be appropriate, even socially acceptable, in civil cases—matrimonial situations, for example—but it should not be tolerated when ongoing criminal actions are involved or gross miscarriages of justice are perpetrated as a result.

If the executive privilege relents for the president of the United States in situations involving misconduct and the public need for access to otherwise privileged information, as it did in the Nixon tapes case, how dare it not when the privilege claim is based on one church's doctrines?

7

ALL IN THE FAMILY: THE SPOUSAL PRIVILEGE

> The notion that a woman who marries is, as if by some peculiar biochemical process, transformed into something like an extra organ of her husband, as functional and compliant as a healthy kidney, has ceased to exercise much persuasive power among the general public. Few contemporary wives are expected to conform without dissent to the beliefs, interests, and preoccupations of their husbands, and standup comedy would be the poorer if they did.
>
> —Rebecca Mead, *Ladies First,* New Yorker, June 6, 2005

The Rationale

Progressive-sounding rules sometimes have surprisingly inappropriate histories. The spousal privilege, holding that husbands and wives cannot be forced to testify against each other, is one example. Reasonable as this rule may sound, the spousal disqualification evolved from "two canons of medieval jurisprudence," the first that women had no separate legal existence and thus husbands and wives were one, and the second that an accused could not testify in his own behalf.[1]

Marital privacy derived from these antiquated views of marital unity. "The very being or legal existence of the woman is suspended during marriage, or at least incorporated and consolidated into that of the husband," the eighteenth-century British scholar Sir William Blackstone reported.[2] No less prestigious an authority than Sir Edward Coke wrote, in 1628 in his *Commentarie upon Littleton,* of "ancient notions that women were chattels of their husbands, and had no independent legal existence." This doctrine of *femme couverte* considered women to be absorbed into their husbands' person (but not vice versa) and thus metaphysically unable to testify for or against them.

By entering into marriage, men and women were deemed to be transformed by these coercive metaphors and images drawn both from dated English common law and prevailing theology, according to histories of marriage. These images were based on formalisms that are radically inconsistent with the real lives led by American couples today.

Spouses were incompetent witnesses under this thinking. When, centuries later, that dated underlying notion was rejected and wives were considered competent to testify, a more benign approach to spousal relations gave rise to a legal privilege not to testify, though wives were deemed competent to do so. The spousal privilege that later evolved was based on the notion that "limitless confidence" between essential family members was required for a "well-ordered civilized society," a very different predicate from that of ancient rulings and one that prevails today. Lord Coke thought that a spouse's breach of confidentiality would cause "implacable discord and dissension"; Lord Chancellor Hardwicke, no doubt a married jurist, thought the spousal privilege was necessary to "preserve the peace of families."[3]

Dean Wigmore quoted commentaries from the late 1800s by English common-law judges about the nature of married life, which warranted making spousal communications privileged from forced disclosure. "So much of the happiness of human life may fairly be said to depend on the inviolability of domestic confidence that the alarm and unhappiness occasioned to society by invading its sanctity and compelling public disclosure of confidential communications between husband and wife would be a far greater evil than the disadvantage which may occasionally arise from the loss of light which such revelations might throw on questions in dispute," pronounced one wordy judge.[4]

The law loves happy marriages. One jurist referred to the "bond of mutual confidence and unquestioned trust that is essential to the peace and happiness of the most sacred of all domestic relations." Another judge proclaimed that confidence "is the charm of domestic life" and that if spousal conversations are "made in the bosom of their families," they must remain sacrosanct. Spouses must be free to "think aloud in the presence of each other" without "apprehension in the intercourse of one's own fireside," that judge mused. He would not "trench" upon such freedom. An early U.S. Supreme Court decision described the marital relationship as "the best solace of human existence." Spouses, the Court instructed, should not violate "the sacred confidence and intimacy of married life," which preserves personal harmony, and the peace of families.[5]

Not all scholars had such a rosy perspective about married life. One commentator suggested that the traditional rationale for the spousal privilege is "highly suspect" and based on a fallacious presumption about the "psychology of married persons." The anticipation of having to testify at some later date in a contentious dispute is not a consideration that will "materially influence in daily life the degree of fullness of marital disclosures," one treatise on evidence posited.[6] One federal appellate court noted that the spousal privilege "has been strongly criticized as of obscure origin, uncertain rationalization, and unfortunate results in limiting judicial search for truth."[7]

More recent interpretations of the spousal privilege accepted the premise of disqualification as one that fostered the harmony and sanctity of marriage. But Wigmore sounded like the most extreme antifeminist when, disparaging the idea of a spousal privilege, he wrote, "In an age which has so far rationalized, depolarized, and de-chivalrized the marital relation and the spirit of Femininity as to be willing to enact complete legal and political equality and independence of man and woman, this marital privilege is the merest anachronism, in legal theory, and an indefensible obstruction to truth in practice."[8]

Jeremy Bentham chided that the rule went beyond the need that one's house be considered his domestic castle and permitted people to convert their homes into a "den of thieves." "It secures to every man, one safe and unquestionable and ever ready accomplice for every imaginable crime." By adding "heroic dimensions" to "the conjugal flare," that old-fashioned critic argued, "the sentimentality of English lawyers" in effect provided an asylum and created criminal accomplices. The nonsensical marital privilege encouraged concealment, if not fraud, in this view. Reaching dramatic levels of criticism of the marital privilege, this florid jurisprude claimed: "It debases and degrades the matrimonial union; converting into a sink of corruption what ought to be a source of purity. It defiles the marriage-contract itself, by tacking to it in secret a license to commit crimes." The antiquated rules of feudal law that merged the identity of husband and wife for self-incrimination reasons and to ensure domestic peace gave rise to an immoral rule that converts marriage from a "sacred condition into a nursery of crime," Bentham concluded.[9]

Whatever the historical basis for the spousal privilege, in 1839 the U.S. Supreme Court adopted the privilege as an essential principle of domestic life. The Court held that a widow could not be forced to disclose a fraud by her deceased husband.[10] Even in more recent times, considering loyalty and security scares, the high court refused to order a husband to disclose his wife's whereabouts to a grand jury investigating the Communist Party.[11]

Although American law initially followed English common law with respect to the marital privilege, American notions about the nature of marriage evolved, faster even than the law in this regard. By the middle of the nineteenth century, there were voices that challenged the understanding of marriage as a fixed hierarchical relationship governed by the states.

By the late twentieth century, American courts began to recognize that cohabitation—unmarried people living together—could give rise to economic obligations.[12] By the 1980s, about 50 percent of all marriages ended in divorce, and there was a growing diversity of family forms.[13] With renegotiations in what some still assumed were traditional roles and obligations, marriage became a private choice more than a state-defined formalism.

Stephanie Coontz, a history professor who has written about the connection between marriage and the state remarked that "the marriage license no longer draws reasonable dividing lines regarding which adult obligations and rights merit state protection." Professor Coontz reports that state control over marriage is a relatively recent (late-nineteenth-century) historical phenomenon that began to change in the mid-twentieth century when states began "to get out of the business of deciding which couples were fit to marry." More recently, marriage licenses have served a new purpose—to distribute resources, benefits, and privileges such as Social Security, pension and health benefits, and inheritance. But given the number of unmarried couples (about half) and the number of children born out of wedlock (about 40 percent), marriage is an imperfect test for interpersonal relationships, she points out.[14]

The current federal rule, Federal Rule of Evidence 501, leaves it to the federal courts to determine the extent of this privilege according to common law, reason, and experience. That is what the federal courts have done, in contrast to the states, whose legislatures have passed laws governing local practices.

The spousal privilege has been followed, but not unquestionably. The marital privilege has been called one "of obscure origin, uncertain rationalization, and unfortunate result in limiting the judicial search for the truth."[15] Justice Potter Stewart called it a "sentimental relic," asserting that it is "the product of a conceptualism long ago discarded, is universally criticized by scholars, and has been qualified or abandoned in many jurisdictions."[16]

Dean Wigmore reported that the spousal privilege was the second privilege (after the attorney-client privilege) enforced at common law but the last to be recognized in America. First mentioned in the 1600s, the privilege was not made the law until the late 1800s. The modern privilege, based on the social need for marital harmony, may be waived, but it survives death (as disqualification did not). The privilege is presumed, but it may be disputed by proof of a contrary intent, such as including a third party in the conversation, or a showing that no valid marriage existed. The privilege ends when the marriage does, but it survives after the death of one partner, but only covers confidential communications, not noncommunicative acts.[17] What courts have called a "bright-line" rule governs the applicability of the spousal privilege: the privilege rests on "the foundation of a valid marriage."[18]

Exceptions to the Spousal Privilege

Despite the flawed ancient sources of the privilege, courts have adopted the spousal privilege because the rule tended not to alienate marriages or "inflame domestic differences." Marital privacy provided "the best solace of human existence," the U.S. Supreme Court stated.[19]

Courts and legislatures have noted that not all marital relations are solicitous and have thus exempted some situations from the spousal privilege, particularly when the wife is the victim of her partner's crime, or where injuries to children are involved. In a Mann Act (prostitution) case, for example, the Supreme Court asserted that "it cannot be seriously argued that one who has committed this shameless offense against wifehood should be permitted to prevent his wife from testifying . . . by invoking an interest founded on the marital relation.[20] The Court ruled that although the wife could decline to testify, she couldn't be prevented from doing so by her husband.

Several cases have dealt with the applicability of the spousal privilege in white-slavery cases in which husbands who exploited their wives by prostituting them sought to silence them from testifying in criminal prosecutions. "Here I am two days married, and he wants me to hustle," one sad woman complained in an Idaho case.[21] The court permitted her to testify against her husband. Another court also allowed a wife to testify against her husband in a prostitution case, noting that white slavery is not only a crime against interstate commerce but is also a "shameless offense against wifehood."[22]

Every state has a law governing the spousal privilege, including rational exceptions. In a crime against one spouse—for example, bigamy, polygamy, unlawful cohabitation, domestic violence—the defendant cannot prevent the spousal witness from testifying on the basis of their confidential relationship. One jurisdiction, the District of Columbia, has a statute that permits spouses to testify against each other where "disclosure is required in the interests of public justice." It has been applied in cases of child abuse and domestic violence to skirt the medical and spousal privileges.

In a manslaughter case in which an eight-month-old infant was killed by his father, the court applied the public-interest exception to the spousal privilege. The marital privilege, a vestige of abandoned medieval jurisprudence, has been revived to foster the harmony and sanctity of marriage, the court noted, but that privilege has exceptions. Spouses have no immunity to injure each other, or to injure children, and hide behind a statutory privilege to foreclose evidence of their offenses. "The welfare of the children takes precedence over the marital privilege," the court concluded.[23] Thus, in the father's prosecution for killing his child, his conversations with his common-law wife were proper evidence at the trial. Of necessity, the parent is the only voice of the victimized child, and that voice should not be silenced by a general rule of evidence that shields spousal conversations. Under these circumstances, there is no marital harmony to preserve nor any fundamental family peace and solitude to protect. Any other tipping of the balance of interests would frustrate justice.

In a 1980 case, *Trammel v. United States*, the Supreme Court formulated the modern American rule.[24] A group of drug traffickers were arrested and indicted for importing heroin from the Philippines to the United States. They were caught at customs in Hawaii. Mrs. Trammel was offered a deal by the government—testify against the others and avoid prosecution. Preferring self-preservation to the preservation of her marriage, Mrs. Trammel talked. Her testimony was challenged by her husband at his trial. A unanimous Supreme Court held, in an opinion by Chief Justice Warren Burger, that a witness may not be compelled to testify against his or her spouse nor foreclosed from doing so. The spouse-witness has the privilege to refuse to testify adversely in a criminal case. But if one is willing to testify, he or she may. Otherwise, in domestic disputes one spouse could escape justice at the expense of the other, and the marital relationship would be frustrated and inharmonious. Self-protection thus becomes another reason for marriages to stay felicitous. The modern trend is to expand the exceptions to the marital privilege.[25]

Modern Cohabitation: Who Is a Spouse?

Will the dated notions underlying legal privileges based on marital solemnity survive? Should they apply to civil unions and other modern marriage-like arrangements of cohabitation? What about couples who live together but do not marry officially? Should their conversations be privileged? Census reports indicate growing trends away from traditional marriage arrangements, suggesting the need for new approaches for measuring appropriate standards of justice to apply in these new living arrangements. Justice Anthony Kennedy noted that conventional notions about nuclear families and "normal" domestic relations are unrealistic.[26]

What about homosexual unions, now legally ordained in some states—if exceedingly controversial? Should conversations between gay couples be protected from legal processes on the basis of their evolving marital nature? A Government Accountability Office study in 2005 identified over one thousand federal legal rights and responsibilities based on marriage (state and local laws add more), one of which is the spousal privilege.[27] Should new relationships receive all or some of these rights?

A law professor who specializes in family law noted that the law lags behind in "taking account of nontraditional family forms." Legislatures, he concluded, are "slow in reacting to changes in society," and courts are "skittish about reshaping social issues."[28] A 1997 New York case, for example, held that the phrase "husband and wife" does not extend "to homosexuals in a spousal relationship" for purposes of the confidentiality privilege.[29]

A recent book about the history of marriage reports that over thousands of years, the social institution of marriage developed to provide care for offspring through a family-based household. The current cultural debate about same-sex marriage has been based essentially on other considerations—equal civil rights, tolerance, gender equality—all of which are aside from the anthropological point of the family. Some homosexual relations include the feature of child rearing; many do not.[30] If the essence of the husband-wife privilege is the family-based element of their cohabitation, then in the absence of that feature, homosexual couples could be compared to friends or roommates, whose relationships may be important or intimate but are not deemed privileged. The extension of the spousal privilege remains to be determined definitively by courts and legislatures; but if extensions are frowned on, this one can be expected to receive a conservative official reception.

The applicability of the old-fashioned rationale for spousal privilege in today's world of divorce, cohabitation, and homosexual "marriage" is uncertain. The legal status of same-sex couples is in flux and is so controversial that it is not likely to be settled soon. Several states (Massachusetts, Vermont, California, New Jersey, and Connecticut, as of mid-2006) as well as the District of Columbia, authorize civil unions or domestic partnerships that provide some or all of the state rights applicable to marriage. Many more states have laws prohibiting same-sex marriages, and major churches are divided over the question whether their clergy should preside over such marriages and whether the churches should recognize them. Because family structures are changing—there are stepfamilies, reconstructed families, mononuclear families, homosexual couples—new ethical questions about their legal status will require fresh perspectives.[31]

The federal courts have ducked the issue of the availability of the spousal privilege to same-sex partners, but two states have allowed same-sex couples to claim the privilege (California and Vermont) and one has denied the privilege to same-sex couples (New York). Several commentators have urged its application.[32]

As Justice Sandra Day O'Connor wrote in a Supreme Court opinion dealing with visitation rights of grandparents, "The demographic changes of the past century make it difficult to speak of an average American family. The composition of families varies greatly from household to household."[33] In language appropriate to the present question, she noted the changing reality of modern family life. Justice O'Connor may have been prescient. Scattered cases and laws have imposed legal obligations on sperm donors, prompting one expert to wonder whether egg donors and gestational surrogates might join sperm donors and homosexual couples as "parents."[34]

The marriage rate in the United States has dropped by nearly 50 percent in recent decades, and "the number of unwed cohabiting couples continues to rise," according to the *State of Our Unions* report by the National Marriage Project.[35] There are about 600,000 same-sex couples living together, according to a recent census.[36]

A New York court considered a claim that the state's statutory marital privilege should apply on a gender-neutral basis to same-sex couples. The case involved a gay couple who had lived together for thirty-three years and had registered as domestic partners. Both were convicted of embezzling from the Roslyn, New York, school system. One of the men argued that his lover's testimony against him could not be considered by the court, but the judge ruled that the question needn't be answered, because the spousal privilege does not apply to communications related to joint participation in a criminal venture.[37]

Television celebrity Rosie O'Donnell sought a San Francisco wedding with her girlfriend and business partner after a judge denied her claim that their conversations were protected by the spousal privilege in a commercial civil litigation for breach of contract. A civil union does not provide that protection or "over one thousand federal rights that you'll never have," O'Donnell complained.[38] The National Gay and Lesbian Task Force has reported that under federal law, "marital status determines 1,138 benefits, and protections from Social Security to employment to health and medical benefits, tax benefits, and many other legal benefits, including the right not to testify against one's spouse."[39]

The centrality of a husband-wife relationship was explained by the skeptical Dean Wigmore. "The privilege concerns solely the relation of husband and wife; it cares nothing for family as such—nothing for parent and child, nothing for brother and sister, nothing for master and servant. It is the peculiar interest in the marital relation, and of that alone, which requires unrestricted confidence. . . . Domestic conduct, therefore, may doubtless be private and confidential. . . . It is only so far as there has been a special confidentiality of it to the wife (or husband) that it comes within the privilege."[40]

That said, it is a perverse application of policy and jurisprudence that denies the comparable treatment of the confidentiality of intrafamily communications, particularly those between parents and children. People can change marriage partners, but not natural parenthood. U.S. courts (and legislatures) have generally declined to protect familial confidences by making communications privileged—only five states have extended the privilege to other family members through lower-court decisions—though the rationale for such a privilege is clear. Professor Imwinkelried has reported that ancient Roman and Jewish law provided and the laws of many modern legal systems in Western Europe provide privacy privileges to communications between family members.[41]

Our courts recognize the more questionable and more limited spousal privilege while denying a privilege between parents and children, though most people would consider violating a child's confidences to be an immoral, personal betrayal. Who can a child turn to for private counseling? Children ordinarily don't hire lawyers, see psychiatrists, or go to confession to assuage their concerns. They have only their parents to turn to. Family loyalty and emotional well-being would argue in favor of a parent-child privilege, a majority of experts have urged.[42] Yet the law provides uncertain protection of the confidentiality of those communications, allowing protection in some instances, denying it in others.[43]

Limitations on the spousal relationship are predicated on dated notions about family. The rationale for and policy behind the spousal privilege applies with equal good sense to privileges for others in the family, especially children. The family hearth should be wide enough to include others directly engaged in family communications. Because there are so many permutations of "family" relationships, courts should consider appropriate ratiocinations, insist on receiving the testimony, and weigh the admissibility of the evidence on the basis of its case-by-case credibility.

Given that the spousal privilege has roots in outdated theories about women being their husbands' property—though the rationale for the privilege is couched nowadays in sentimental modern homilies about marital harmony—it is unrealistic to believe that marital behavior is predicated on notions of the potential for disclosure in subsequent litigation. A distinction might be drawn between forcing spouses to testify against one another in criminal cases where life and liberty are at stake and protecting confidentiality in civil cases where economic and social interests are involved.

A rational and humane social policy would recognize powerful privacy interests in confidential communications between all family members—*family* defined broadly. If there is a harmonious marital relationship, a spouse simply will not testify to the disadvantage of his or her mate. If it is an unhappy relationship, a spouse will. Thus, in many cases, the de facto realities are likely to govern. The law already provides uncertain protection of the confidentiality of those spousal communications, allowing it in some instances, denying it in others.[44] Courts should be left to decide whether a privilege applies to other family members on a case-by-case basis, balancing the presumption favoring family privacy against the competing public interest at issue in given cases.

8

CONFIDENTIALITY IN BUSINESS

> Leaders of the Smithsonian in the past seven years took extraordinary steps to keep secret the amount of top executives' compensation, lavish expense-account spending, ethical missteps and management failures, an independent report released yesterday shows.
>
> —James V. Grimaldi and Jacqueline Trescott, *Secrecy Pervaded Smithsonian on Small's Watch,* Washington Post, June 21, 2007

> A top Smithsonian official has resigned after he destroyed records from a key Smithsonian Board of Regents meeting. . . . The transcript of the January meeting included discussion about how to respond to a confidential report. . . . Officials said they would not discuss personnel matters. Officials who asked not to be named said that . . .
>
> —James V. Grimaldi, *Smithsonian Official Quits after Records Destroyed,* Washington Post, August 8, 2007

Earlier chapters focused on relational rationales for protecting the confidentiality of professions and families. A broader universe in the business world also claims confidentiality for its participants. From Main Street to Wall Street, in this country and globally, for good reasons and bad, businesses attempt to keep their affairs confidential. These attempts at confidentiality are common, affect many people, and have important social consequences.

Businesses claim that their need for confidentiality is as deserving as that of lawyers and doctors, even if the law has not recognized it as warranting privileged status. If personal autonomy is the basis for conventional claims of confidentiality in medical and legal and pastoral settings, commerce and money is the fundamental source of high-stakes claims for confidentiality in the business setting.

Confidentiality issues arise in business settings in a variety of ways. Courts have enforced explicit agreements of confidentiality and imposed implicit confidentiality requirements where equity and fairness warranted doing so. Confidentiality controls regularly arise in fiduciary arrangements and agents' relationships. Statutes have imposed rules requiring confidentiality in certain business arrangements (banking records, for example) and have mandated exceptions to those instances as well (in cases of money laundering, for example). Professional codes governing members (accountants, engineers, architects, for example) impose duties of confidentiality in their business arrangements. Private confidentiality agreements are common in litigation settlements, often involving public-policy considerations (defective products and hazardous conditions, for example). Private and public organizations (universities, for example) strive to maintain the confidentiality of their inner workings—such as peer review or research—sometimes successfully, sometimes not. This chapter explores these diverse and varied situations of confidentiality in business settings.

Business Law

The need for confidentiality in business dealings has been widely recognized in private agreements, statutes, and court decisions—though confidentiality is not absolute and may be overcome by countervailing claims. It is the essence of the free-enterprise system that businesses should be able to protect their investments. It is also part of that same democratic free-enterprise system that participants in the competitive marketplace be free to compete and that public information be available to people on an equal basis. That inherent conflict keeps judges busy and lawyers rich. It arises in infinite and consequential circumstances: the protectability of confidential customer lists, software design, sales strategies, manufacturing processes, formulas, programs, and other items.[1]

Fair business practices require protections if the freewheeling marketplace is not to disintegrate into anarchic chaos. Corporate espionage is common. The sanctity of confidential client and customer lists, trade secrets, inside information and strategies, intellectual property, competitive planning, deal making, marketing data, all require an equitable climate of confidentiality if business is to prosper in a global economy as our more high-minded social-policy planners and law enforcers would encourage. Although the law is not as protective of the sanctity of business relations as it is of traditional professional relations, it does recognize some public-policy standards of business confidentiality.

The need for confidentiality in business contexts is extensive and palpable, and business confidences are as insecure as other confidences. For good reasons, and for evil ones, aggressive businesspeople prefer to work in the shadows of secrecy. Surreptitious monitoring of competitors, eavesdropping, wiretapping, industrial espionage, and other ingenious uses of evolving technologies have been exploited imaginatively, corruptly, and in a seemingly infinite number of ways in the competitive and high-stakes world of business.

The problem is historical and contemporary. Professor Westin's 1960s privacy study recorded examples of high-level transgressions involving confidential communications in the business community—in stock offerings and proxy fights, in construction-contract biddings, in real-estate dealings, and in other major businesses' and industries' competitive dealings.[2] Information is "the lifeblood of business and industry," one expert has noted, and the competition to preserve it and to obtain it is in constant competition.[3] The economic stakes can be profound.

The daily modern demands for confidentiality in business dealings illustrate the pervasiveness of the problem. In 2007, the global entrepreneur Rupert Murdoch's offer to buy Dow Jones & Company demonstrated the financial dimension of confidentiality in business settings. Murdoch first approached Dow Jones's chief executive over a private breakfast to express his interest in buying the company for $5 billion. He followed with a written proposal to the company's board, and then a confidential e-mail to the editor of the *Wall Street Journal* to assure the editor of his commitment to the newspaper's editorial independence. The editor honored the requested confidentiality and, as a result, the *Journal* was beaten by CNBC in reporting the offer publicly.

As soon as the proposed sale was made public, Dow Jones's stock price rose 50 percent. There were immediate SEC inquiries into stock options purchased before the sale, to examine potentially illegal activity. Lawyers and financial advisers of both Murdoch and Dow Jones, as well as insiders at both companies, knew of the imminent offer. Options purchases yielded a profit of $4.6 million for one investor when the news broke.[4]

In 2006, a major scandal at Hewlett-Packard raised corporate confidentiality questions. The leaking of confidential information about discussions by the board of directors led to one director's resignation and to SEC, congressional, and state criminal investigations. Top officials were indicted.[5] "There is no general duty of confidentiality for directors, only a duty of loyalty to act in the best interests of the corporation and its shareholders," counsel for one of the directors argued.[6] The directors had made a private mutual commitment of confidentiality among themselves.

The goings-on at board meetings—like government deliberations discussed earlier—ought to be confidential to encourage collegial give-and-take, the freewheeling exploration of ideas, and the uninhibited sharing of critical business information. When these confidential communications are made public, it is not surprising that the corporation would investigate the source of the leak. In this case, along with directors, nine journalists were investigated by private investigators hired by the corporation. The investigation itself prompted complaints about the invasion of the privacy of the journalists (several have sued Hewlett-Packard) and board members who were investigated. The corporation had hired private investigators, who reportedly used questionable tactics—pretexting of phone records, for one.

Litigation in St. Paul, Minnesota, involved a newspaper executive who moved to a rival newspaper in violation of a noncompete agreement, taking with him confidential business documents from the computer files of his prior employer. The executive testified that he copied proprietary documents from his old computer and transferred them to his new computer at his new employer's office and shared the information with his new colleagues. He "had profit numbers, revenue numbers, and expense numbers," along with sensitive information on advertisers and personnel, a press account of the trial reported. One wonders what he had in mind. His defense was an oral release from the noncompete agreement and his claim that he intended to use the spreadsheets only as templates. The local court barred him from working for his new employer for a year, in accordance with state law and "his common law duty of loyalty." A trial for monetary damages will follow.[7]

Courts have protected employers in various contexts in which former employees used confidential information gathered in the course of their employment to profit personally in competition with their former employers. Courts have been conservative in enforcing noncompete agreements against former employees, viewing such agreements as against public policy, but they have more readily enforced nondisclosure agreements as proper forms of protecting against unfair competition, wrongful appropriation of confidential information, and breach of expressed or implied loyalty. Trade secrets are an example of business confidentiality that courts will protect.

Not only do businesses endeavor to protect the confidentiality of their inside information; they also must protect their clients' confidentiality. Most businesses have programs and practices designed to protect their clients' confidentiality. For example, major brokerage houses store vast collections of their investors' most private and personal financial information. They promise, and laws require them, to safeguard this confidential information and limit access by third parties. Investors may opt to instruct that the brokerage company not share their confidential records with other companies.

Despite these protections, within a brokerage company a small village of people aside from one's broker have access to clients' records—sales assistants, cashiers, operations-department and management personnel, other collaborating brokers and assistants, regional management, compliance officers, trade-desk operatives. Most brokers work at multiple organizations during their careers, so the number of people with access to a client's files is further increased when, as is often the case, clients move their accounts to their broker's new firm. For audit and compliance purposes, and because of legal requirements, each company keeps client records for several years after an account is closed.

Access to people's confidential information is expanded when nonaffiliated organizations and personnel provide supplemental services. And financial institutions often allow clients to conduct transactions over the Internet, which is less than completely secure. Brokers ask, sincerely, how might they provide their services otherwise? Investors may ask, how confidential are my records?

A major insurance conglomerate advises its customers that it may need to know more information about them than they provide. Thus, it may seek information about them from "relatives, employers, consumer reporting agencies, health care providers and others." To serve you better, the insurance company may need to "disclose it [the information] to our affiliates and others," if the company deems it "reasonably necessary." Do not worry, the company says, those to whom information about you is disclosed "are required to take appropriate steps to protect this information."[8] Those who read this privacy notice are expected to feel comfortable about the confidentiality of their files.

Businesses sometimes are self-conscious or defensive about their obligations to maintain customers' privacy. Google's annual report in 2007 noted that their Web-based products and services could create problems concerning the confidentiality of their customers' data. Those problems would "harm our reputation and brand, and therefore our business," the report commented. Thus Google promises to "strive to comply with all applicable data protection laws," however uncertain and in flux they may be. Confidentiality must be on its corporate mind because all online searches are traceable to a personal Internet address. Google's database includes information about all aspects of its customers' lives—health, financial, personal, and professional.

It is not only the vast global companies who must deal with confidentiality. Small-business owners and other professionals as diverse as real-estate agents and sports professionals, physical therapists and executives at nongovernmental organizations, have told me that they and their colleagues operate under some, often ill-defined, constraints about the confidentiality of their conversations with clients and other client records. Florida condominium associations are governed by a statute that requires certain condominium records to be confidential, but state sunshine laws demand that some of these records be accessible to the public. As a result, condominium operations involve a riptide of competing interests—for confidentiality and for openness.

Confidentiality issues arise often in diverse business situations. When a letter from a museum curator to top museum officers complaining that they had acted improperly toward her in a public dispute was leaked to the press, her lawyer asserted that the letter was "a private document"[9]—whatever that means.

Showtime entered into a joint venture with the Smithsonian Institution for exclusive network rights to present documentaries using Smithsonian materials. Independent documentary makers protested that they were excluded. When they challenged contract procedures, one Smithsonian official claimed that its contract terms were "confidential." Curators who were interviewed would only speak anonymously for fear of recriminations.[10] The Smithsonian eventually backed away from its position after facing a public furor. The dealings were confidential, until they weren't.

So was the transcript of a controversial conversation with O. J. Simpson that was filmed for what turned out to be an aborted television interview. Despite a confidentiality agreement signed by the parties, the *New York Times* received the transcript from an anonymous source.

A Hollywood movie producer sued the Academy of Motion Picture Arts and Sciences and the Producers Guild of America for denying him credit as a producer of the 2005 Academy Award–winning film *Crash*. He challenged as unfair both organizations' confidential procedures for secretly arbitrating such claims. The confidentiality of the procedure was justified as a way to encourage witnesses to speak freely without fear of retribution. One observer remarked that if testimony by witnesses from the film industry was disclosed, powerful protagonists could ensure that "they're never going to do lunch in this town again."[11] As a practical matter, that fear may be real. But due process of law based on fair procedures is as important as self-protection, especially when matters of consequence are involved. All witnesses are subject to stress and intimidation when they testify; but the law requires that witnesses endure such vicissitudes as a necessary civic responsibility for a greater social good, namely, getting to the truth of a matter in dispute.

Employers and employees have different motives and needs regarding the confidentiality of employee records. One of the country's largest corporations, Wal-Mart Stores, Inc., instituted a sophisticated electronic surveillance operation to screen its employees. One employee reported that the company's computer network was spied upon regularly by a special group of security employees who worked in a secure office called the "Bat

Cave." They trolled e-mails looking for evidence of theft or misbehavior. But, through this monitoring, screeners picked up information about shareholders and communications with the press, and intercepted phone and pager communications—all inappropriate actions. Employees have "no expectation of privacy" on the premises when they use company computers and phones, the company admonished, challenging the reports about its spying.[12]

A business's noble aspirations and its commercial needs may conflict. Self-interest and public interests can be antagonistic, as when business efficiency is at variance with humane concerns. (When, if ever, should a prospective employee's medical condition or that of an employee's family member be disclosed to an employer?) Secrecy and transparency are in regular opposition to each other in the competitive commercial marketplace.

New technologies magnify the potential for invasions of confidential information. An example of the technological aspect of industrial espionage involved Reuters, a major supplier of financial information. When it learned that a competitor, Bloomberg, had taken over a significant segment of the $6 billion annual market, Reuters commissioned another company to conduct electronic break-ins of Bloomberg's computers to obtain confidential information and enable it to develop a competitive product. What was called Bloomberg's "holy grail," "the central nervous system of the software" that serviced institutional investors, was stolen. A confidential informant helped a yearlong government investigation.[13]

Claims of confidentiality may be based on explicit or presumed agreements in various business dealings. Courts treat these situations as matters governed by the general law of agency or the law of trust and fiduciary relations.

Confidentiality questions may arise in cases construing codes of ethics governing professionals who historically have not been covered by recognized privileges—accountants and engineers, for example. Confidentiality issues arise in interpreting agreements by parties settling claims and litigation. Confidentiality also comes up in evolving institutional claims for privilege—universities in their peer-review procedures, for example.

Statutes and court decisions do not always make clear what is and what is not public information. Businesses have internal rules and intraorganizational codes of ethics, which may or may not be enforced by courts. Some business information is protected through private agreements, which may create a just resolution between the agreeing parties but for reasons that are explored in this chapter, may have social impacts that are not in the public interest.

Business, government, employment, and educational relationships, and even private commercial relationships between strangers or friends, require participants to honor the confidentiality of communications in order to encourage communal integrity and full and open participation. If participants thought that there would be no confidentiality, they might not participate. Confidentiality should therefore be encouraged. Only when public disclosure is required for a strong public purpose is there a question whether confidentiality should be breached.

Professional Codes

The American Institute of Architects (AIA) Code of Ethics and Professional Conduct requires architects to "safeguard the trust placed in them by their clients." Practitioners are instructed not to disclose information "that they have been asked to maintain in confidence" or that "would adversely affect their client." The requirement is intended to help safeguard clients' trust. The AIA code recognizes the distinction between a privileged communication and confidentiality: "Members must recognize and respect the sensitive nature of confidential client communications. Because the law does not recognize an architect-client privilege, however, the rule permits a Member to reveal a confidence when a failure to do so would be unlawful or contrary to another ethical duty imposed by this Code."[14]

Similarly, engineers and accountants have intramural policies regarding the confidentiality of their dealings with clients. They are guided by rules describing when they are excused from maintaining confidentiality and when they may be mandated to disclose information. But the law, so far, does not provide these professions with privileges not to testify if their testimony is required and appropriate.

At the end of the twentieth century, there were half a million engineers in America. The American Institute of Electrical Engineers and the Engineers' Council for Professional Development admonish engineers that they have a duty to the public as well as to their clients. The consequences of this public duty can be quite serious, as they were in a 1971 case involving engineers who disclosed—first to their employers, then to organization managers, and finally to the California Society of Professional Engineers—that the BART rapid system had flaws in its design that endangered public safety. Their fears were realized when a train overran a station and injured passengers, as the engineers had warned could happen. For their social responsibility, they were fired, then vindicated, but they ultimately paid a personal price, as whistle-blowers generally do.[15] The catastrophic nature of engineering disasters—like medical epidemics—certainly justifies exceptions to general professional rules of confidentiality.

Accountants are licensed and regulated by professional associations (the American Institute of Certified Public Accountants (AICPA), and the Institute of Management Accountants)) whose codes encourage confidentiality but note that the public interest may warrant disclosure of confidential information, such as when one client is defrauding another,[16] or when a general partner is defrauding limited partners. The AICPA Code of Professional Conduct mandates confidentiality.[17] However, reliance on private advice from accountants—like stockbrokers, financial advisers, and insurance counselors—is generally not a basis for privilege in American law. Accountants' work is not fiduciary, and much of it is required to be disclosed. Although there may be a general preference for financial confidentiality, there is no justified expectation of privilege. For audits, the presumption is that they will be made public.

The U.S. Supreme Court has ruled that there is no accountants' privilege under federal law, nor under the Fourth and Fifth Amendments, "and no state-created privilege has been recognized in federal cases." The Court asserted that "there can be little expectation of privacy where records are handed to an accountant," and accountants can be indicted for preparing a false return. Indeed, the Court reminded us, the tax system is "dependent upon honest self-reporting even to survive."[18] The rationale is that "the accountant's workpapers are not the taxpayer's. They were not prepared by the taxpayer, and they contain no testimonial declarations by him."[19]

Justice William Douglas urged that people's personal possessions should be "sacrosanct from prying eyes, from the long arm of the law, from any rummaging by police." Voicing lofty sentiments that today seem naive, Justice Douglas claimed that "privacy involves the choice of the individual to disclose or to reveal what he believes, what he thinks, what he possesses." He added: "Those who wrote the Bill of Rights believed that every individual needs both to communicate with others and to keep his affairs to himself. That dual aspect of privacy means that the individual should have the freedom to select for himself the time and circumstances when he will share his secrets with others and decide the extent of that sharing."[20]

This notion reflects the inherent dynamic of the broad question of confidentiality—people divulge information but still want to control its distribution. Whatever one may think about Justice Douglas's philosophical point of view, it is hard to deny law-enforcement officials access to accountants' records in a criminal case. Justice Douglas thought that "one's privacy embraces . . . what he tells any confidant," including his accountant. Otherwise the Constitution is violated and a too powerful government "may reduce people to digits."[21]

Although accountants and their clients have a confidential relationship, often involving conversations and documents of a very personal and financially consequential nature, the accountant-client relationship has had uncertain protections. About a third of the states do provide some form of an accountant-client privilege.[22] In some limited situations, the attorney-client privilege will protect the work of a collaborating accountant. In one limited situation, the attorney-client privilege has been extended to accountants by statute.[23] Under this exception to the rule requiring accountants to testify and produce documents in legal proceedings, accountants providing tax advice in a noncriminal matter at the IRS or in federal court may claim the attorney-client privilege. In all other instances (including assistance in preparing tax returns), they have no privilege.

The attorney work-product privilege is lost when information is disclosed to third parties who do not share a common interest. Disclosures to a corporation's auditors and accountants may or may not be a basis for waiving the privilege. Indeed, the Sarbanes-Oxley Act requires corporate management to provide an assessment of internal controls and the procedure for financial reporting,[24] and the courts should not discourage such self-analysis. Corporate clients should be encouraged to share information with their auditors without fearing perverse consequences. Applying that value judgment, a district court ruled that Merrill Lynch need not provide a "roadway" to its adversaries by being made to disclose its counsel's impressions and opinions.[25]

The nature of the service provided by tax practitioners to taxpayers is not privileged.[26] When, in the course of investigating certain tax shelters, the IRS sought names of an attorney's clients, the claimed privilege was denied. "The general nature of the services is not privileged," the court ruled. Client identifications are not the same as confidential communications about tax shelters. The client's very retention of the accounting firm envisioned the information being disclosed to the IRS on its returns. Thus, no confidentiality of the fact of their having the tax shelter could have been presumed; quite the contrary.[27]

The theory of extending the attorney-client privilege to accountants is that ordinarily privileges are lost if the communication is made in the presence of a third party, unless that third party is a necessary adjunct of the attorney doing his professional work for the client. The use of auditors would seem to qualify as a necessary part of an attorney's work for a client, and extending the attorney-client privilege to auditors would encourage corporate cleansing, a valuable concomitant social policy.

A 2004 case set out the ground rules for such cases. The decision dealt with a litigant's claim for access to reports of an internal investigation by Merrill Lynch's auditors completed under the supervision of its in-house and outside counsel. Merrill Lynch conceded that it had waived the attorney-client privilege but claimed that its work-product privilege covered the auditor's reports. The court explained that the work-product privilege promotes the adversary system and covers materials prepared in anticipation of litigation. A "zone of privacy" is created and materials within it are not discoverable by adversaries. Disclosures to corporate accountants and auditors do not waive the work-product privilege. In this case, the corporate client and its lawyers and accountants shared a common interest, and the court held that their work product could not become "a conduit to a potential adversary." Another interpretation would, the court pointed out, "discourage corporations from conducting critical self-analysis and sharing the fruits of such an inquiry with the appropriate actors." Such a practice would be a "perverse incentive" that would provide adversaries with a "roadway" to their opponent's strategy.[28]

Recent attempts to hold attorneys and accountants accountable for corporation misconduct have forced a reevaluation of confidentiality rules. One observer argues that "the rationale for strong confidentiality evaporates completely in those areas of corporate practice covered by regulations like the SEC's noisy withdrawal proposal." The client, not the managers, is the corporation, and corporations can waive the privilege, protect the corporation, and hold the managers accountable. The managers need to consult attorneys in order to have an advice-of-counsel defense.[29]

Agents and Employees

Employment relationships have also been encumbered by legal limitations that are reminiscent of but different from privilege. The law of agency subjects an agent to a duty "not to use or to communicate information given him by the principal or acquired by him during the course of . . . his agency," in order to compete with, or if it would injure, the principal.[30] Standard legal authorities all note that the laws of agency provide that agents are required to keep confidential all information about their principals. "An agent's duty of confidentiality extends to all such information concerning a principal even when it is not otherwise connected with the subject matter of the agency."[31] The means by which the agent appropriates a principal's information are irrelevant. The duty of confidentiality is highly regarded, but it is not absolute. Nonetheless, confidentiality may be breached only in extreme circumstances—a crime about to be committed or a person injured.

An agent is treated like a trustee. The agent's duty may be agreed upon explicitly, as a term in an employment contract, or may be implied by the law.[32] Agency arrangements are sometimes referred to as master-servant relationships.

Agents are deemed to have fiduciary relationships with their employers, and these relationships should not be exploited to the detriment of past employers, though the encouragement of competition in a capitalistic society does afford employees the right to strike out on their own in fair and open competition. Courts will, for example, permit employees to leave their jobs and compete against their former bosses, but they will not allow them to appropriate and exploit private or secret proprietary information gathered in the course of their prior employment—a fair and balanced formula. There is an obvious difference, for example, between a securities trader or banking official using confidential inside information for private gain and a salesperson learning a business generally and striking out on his or her own in competition with a former mentor—as long as the salesperson doesn't take client lists or proprietary records.

When a fiduciary relationship does exist, courts will enforce claims stemming from the appropriation of confidential information, even if information is appropriated indirectly, as when a psychiatrist used information gained from his treatment of the wife of a stockbroker to make investments, or when a newspaper reporter tipped a broker of news about to break in his newspaper to gain an investment advantage.

Formal fiduciary or agency relationships are not necessary for obligations of confidentiality to be recognized. In her book *Legal Secrets,* Professor Kim Lane Scheppele analyzes cases in which courts allowed parties in commercial transactions to keep secrets and cases in which courts imposed obligations to reveal secrets to avoid fraud.[33] Caveat-emptor attitudes in a laissez-faire society do not condone an insured's failure to disclose a known medical problem, for example; contract and tort law both require disclosure in such situations.

The legal duty not to disclose information is greater when there is a confidential fiduciary relationship, such as a bank has to a depositor. That duty to maintain confidentiality may be overcome when certain circumstances (transactions related to drug trafficking, money laundering, or terrorism, for example) give rise to special duties to reveal confidential information. Courts have required parties to reveal confidential information, for moral and ethical reasons, in connection with insurance, stock, and real-estate transactions.

Private Confidentiality Agreements

An excessive and often questionable claim of confidentiality is based on the confidentiality clause commonly found in private settlement agreements. A standard clause in most settlements of civil disputes states that the parties agree to maintain the confidentiality of the terms of the settlement. The records are sealed and the parties gagged. It may be logical to sanction such practices, but it raises troubling questions of public policy: Should courts allow the parties to hush facts that endanger others?

Without such confidentiality agreements, the argument goes, parties would lose a crucial reason for settling cases and the judicial system would lose a way to reduce the volume of litigation. When the pop entertainer Michael Jackson was indicted (he was ultimately acquitted) for child molestation in California in 2002, his earlier settlement of a civil suit involving comparable charges was leaked to the press. Jackson cried foul: that 1993 settlement contained a confidentiality agreement not to make the settlement terms public. Jackson claimed that avoiding negative publicity was a major reason for his agreeing to the multimillion-dollar settlement. People who agreed reluctantly to settlements to avoid negative charges being made public might have shared Jackson's feeling of betrayal.

As common as confidentiality agreements are, their social utility is debatable. A 2004 Department of Justice seminar on civil justice concluded, among other things, that the dearth of insightful information about the quality of civil justice is due to the ubiquity of civil settlement agreements, in courts and in mediation, which typically contain confidentiality agreements. "Confidentiality requirements are one of the major impediments to studying civil settlements," the Justice Department report concluded.[34]

Proponents point out that confidentiality agreements foster settlements, which cuts litigants' private costs as well as the public costs of the trial process. Secrecy facilitates compromise; it is "the lubricant to dispute resolution."[35] Settlements save court costs. Nuisance claims can be bought off for the price of secrecy. The parties and their attorneys have only their cases to consider, not the public's interest in them. Courts provide problem-solving functions in such cases. The role of courts is not to supply public information.

However, because of these confidentiality agreements, public misconduct goes undetected and may be repeated.[36] When a highly ranked professional tennis player from Argentina, Guillermo Coria, tested positive for steroid use, he was suspended from the pro circuit for seven months. He lost two seasons of potential prize money and endorsement and appearance fees, worth millions, he claimed, in addition to being labeled a cheater. He claimed that the supplement he used was contaminated and sued the manufacturer. Terms of the settlement were not released. Nor were the settlement terms of a similar suit by a swimmer. Comparable claims have been made by football and baseball players, a bobsledder, and other tennis players against other companies. When the cases are settled with secret agreements, others similarly situated have no idea of potential problems—problems that they might avoid if the findings were public.[37]

The public has an interest in full and open adjudication when, as often happens, private disputes have important public implications—exposing safety problems, medical malpractice, product defects, human- and civil-rights violations, or government misconduct, for example. When cases involve more than private wrongdoing, the public has no way of preventing repetition of such conduct if the result of the case is hidden. Courts can perform public watchdog roles in such instances by publicizing the facts of the settlement.

Yale law professor Owen Fiss is cynical about the public consequences of confidential settlements. He calls them "a capitulation to the conditions of mass society" that encourages private parties to "settle while leaving justice undone." When that happens, he points out, "society gets less than what appears, and for a price it does not know it is paying." In civil-rights cases, for example, he points out that settlements "might secure the peace, but not racial equality." Community peace may not be the same as justice. "To settle for something means to accept something less than ideal."[38]

Another academic commentator reached a similar conclusion regarding environmental disputes. There, confidential settlements may mask the true cost to society, allowing polluters to settle without alerting nonparties who will be affected, shielding producers of harmful products from public scrutiny, and allowing repeat offenders to avoid creation of adverse precedent.[39] The bigger the business interest, the greater the need for confidentiality and the greater the corresponding need for public disclosure.

A related problem arises from the concealment of judicial decisions by judges and court officials. In April 2007, the Florida Supreme Court adopted a rule forbidding court insiders from secreting dispositions from public scrutiny.[40] Under a common practice, judges, lawyers, politicians, and businesspeople regularly concealed files and records of sensitive cases—"super-sealing," it was called. Under the new rule, openness replaces secrecy unless litigants demonstrate a legitimate reason for shielding information (for example, to protect trade secrets or confidential informants).

There may also be private reasons for disclosing confidential settlements. An attorney who represented many victims of sexual abuse by church officials refused to muzzle his clients. "The victims were entitled to talk to who they wanted to," he wrote to me, "as part of the healing process." He added, "confidentiality agreements for victims of sexual abuse can become very traumatic after the fact. Almost invariably, the victim at some point begins to feel that the defendants . . . bought their silence . . . and [victims] beat themselves up severely. . . . I resist confidentiality."

The use of confidentiality agreements in settlements is governed by court rules or statute, or is left to the discretion of judges. About a dozen states—including Florida, North Carolina, Oregon, Texas, and Rhode Island have "sunshine in litigation" rules requiring the publication of settlements unless there is an overriding demonstrated public interest in secrecy.[41] Some states forbid confidentiality clauses in cases involving public officials.

There is a discernable trend—judicial and legislative—toward disapproving secret settlements. The South Carolina Supreme Court, for example, amended its court rules to require a balancing of public and private interests before courts approve secret settlements. Judges are required to consider public harms caused by keeping settlements secret and the public interest in the openness of settlements. And "under no circumstances shall a court approve sealing a settlement agreement which involves a public body or institution."[42]

Several federal circuit courts have articulated the policies behind disclosure of settlement agreements. They have noted the "presumptive common-law right of access to court documents," the need for public access to court records, the public interest in court matters, the secondary nature of the private litigants' interests in settlements involving public issues, and the need to protect the integrity of the judicial process by not allowing courts to be implicated in keeping public information from the public.[43]

Recent cases have decreed that the public's right to know should defeat the private parties' interest in secrecy for personal or business reasons when public interests are involved. Duplicate litigation is necessitated and the public is deprived of a valuable asset when settlements are kept secret. To require repetitive litigation is economically inefficient and, in cases where public interests are involved, can be a hazard to public health and safety, courts have ruled.[44] Secrecy can conceal corruption and should not be sanctioned by courts unless strong reasons require it. Secret settlements are unethical and dangerous to the public. One critic of bar policies and practices recommended that state courts and legislatures and the ABA deal with the problem.[45]

Compromise should not be difficult. In cases involving trade secrets or personal intimacies, there are clear reasons to protect secrecy. In commercial cases involving public misconduct, secret settlements would be mischievous and against the public interest, amounting to no more than hush money.

One expert concluded that "courts should accommodate the various competing interests, both public and private, in determining whether and when to override the litigants' mutual desire or need for privacy and the strong, institutional policy favoring settlement."[46]

Because most cases are settled, the administration of justice is carried out quasi-privately in a large majority of cases, regardless of the public interest involved. The impact of secret justice is profound. A case-by-case, issue-by-issue balancing approach would weigh the need for "public monitoring of the judicial system and its core adjudicative product" against the competing value of private and confidential settlements.[47]

Self-Regulation

Private organizational policies pose an expanding category of confidentiality problems. Some courts have condoned a qualified privilege for university research, peer review, and other academic processes; other courts have denied any privilege; some have purported to strike a balance between the need to protect secrecy and policy reasons not to.[48]

Congress passed laws protecting the confidentiality of census and alcohol and drug studies. However, most scholars and researchers have been rejected when they claimed protection for their scholarly research sources, comparing their claims to those of journalists who have shield laws (see chapter 9). Courts usually reject such claims for a qualified privilege for researchers, though some exceptions have been made. As one survey of these cases concluded, "a researcher can only offer participants personal promises of loyalty and confidence."[49] There is no clear privilege governing scholars. The late senator Moynihan proposed (unsuccessfully) the Thomas Jefferson Researcher's Privilege Act in 1999.[50]

The self-evaluative process that all organizations, corporations, government agencies, and universities engage in is the heart of self-improvement and reform. Questions arise, however, about access to such private and quasi-private institutions' inside appraisals. Like government deliberations, the creative process is encouraged by the sense of confidentiality between participating parties, the security of knowing that their conversations and reports are confidential. But the value judgments rarely end there, and countervailing pressures for access to this kind of insider information often arise. Most state and federal courts have rejected claims for a privilege applicable to self-criticism, inside deliberations, and evaluations.[51]

Encouraging self-regulation by organizations is an important social-policy goal. When the self-evaluation is required by law, courts are less resistant to condoning some privilege to protect the information, though arguably the greater virtue is the voluntary reform, which should not be punished or discouraged. Corporate audits, legal investigations, and other forms of self-regulation are increasing, and with them will come the contentions that the results should be privileged.

Akin to self-regulation by organizations is self-evaluation, a subject that arises in cases involving internal academic proceedings. Universities are centers of learning, but they are big—multibillion-dollar—businesses, too. In 2003, 13 million Americans were enrolled in and 1.4 million graduated from colleges and universities; universities employed 2.5 million people including scholars and working laborers; and their budgets were over $315 billion.[52] Big business it is, giving rise to various confidentiality issues.

A recent book criticizes colleges and universities for conducting their business behind closed doors, where scandals and crimes can be buried or covered up. "Secrecy envelops student and faculty discipline matters, admissions, promotion and tenure, searches and hires, public safety, financial dealings." The culture at universities, that study concludes, is "endemically secret," "Vatican-like," and as authoritarian as the Pentagon."[53] Even archival records are buried to hide past prejudices and injustices.

The confidentiality issue most unique to universities involves the peer-review process. Universities view those confidences as absolutely essential to ensure candor and frankness and integrity. So far, the courts have not agreed, and have been "reluctant to adopt a peer review privilege."[54]

Academic corporations have argued vigorously that their deliberations deserve privileges comparable to those of other professions and businesses, and those arguments have been accepted in some cases but rejected in others. Academic organizations have claimed a constitutional source for their need for confidentiality, not the same as businesses and professions. The college and university claims have been based on academic freedom emanating from the First Amendment, which protects the right to decide who teaches, what is taught, how it is taught, and who may be admitted. Confidential peer review, they argued, is critical to academic freedom and worthy of qualified, if not absolute, protection. It is, one claim urged, "the very lifeblood and heartbeat of academic excellence and plays a most vital role in the functioning of our nation's colleges."[55]

The federal courts have divided on this issue and the question whether Federal Rule of Evidence 501 permits a qualified privilege of confidentiality for academic organizations, be they small liberal-arts colleges like Franklin and Marshall or large universities like Notre Dame. One case acknowledged the business nature of academic institutions; another dealt with the balancing of legal and academic claims in a university setting. The issue was resolved near the end of the twentieth century in a Supreme Court case involving the University of Pennsylvania.

An earlier case involved a University of Wisconsin survey and research organization run by a faculty member in Madison. One part-time interviewer conducting a survey of shoppers' attitudes about a mall protested to his supervisors that their role in the survey was inappropriate. His view not accepted, he leaked survey data to the press, and later a student newspaper picked up the story. He had signed a confidentiality agreement pertaining to his work on the survey and had been admonished about the importance of the confidentiality of the research when the first story appeared in a local newspaper. When he was discharged, he sued, claiming that his First Amendment rights were violated. The Supreme Court of Wisconsin decided that the claimant was not fired for his expressions of views on a matter of public importance. Confidentiality of survey questions is necessary to ensure the integrity of evolving research and the researcher's reputation; thus, the confidentiality agreement was reasonable and enforceable. The employee in effect violated a fiduciary duty to his employer. The court concluded that the university "is no different than any other business enterprise, and was entitled to enforce its confidentiality rules to protect its "profitability."[56]

However, the key case dealing with claims by academic organizations for privileged communications arose from a clash between the EEOC and the University of Pennsylvania.[57] Rosalie Tung was denied tenure. She claimed that she had been discriminated against on the basis of her sex and race. During its investigation of her claim, the EEOC sought but was denied confidential evaluations, the department chairman's evaluation letter (Tung claimed that he had sexually harassed her and took negative action when she rebuffed him), and notes of the faculty committee's internal deliberations regarding her and other candidates for tenure. The university argued that it had a qualified privilege to protect peer-review materials, a privilege based on the First Amendment's protection of academic freedom.

Justice Blackmun's majority opinion upheld the EEOC's right to demand evidence needed to make its decision, noting that Congress did not grant confidentiality to employers dealing with the EEOC, though Congress considered the question. The Court rejected the university's claim that, as a center of learning protected by the First Amendment's protection of academic freedom, the university required confidentiality of its peer-review process. To deny this privilege, the university claimed, would chill and undermine the candor and free exchange of ideas that faculty members require in making tenure decisions. The Court decided that the burden on the university was incidental and that the EEOC's mission would be frustrated if it could not establish proof, or lack of proof, of charges brought to it. The university chose the wrong test case. On balance, the Court favored the search for truth over competing needs for confidentiality, the mission of the government over that of the academy. The Court feared "a waive of similar privilege claims" by other groups if it extended the privilege of confidentiality to universities.

Some laws preclude the disclosure of certain kinds of information. In doing so, they create protections similar to the protection afforded privileged communications. The Freedom of Information Act and the Americans with Disabilities Act preclude access to certain information by the general public. That information, however, might be available in a trial. Treating information as confidential is not the same as, and does not have the same consequences as, privileged information.

In his update of Dean Wigmore's classic treatise, Professor Imwinkelried presents a diagram illustrating the differences between privilege and its comparable cousins—ethical duties, evidence rules, quasi privileges, and constitutional exclusionary rules.[58] As a general rule, confidential business arrangements are not privileged, though courts will protect some arrangements for reasons of equity and fairness.

There is a postscript to the question of protecting the confidentiality of business information: businesses regularly invade the privacy and sanctity of individuals' otherwise confidential communications. For example, an employer's monitoring of its employees' actions and records may be reasonable and prudent from an economic perspective, but it also intrudes upon employees' privacy. That was the issue when Wal-Mart's surveillance of workers, vendors, critics, and consultants was challenged.[59] Employee medical and work records may be relevant to employers' hiring, disciplining, and firing decisions, but employees are rightly concerned about invasive and prejudicial surveillance of their confidential communications. Too often, litigators, insurers, marketers use invasive technology that violates individuals' privacy—practices that are always morally suspect and often illegal. Violations of employees' privacy are enhanced by sophisticated modern technologies, which is the subject of chapter 10.

Ground rules are required to ensure a proper balanced control of business practices, and they should be enforced once prescribed. In this context, confidentiality must be a two-way street; it should be enforced by businesses, as well as for businesses, to appropriate a classic phrase.

9

JOURNALISTS: THE REACH OF THE FIRST AMENDMENT AND THE VALUE OF THE ANONYMOUS SOURCE

> Raymond Rambert . . . came straight to the point. His newspaper, one of the leading Paris dailies, had commissioned him to make a report on the living conditions prevailing amongst the Arab population, and especially on the sanitary conditions.
>
> Rieux replied that these conditions were not good. But, before he said any more, he wanted to know if the journalist would be allowed to tell the truth.
>
> "Certainly I shall," Rambert replied.
>
> "I mean," Rieux explained, "would you be allowed to publish an unqualified condemnation of the present state of things?"
>
> "Unqualified? Well, I must own I couldn't go that far. But surely things aren't quite so bad as that?"
>
> "No," Rieux said quietly. He had put the question solely to find out if Rambert could or couldn't state the facts without altering the truth.
>
> "I've no use for statements in which something is kept back. And this is why I shall not furnish information."
>
> The journalist smiled. "You talk the language of St. Just."
>
> —Albert Camus, *The Plague*

For about a century, journalists have claimed that they should not be forced to testify when doing so would require disclosing the sources of their information. They have based their claim on the First Amendment and on the public-interest-based pragmatic ground that without the ability to promise anonymity, they could not perform a vital part of their work. Both premises—the right and the need—are discussed in this chapter.

The Privilege

Should news gatherers and writers in general have a privilege not to disclose confidential communications, a right that has historically been denied other citizens? The claim that citizens may not, as a point of honor, be forced to disclose confidential information they had promised not to divulge has generally been denied by courts in their search for truth. The Sixth Amendment guarantees those accused in criminal prosecutions the right to a fair trial, including the right "to have compulsory process for obtaining witnesses in his favor." That constitutional right is explicit and unequivocal.

In the United States, where journalists have some protections deriving from the First Amendment, they have also claimed a constitutional right not to reveal their anonymous sources; indeed, they have operated as if they had such a privilege, which they view as a fundamental canon of their ethics and a professional, principled article of faith. They have done so with mixed success, often in high-visibility cases involving notorious parties. Their claim of privilege was very much in the news at the start of the twenty-first century. The question of confidentiality is relevant not only to print and television journalists but also to scholarly authors, students, novelists—indeed, to all writers, including the new breed of commentators on the blogosphere.

The underlying premise relied on by reporters and press organizations in claiming a constitutionally based privilege is that journalists perform an important public service by ferreting out misconduct. It is in the public interest that their information gathering be protected.[1] That public-information function is based on and protected by the First Amendment, the argument continues. Without the gathering of information, according to this argument, there can be no reporting of valuable but unavailable news. To complete the syllogism, the press points out that if it cannot promise anonymity to news sources, it cannot acquire the news that it is in business to print and broadcast, and cannot report it to the public. The press is a critical check on governmental power, and sometimes the only one; its watchdog role is in the public interest. In this respect, the press is the alter ego of the public.

The strong intersecting policy considerations involved in this continuing dispute were suggested in a recent review of a book dealing with the use of performance-enhancing drugs by professional athletes. In her review of *Game of Shadows,* by two San Francisco investigative reporters, the influential *New York Times* critic Michiko Kakutani noted the riptides of social policies that underlie journalists' claims that they should not be forced to disclose their sources. Kakutani noted that the authors' articles "helped galvanize the national debate about steroids and contributed to the push for Congressional hearings." She also noted the authors' use of questionable sources. Their groundbreaking reporting, Kakutani revealed, was based on "secret grand jury testimony . . . confidential memorandums detailing federal agents' interviews with some of the principal players in the case; and unredacted versions of affidavits filed by the Balco investigation."[2]

The book caused a public furor and generated further investigations—classic examples of the justification for protecting reporters' sources. But those grand-jury sources Kakutani mentioned are legally protected and for good reasons that are themselves grounded in important social policies. On the one hand, the book is "necessary reading" for understanding "the fallout on sports history" of the use of steroids by athletes, according to the Pulitzer Prize–winning reviewer. At the same time, it should be understood, it is against the law to disclose secret grand-jury and confidential prosecutorial investigative information—and for good reasons of public policy.

To make the conundrum more complex, it was discovered months later that the source of the leak was none other than the attorney for one of the officials being investigated by the grand jury. He leaked the grand-jury record not because the grand jury was not doing its work properly—it was—but in an attempt to have the charges against his client dismissed by blaming the prosecutors for the leak and arguing that his client could not get a fair trial. He leaked a second time, claiming that the prosecutors were smearing his client. The reporters knew that he was their source, but they printed the accusations, which, it turned out, were wrong and self-serving. The attorney was indicted and pleaded guilty to the charges.

A press critic argued that when reporters are complicit in assisting a leaker's private agenda—and a questionable one at that—they are in an "ethical mess" and in no position to claim a constitutional right to protect that source. Indeed, it could be argued that they should have exposed the leaker's morally and legally wrongful leak.[3]

Therein lies the heart of the historic battles between journalists and courts, between the overarching and at times competing rights of the First Amendment's freedom of the press and the Sixth Amendment's guarantee of a fair trial. The Sixth Amendment guarantees defendants in criminal trials several rights—the right to a speedy and public trial, the right to an impartial jury, the right to counsel, and, particularly relevant to this book, the right to confront witnesses testifying against them and to have compulsory process for obtaining witnesses in their favor. Together these rights constitute the constitutional right to a fair trial. But these rights may conflict with the press's claims of privilege, and when they do, there arises a classic constitutional conundrum, the so-called free press—fair trial conflict.

Rodney Smolla, dean of the Washington and Lee University School of Law, has made an interesting point about the nature of privileges in the legal system. Whereas the traditional privileges, like those of attorneys and doctors, derive from formal confidential relationships in which candor is necessary, he suggested, a journalist's privilege "might apply to everyone a journalist meets in reporting a story," and could be made on the spot, as needed. "The courts are loath to hand that kind of power to journalists to put information off limits."[4] A former editor of the *Des Moines Register,* Gilbert Cranberg, made a similar point about the critical difference between the journalists' claim for privilege and that of doctors and attorneys. The latter "do not publicize what clients tell them, whereas reporters do. Because they do, the public has an interest in knowing the identity of sources so they can assess the reliability of the information the sources provided."[5]

Early-nineteenth- and twentieth-century American cases uniformly rejected journalists' claims that they have the right not to disclose their sources. "As the law now is, and has for ages existed," a New York state judge wrote in 1874, "no court could possibly hold that a witness could legally refuse to give the name of the author of an alleged libel, for the reason that the rules of a public journal forbade it." A California judge in 1897 said that a newspaper reporter's claim of privilege "scarcely merits comment." A Mississippi judge wrote, "Individual standards of elevated principles of social duty cannot be permitted to terminate investigations so absolutely essential to public welfare." And an early-twentieth-century Georgia court explained the judicial lack of sympathy for reporters' claims: "A promise not to testify when so required is substantially a promise not to obey the law"; such a notion would "render courts impotent" and justice a mockery.[6]

The problem emerged after the Civil War, when muckraking journalism led to the practice of protecting anonymous sources in order to cover sensational cases. As one evidence treatise reported, claims of testimonial privilege were rare, historically. Earlier, Benjamin Franklin's brother was jailed for refusing to name a source for a story in his newspaper. But no case on the subject reached the courts until the mid-nineteenth century, when the Senate imprisoned a *New York Herald* reporter who would not name the source of a leak about a pending treaty. During the Depression, critical press stories led to legal battles over access to press sources. Journalists claimed privilege on various grounds, asserting that forcing their testimony would violate journalistic ethics or their employer's regulations, would violate their rights against self-incrimination rights, or would impinge on the freedom of the press.[7] Courts were uniformly unreceptive to these claims. But jailings were short and ritualistic, creating a de facto privilege, some claimed, that preserved judicial superiority without generating institutional antagonisms.

In the second half of the twentieth century, cases proliferated as a result of the clashes between aggressive journalism and equally aggressive prosecutions, and expanding interpretations of the First Amendment. "About all litigation on this controversy in the federal courts has occurred within the last forty-five years," a 2005 law-review article notes, probably as a result of clashes between the press and the government arising from Watergate, Vietnam, and the civil-rights revolution. These battles moved the press-court conflict "out of the law reviews and into the political arena."[8]

The governing principle, one that has consistently been upheld, was articulated in a 1958 defamation case. The singer Judy Garland was offended by a column quoting a CBS official saying that she was too fat. Garland demanded the identification of a *New York Herald Tribune* reporter's source at CBS. The reporter claimed a privilege to protect her source. The trial court denied her claim of privilege and ordered her to state the name of her source. The Second Circuit Court of Appeals affirmed, explaining,

"At the foundation of the Republic the obligation of a witness to testify and the correlative right of a litigant to enlist judicial compulsion of testimony were recognized as incidents of the judicial power of the United States." This citizen's duty is essential "to the fabric of our society." The right to sue and defend in court "is the alternative of force. . . . It is the right conservative of all other rights, and lies at the foundation of orderly society."[9] Justice Felix Frankfurter had said in an earlier case that the obligation to testify "has to do with the power of the state to discharge an indispensable function of civilized society, that of adjudicating controversies . . . through legal tribunals . . . with their historic procedures."[10]

In 1961, the Supreme Court of Hawaii explored the constitutional dimension of this conflict in a case dealing with a reporter who refused to divulge his source for a story about the firing of a Civil Service Commission official. The reporter claimed that exposing his source would be "a very grievous breach of my professional ethics."[11] The Hawaiian high court reviewed the First Amendment theory underlying this claim and the policy reason for denying it. There is a fundamental societal need, the Hawaii court observed, to, as U.S. Supreme Court decisions had historically held, preserve an "untrammeled press as a vital source of public information."[12] The country needs its public affairs publicized to prevent misgovernment. A free press is necessary for a free society; thus it should be given "the broadest scope that could be countenanced in an orderly society."[13] The freedom to gather news is inseparable from the freedom to print news. Any government action that interferes with the collection of news is an interference with the press.[14] But this press power is not absolute, the analysis continued. There is a corresponding and prevailing duty of all citizens, journalists included, owed to the government "to support the administration of justice by attending its courts and giving [their] testimony whenever [they are] properly summoned."[15] That duty too is based on the welfare of the public. Journalists are afforded no exception to this duty, American courts have traditionally ruled.

Despite consistent court rulings following these precedents, reporters have persisted in claiming that the inherent nature of their public service warrants extending the guaranty of confidentiality to their sources. Reporters assure their sources that although the information they provide may be made public, their identification as the source of the information will be protected. Only then are reporters able to provide public information of real value. If reporters could not assure their sources that their identities would remain confidential, the sources would dry up for fear of retribution.

No doubt, anonymous sources are useful to journalists. And if sources are not protected, public enlightenment in these situations might suffer and government abuse might go undetected. The free press ensures the success of self-government, and it exists to bare the secrets of government and inform the people. Reporters are no better than their sources of information. Without good and reliable sources, "the real news simply dries up, and the whole truth steadily recedes behind a wall of image-mongering, denial and even outright lies."[16] In the words of First Amendment absolutists Justices Hugo Black and William O. Douglas, there is nothing to balance; the Amendment's protection is absolute.

In 1971, the University of Michigan law professor Vince Blasi conducted a survey of journalists' practices regarding confidential sources. Professor Blasi questioned big-city newspaper reporters, magazine reporters, network and radio news editors, and underground reporters about the workings of the journalists' privilege. Many of his interviewees were or became prominent in their work. His conclusions are illuminating. Professor Blasi's study concluded that good reporters use confidential sources to assess and verify more than to uncover news; legal subpoenas make interviews difficult but do not dry up sources; reporter-source understandings are often "unstated and imprecise"; reporters not surprisingly resist repeated judicial control of their practices; they prefer "a flexible ad hoc qualified privilege"; the anonymity of sources' identity is more important than the contents of their confidential information; and most important, they feared rejection of the privilege by the Supreme Court and viewed an upcoming case as "of utmost importance."[17]

In 1972, the Supreme Court issued the landmark decision *Branzburg v. Hayes,* holding that there is no First Amendment–based reporter's privilege.[18] *Branzburg* consolidated several cases from Kentucky, Massachusetts, and California in which investigative journalists challenged, on First Amendment grounds, grand-jury subpoenas seeking their testimony and records. Not surprisingly, their position was supported by amicus briefs from press organizations and opposed by the Association of District Attorneys.

The Supreme Court was divided: three justices joined Justice Byron White's opinion for the Court, four others dissented, and Justice Lewis Powell wrote a brief and often cited concurring opinion, making the White opinion a majority. The Supreme Court split 4 to 4 on the question whether there should be such a constitutionally based reporter's privilege. Justice White's plurality opinion held that the First Amendment did not inhibit federal or state grand juries from subpoenaing reporters.

The Supreme Court traced the history of privileged communications and denied that reporters had such a claim based on the First Amendment. The more compelling public interest, the Court ruled, was in ferreting out crimes. "Agreements to conceal information relevant to the commission of crime," the Court stated, "have very little to recommend them from the standpoint of public policy." If that conclusion results in an "incidental burdening of the press," so be it.[19] The Court noted that the evidence that this rule would constrict and inhibit the necessary flow of information was anecdotal and speculative.

To the request that the Court create a testimonial privilege for reporters, Justice White replied, "This we decline to do." The public interest in law enforcement and effective grand-jury proceedings takes precedence over the "consequential, but uncertain burden" on reporters. Responding to the argument that freedom of the press would be undermined without this privilege, Justice White asserted, "This is not the lesson history teaches us." Without the privilege historically, "the press has flourished," and no obstacle to confidential news sources has resulted, Justice White wrote. Indeed, Justice White noted, the informative function upon which the press rationalizes its claim for privilege "is also performed by lecturers, political pollsters, novelists, academic researchers, and dramatists." Change should come from the legislature, not the Court.

In a brief concurring opinion—"enigmatic," one jurist called it[20]—Justice Powell asserted that there should be a balancing test to determine whether to protect sources. The Powell test would weigh the availability of alternatives to forced disclosure, the importance and exclusivity of the reporter's information, and the public's need for that information.[21] These are rational factors, but reasonable observers have differed about where to strike the balance in individual cases. And it affords no reliable predictability to reporters or sources in their high-stakes dealings.

Justice Powell's much analyzed and variously interpreted opinion stated that the Court's ruling did not mean that reporters could be annexed as an investigative arm of government, or that they were without constitutional rights. Courts must strike a balance between the freedom of the press and the obligation of all citizens to give relevant testimony. That must come, he suggested, on a case-by-case basis, after considering the importance of the investigation and the needs of law enforcement. Questions that courts have considered in these cases include, Is the information sought relevant and critical to an important government inquiry? Does the witness uniquely have the information sought? Is there a way to get the information that is less invasive to the First Amendment liberty?

Justice Potter Stewart described the Court's opinion as "a crabbed view of the First Amendment," and Justice Powell's now influential concurring opinion as "enigmatic" and offering hope for "a more flexible view in the future."[22] The right to gather news is inextricably part of the right to report it, and is a means to enlighten society. Invading confidentiality would lead to self-censorship, he predicted. Thus, where government action impinges on First Amendment guarantees, it must be shown that the inquiry is of compelling and overriding importance, that the information sought is directly related to the inquiry, and that there is no other access to it through means less invasive to the First Amendment.

Consistently denying First Amendment–based privilege claims by reporters, courts have applied balancing tests like the one Justice Powell recommended in *Branzburg*. If reporters can demonstrate that a case is not meritorious or that there are other sources for the information sought or that the information is not important, they may, as a matter of comity, not constitutional law, be relieved of the obligation to reveal their sources.[23]

I represented a writer in such a case, and we found that the balancing test worked. My client wrote a book about lobbyists. He was subpoenaed and asked to identify a source. He thought that identifying his source would result in that person's being killed. Because the source was an embassy official who could claim diplomatic immunity, I argued to the federal district court judge that forcing my client to identify his source when ultimately the source could not be forced to testify would be mischievous and, at that, would not lead to the disclosure of the information sought. The judge ruled, in camera, in our favor because on balance it was the sensible course. Indeed, the Department of Justice has an in-house guideline that restricts the subpoenaing of reporters unless *Branzburg*-like criteria are met. But leaving the decision about balancing competing interests to later adjudication is stressful, expensive, and uncertain.

Branzburg led to decades of debate and divergent rulings. Since then, the Reporters Committee for Freedom of the Press noted thirty-five cases of reporters jailed or fined for refusing to identify sources.[24] State legislatures have been more receptive to the press, and some have granted a reporter's privilege—Maryland was the first, at the end of the nineteenth century.

Branzburg was hardly the beginning or the end of the matter. The press continued to act as though it had a reporter's privilege, so the culture of the anonymous source, and the occasionally imprisoned reporter, persisted. Dean Smolla remarked that the press spun a win out of a loss by persuading lower federal courts to adopt the balancing test in Justice Powell's concurring opinion rather than follow Justice White's majority opinion.[25] As a result, the balancing test remains an option, if not a guarantee. Some courts have ignored *Branzburg* or treated it as a plurality opinion; some have referred to reporters as having "a qualified privilege" and have protected them when extenuating circumstances existed or when there were rational ways to elude the absolute application of *Branzburg*, though not when they were witnesses to the perpetration of crimes.

In the highly publicized turn-of-the-(twentieth)-century case involving the jailing of *New York Times* reporter Judith Miller, D.C. Circuit judge David Tatel, affirming the trial judge's ruling against Miller's claimed privilege, opined that a common-law rebuttable privilege does exist based on post-*Branzburg* experience—to wit, states adopting shield laws, and the Department of Justice following self-imposed guidelines respectful of press rights.[26] The conservative federal judge and prolific author Richard Posner, writing earlier in a federal case in Chicago, warned that federal courts that viewed *Branzburg* as authorizing a privilege for nonconfidential sources were "skating on thin ice."[27]

Many cases since *Branzburg* have wrestled with the problem, with varied results. Since 1896, when Maryland enacted the first reporter's shield law, the legislatures of thirty-three states and the District of Columbia have passed shield laws protecting reporters in certain situations, and the other states have provided some limited protections through court decisions interpreting *Branzburg* liberally in favor of the press. Wyoming alone has not adopted any protections for reporters. In thirteen of the states, the privilege is absolute; it is qualified in the other thirty-six. Some states—New Jersey and Ohio, for example—use a balancing test, as Justice Powell's concurrence in *Branzburg* suggested. Congress periodically addresses the question (one hundred bills in the aftermath of *Branzburg*) but has not yet passed a federal shield law (the Free Flow of Information Act of 2007 is pending[28]).

Although constitutional interpretation is the province of the courts, the Supreme Court has not interfered with state legislatures experimenting with shield laws that provide various forms and degrees of protection for confidential sources. Justice White specifically noted that Congress has the freedom to determine the necessity, desirability, and standards for a federal shield law, as do state legislatures. The states have done so, but the U.S. Congress has not.

The *Branzburg* criteria are followed in state shield laws. Reporters are required to testify only if the information is necessary to the progress of the case, is not obtainable from other sources, and is needed for an important and compelling purpose. Only the reporter, not the source, may claim the privilege, and it may be waived. The state shield laws are strictly construed. They vary as to who is covered and in what situations. In some states, it is the source's identity that is privileged, not the information itself. Observations of (in contrast to communications to) the reporter are not shielded. There have been hundreds of cases interpreting the extent of the coverage and applicability of state shield laws.[29]

The early-twenty-first-century case involving the syndicated columnist Robert Novak, and its fallout with other well-known journalists who also were involved in the same incident, gave rise to heightened public consciousness of the issue of privilege and anonymity. A poor test case, the flap began when Novak wrote a column in July 2003 stating that "two senior administrative officials" told him that former ambassador Joseph Wilson's wife, Valerie Plame, was a CIA operative. Several other Washington reporters were also leaked the story, but they did not report the disclosure. Wilson had discredited President Bush's claim about weapons of mass destruction in Iraq. He later charged that "outing" his wife was a retaliation against him and a violation of the federal law prohibiting officials with access to classified intelligence from disclosing the identity of covert CIA agents. Secretary of Defense Donald Rumsfeld told journalist-scholar Marvin Kalb, "Officials who leak information have violated federal law and should go to jail. . . . [They] frustrate efforts to track down and deal with terrorists. It can cost people's lives."[30]

There were calls for a congressional investigation. The CIA asked for a Justice Department investigation, and the attorney general appointed a special prosecutor, whose investigation continued for years and cost millions of dollars. Even President Bush reportedly retained a lawyer to represent him if he was to be questioned by the grand jury. One is reminded of President John F. Kennedy's wry remark that the ship of state leaks from the top—President Bush's chief political adviser was called before the grand jury several times, and Vice President Cheney's key assistant was convicted of obstructing justice and lying to investigators (his sentence was later commuted).

Ironically, Novak reportedly testified about his source, but the other journalists who did *not* write the story, but wrote follow-up pieces about it, were subpoenaed and refused to testify as to who their sources were. Two were held in contempt as a result, and one, Judith Miller, was jailed for eighty-five days for her professionally honorable—if legally questionable—claim of privilege. She agreed to testify when her source released her from her promise of confidentiality. According to an article in *Vanity Fair*, the unapologetic instigator of the crossfire, Novak, said that he had no regrets.[31]

Other national reporters were also involved. *Washington Post* reporters Walter Pincus and Glenn Kessler, *NBC News* reporter Tim Russert, and *Time* magazine reporter Matthew Cooper were also subpoenaed. Several of them were released by their sources and negotiated deals with the special prosecutor permitting them to answer questions without revealing their sources. At the last minute, Cooper's source allowed him to testify, and *Time* magazine turned over his records, conceding that corporate press organizations are not above the law. Cooper's editor, Norman Pearlstine, remarked that they had paid millions to fight this case in the courts and lost. When the Supreme Court turned down their plea, they conceded. The decision was unpopular, but right, he argued.

Time magazine concluded that reporters, who too often "fall in love" with their sources and trust them too much and too often, and can thus be manipulated, needed clear guidelines. Pearlstine noted, "Sources are rarely altruistic. They usually have an agenda." *Time* now has guidelines. Reporters are instructed to use all efforts to conduct interviews on the record, obtain verification, demand a compelling reason for anonymity, and identify all anonymous sources to one responsible editor, who must approve confidentiality. Even when confidentiality is promised, the source must be advised that the privilege is not absolute. The journalist "cannot legally promise more than the law allows," and no privilege of confidentiality is absolute. "Journalists aren't above the law, and we have to stop acting as though we are."[32]

Miller never wrote a story on the subject at issue, and one of her sources had waived his anonymity. Sticking to her position (some said preferring to be martyred), she nonetheless refused to testify, as a matter of principle, and was incarcerated at a local jail. Miller argued that blanket waivers by government officials were intrinsically coercive; she ultimately relented and testified when her source specifically released her. After her release, she left the *New York Times,* and observers were left to wonder what the point of her adamancy and the prosecutor's pursuit was. Novak's source had told the FBI of his involvement before the special prosecutor was appointed, information the prosecutor must have known as he began his investigation.

The case was much ado about something: the legal and policy considerations concerning the reporter's privilege received an extensive airing. In 2004, the District of Columbia federal district and appellate courts endorsed the post-*Branzburg* jurisprudence. Miller's position was supported by eighteen news organizations and reporters' groups who circled the wagons as amici. Miller based her refusal to respond to a grand-jury subpoena on federal common law and Federal Rule of Evidence 501, which was passed by Congress in 1975—several years after *Branzburg*.

The fundamental maxim, the district court declared, is that the public has the right to everyone's evidence. Exceptions to this general rule are made only when required by some transcendent public good, a good that outweighs the benefits of cooperation in criminal investigations. The need to protect society from crime is more important than the burden this need puts on the news-gathering function. The trial court reminded journalists that there is no blanket privilege against testifying, under the Constitution or the common law.

The appellate court unanimously affirmed the trial court. Each of the three judges wrote a separate opinion. There is "no reason to believe that Justice Powell intended to elevate the journalistic class," Judge David Sentelle wrote, referring to Justice Powell's concurring opinion in *Branzburg*. Judge Sentelle suggested that the ways to deal with the balance of competing rights "smack of legislation rather than adjudication."[33] Judge David Tatel noted that the case involved "a clash between two truth-seeking institutions: the grand jury and the press." Because both are basic to a free society, a categorical approach is inappropriate. In this case, the gravity of the investigation outweighed "the low value of the leaked information."[34] All the judges alluded to the various state shield laws, suggesting that a legislative solution is the better course than a blanket judge-made constitutional privilege.

Thirty-four state attorneys general urged the Supreme Court to clarify confusion caused by post-*Branzburg* decisions, as did forty media companies. But the Supreme Court did not accept Miller's appeal and let stand the court of appeals decision upholding *Branzburg*. That case remains an important precedent, and as a result, confidential sources have lost their automatic heroic status and reporters continue to risk being penalized for their protection of confidential sources.

Since the *Miller* case, federal prosecutors have been more aggressive in pursuing reporters' records in criminal investigations. Ten of the nineteen witnesses in the later trial of Cheney aide I. Lewis "Scooter" Libby were journalists. The truce between the government and the press had been breached, critics feared. One media lawyer complained that the whole culture of the independent press is under attack, and that the press is in danger of becoming an investigative arm of the government. In an eighteen-month period, she noted, her media company had received eighty subpoenas issued to broadcasters and newspaper and magazine reporters, compared with a handful in the prior two years. The consensus in the news business is "that the roof is caving in on the legal protections for working journalists."[35] Journalists are "drowning in a sea of subpoenas," the Reporters Committee for Freedom of the Press complained.[36] Viewed by the public as heroes in the post-Watergate era, they are now seen as elites and villains, another observer suggested.[37]

The Blogosphere

The problem will not go away. Indeed, it is likely to proliferate. There is a whole new feature to this age-old conflict. Early in the twenty-first century, there were over 50 million blogs globally. The question has been raised: Are bloggers on the Internet to be considered journalists and as such appropriate protectors of their confidential sources?

A California case (no surprise, as California is central to the computer world) dealt with the applicability of the state's shield law to an online newsmagazine. The magazine had published inside information about a planned new Apple product for digital audio recordings, and the company understandably wanted to find out who disclosed this confidential information. The case "generated widespread interest within the technology sector, the digital information industry, internet content providers and web and e-mail users," the California Court of Appeal reported.[38]

The California court ruled that the shield law applied to the online magazine publishers, as well as its e-mail service provider. "Courts ought not to cling too fiercely to traditional preconceptions" in deciding what a news gatherer is, the court ruled. The operator of a Web site is a "publisher" under the protective law, even though the information it published was in an electronic presentation file and not a traditional print magazine. The California court also held that the e-mail provider was not required to reveal its clientele, on the theory that the provider is a data bailee for delivery and storage. Accordingly, the subscriber must consent to disclosures or be the exclusive party to respond to the subpoena.

Anyone can write anything online and with immediate access to vast audiences. Understandably, at first bloggers were not taken seriously in the world of professional journalism (which is not licensed). Over 80 percent of professional journalists deny that bloggers are journalists. Elitism or professionalism? One law professor concluded that "there is no principled distinction between a *New York Times* reporter and a blogger. . . . Both operate as news sources for wide swaths of the general public"; a strictly functional test should apply to the right to invoke the privilege.[39] One recent analysis concluded that in the context of the YouTube age, "the rules of the game have been redefined by technology." Citizen journalism is good for democracy, but it has its pitfalls regarding quality and the "rules of engagement" between the informal part of the press and the public.[40] An analysis of "the life and death of the American newspaper" in 2008 called the birth of the blogosphere "a revival of the Deweyan challenge to our Lippman-like understanding of what constitutes news."[41]

In its *Branzburg* opinion, the Supreme Court noted that the First Amendment protects "the lonely pamphleteer" as well as "the large metropolitan publisher"; it covers "pamphlets and leaflets" and "every sort of publication," including "lecturers, political pollsters, novelists, academic researchers, and dramatists."[42] Nonetheless, deprecators referred to bloggers as amateurs working at their kitchen tables, distributing uncurated information. They were denied access and preferences that mainstream reporters received.

But perceptions are changing. In the Libby perjury trial, bloggers were given limited press credentials for the first time in a federal case. About 10 percent of the one hundred credentialed members of the press were bloggers; the rest were reporters from major news organizations. The *New York Times* called this "a coming of age," and the president of the Media Bloggers Association claimed that it demonstrated that bloggers are "citizen journalists who should get the same protections as other journalists get." Their relations with mainstream journalists were wary, as they occasionally collaborated and at the same time challenged each other's roles.[43] In 2006, an organization of professional and amateur journalists, New Assignment.Net, was launched, perhaps a sign of self-regulation and professionalism by bloggers.[44]

Networks now regularly receive tens of thousands of videos and photographs from volunteers—citizen "journalists"—who are, as one observer put it, empowered by their access to the public. They all have programs to receive and vet on-the-spot photos of natural and human disaster. "They really make the viewer feel they're at the story," one network producer commented. One media critic concluded, "The rise of citizen newsgathering is changing the news business in subtle ways. It's an extension of the Facebook culture . . . and the You Tube ethos." Citizen journalists have also been quite influential, as demonstrated by the election-affecting report of Senate candidate George Allen's "macaca" remark, the student photos of the Virginia Tech tragedy broadcast by cable networks, and the cell-phone-camera footage of the comedian Michael Richards's racist remarks.[45]

In an age of vast, pervasive information exchange, the potential global expansion of the reporter's privilege raises serious public-policy questions. Is today's blogger the modern equivalent of the colonial pamphleteer? One Web site's commentary about a 2008 presidential candidate, which was quickly discredited but widely circulated by media, highlights how dangerous the use of anonymous sources on the Internet can be. It is a "business model that is designed to manufacture mischief in large volume," one journalism professor remarked.[46]

However, as Abraham Zapruder demonstrated, and thousands of young cell-phone photographers have shown since, the next generation is likely to expand traditional notions of who qualifies as a journalist.

Extensions of the Privilege

With membership in the journalistic world will come claims of privilege. Already the claims have arisen in high-stakes commercial litigation. In the course of the Microsoft antitrust litigation, the embattled company sought research records of two academic authors who had written a book about the "browser war" between Microsoft and Netscape. The authors had interviewed Netscape employees, promising them both confidentiality and the right to correct remarks attributed to them. Microsoft's discovery request was denied.[47]

The federal appellate court ruled that the need for confidentiality outweighed the need for disclosure. Scholars and academicians desire the same protection as journalists; both gather and disseminate information for the public's enlightenment and to do so must rely on their confidential sources. The media and the academy have First Amendment protections for their work, including outtakes, notes, and other unused information. But, as with journalists, the protections afforded scholars are qualified, and uncertain, as the *Cusumano* court noted. Courts balance, on a case-by-case basis, the relevance of and the need for the information as well as the reasons for withholding it, reviewing the information in camera if necessary to ensure confidentiality.[48]

Behind this conflict—a clash between one right and another, not necessarily between rights and wrongs—is an important social issue. Is the public's right to every person's evidence—testimonial and documentary—superseded by the policy of protecting news sources? It concerns not a technical legal issue, law professor Ronald Dworkin has said, but an important question of "political principle."[49]

Political or legal, it is not a question without complications. Is it better to write about a crime than to do something about it, the *Branzburg* majority opinion asked? Are all claims of press privilege entitled to the same protection? If a whistle-blower exposes wrongdoing in a government agency, should not his or her identity be accorded broader protection on public-policy grounds than that of a mischievous leaker whose remarks are aimed at hurting a member of the public or prejudicing an insider with antagonistic views? Who should make such a determination—courts or the legislature? Should cases be decided on a case-by-case basis as *Branzburg* concluded? Would it not be preferable that the press and the public know in advance, and clearly, what the policy is before they act, or decide not to? Should states be permitted to make their own rules, or is the First Amendment the prevailing guide? Which writers are covered by such a privilege—book authors, bloggers, freelance writers?

Federal courts have recognized eight privileges under Federal Rule of Evidence 501—none protecting journalists. As one study noted: "Congress declared that the development of privilege law should not be codified by the legislature, but instead should be continually developed and modified by the courts."[50] The rationale is that courts are better able to avoid political pressures from special-interest groups and to be discriminating about the operation and fairness of proposed privileges. Accordingly, *Branzburg* is likely to continue to be the federal rule, though state legislatures have passed statutes that attempt to strike a reasonable balance between the competing interests of the press and the courts.

The Anonymous Source

Journalists have gone to jail to protect sources. Journalists claim to have a vital constitutional right to protect their sources without having to, in effect, engage in an act of civil disobedience. Thus, the reach of the

First Amendment is tied to the ability to protect a source's anonymity. "Confidentiality is the lubricant of journalism," a *Time* magazine reporter urged, voicing her institution's mantra. *New York Times* executive editor Bill Keller has said that "the ability to offer protection to a source is an essential of our craft," though one "not to be used lightly."[51] Granting anonymity should be a last resort.

The quandary arises because not all anonymous sources lead to the exposure of valuable truths; indeed, some may engage in mischievous manipulations of the press, making it an agent of government misconduct rather than a valuable beam of light on government transgressions. Anonymity is also granted in routine cases where there is no public interest or right-to-know aspect to the protection.

Despite the costly battles for a journalistic privilege and the Supreme Court's refusal to find one in the words of the First Amendment, the use of anonymous sources by newspapers and television has continued in recent years in considerable numbers. One former White House press secretary reported that 80 percent of the reporters who contacted him regularly pledged not to name him as their source.

Legislatures have been more amenable to press claims for a privilege than have the courts, perhaps because of their susceptibility to press influences on elections, which is not a consideration for appointed (all federal and some state) judges.

The view among knowledgeable journalists about the virtue of anonymous sources is not unanimous. An experienced journalist and editor told me, "I did not grow up believing that reporters could defy a court order to give up their information." That writer-editor, now scholar, thinks that reporting was not hampered before there were shields or First Amendment protections. "I didn't feel that testifying in criminal cases about information I had obtained as a reporter somehow meant that my First Amendment freedoms had been infringed. I always figured my duties as a citizen came first and claiming special privilege was a good way to enrage the citizenry from whom all such rights arose."[52]

A sympathetic press critic noted that confidentiality agreements are not of "transcendent importance" and need not be observed at all costs. "Other obligations may matter more."[53] A recent case in Brooklyn provides an example of the type of dilemma journalists may face. A quadruple murder case was dismissed against a former FBI agent when a reporter presented the court with his taped interview with a key government witness that was inconsistent with her testimony. The reporter (who was writing a book on the case) had interviewed the witness years earlier. When he realized that her inconsistent testimony could convict an innocent man, he divulged his earlier interview on the *Village Voice* Web site. "No journalist wants to go against a source. But life trumps almost any promise you can make," he said about his agonizing decision to break his promise of confidentiality to his source.[54]

A veteran *Washington Post* journalist said that he is skeptical of the standard press argument that subpoenaing reporters could have a chilling effect on legitimate news gatherers. In his experience, many sources provide bad information, many should not be offered promises of confidentiality, and too much anonymity-granting creates bad habits in reporting.[55]

Their views are not typical among reporters. The famous television anchor Walter Cronkite submitted an affidavit in one case saying that he relied on confidential sources who are "essential" to his investigative work.[56] But the majority opinion in *Branzburg* noted one academic survey of 975 reporters who said that they relied on confidential sources in 10 percent of their stories. Of the 975 reporters, only 8 percent felt certain that their work would be adversely affected by threats of subpoenas.[57]

Geneva Overholser, a former newspaper editor, press ombudsman, *New York Times* board member, and journalism professor, concluded that Novak's disclosure was an ethical lapse that "raises disturbing ethical questions. He apparently turned a time-honored use of confidentiality—protecting a whistle blower from government retribution—on its head, delivering government retribution to the whistle blower instead. Worse, he enabled his sources to illegally divulge intelligence information."[58] For this, dispassionate observers might ask, reporters must go to jail? For this, press organizations should go to battle?

Former *New York Times* editor Max Frankel described what he called "the mysteries of the capital's information traffic." The most celebrated journalists grant anonymity, Frankel reported, "just to hear whispered propaganda and other self-serving falsehoods," and public officials "wantonly leak" wartime secrets, "to manipulate public opinion, protect their backsides or smear an adversary." Debunking the myth of the high-minded exposés of government misconduct portrayed in *All the President's Men,* Frankel explained that anonymous sourcing is often the result of "one continuing round of professional and social contacts and cooperative and competitive exchanges of information" by which government officials "shape a story" and "advance their interests." The realpolitik of all this ritualistic give-and-take, Frankel candidly revealed, is that "the government hides what it can, pleading necessity . . . and the press pries out what it can, pleading a need and right to know." Frankel endorsed Justice Stewart's assessment of the institutional clash of competing interests, that the Constitution is neither a freedom-of-information act nor an official-secrets act, and the result is a continuing political tug-of-war.[59]

Another veteran editor, W. Hodding Carter III, offers a skeptical view of the coziness between government officials and reporters. "The dirty little secret of that incestuous closed circle of beat reporters, well-placed columnists and official sources who do their horse-trading out of sight," Carter wrote, is that "officials place their propaganda and reporters get their hot story." This happens, as in the Novak case, when what Carter called "horseback declassification" occurs—"it's unclassified when I say it is," say powerful officials operating a "hidden hand" government.[60]

Edward Wasserman, a professor of journalism ethics, also criticizes beat reporting, whereby reporters rely on anonymous insiders on their beat for cooperation. The practice is necessary but "profoundly corrupting" because the reporter's success depends on the goodwill of the very officials he or she is supposed to be holding accountable to the public. This phenomenon occurs in police precincts and the White House, and all stops in between. Professor Wasserman, a sympathetic press critic, has noted "the perils of a chummy camaraderie among supposed adversaries in officialdom and the press."[61]

Martin Kaplan, a former federal official and currently a professor at the USC Annenberg School for Communication, charged that reporters regularly become "enablers of a smear campaign" by protecting government officials in cases like the Valerie Plame incident. "Anonymous sourcing in Washington exists today much more to protect government spinners than it does actual whistle-blowers."[62] The *Washington Post* columnist Richard Cohen described the Washington leaker as "a poltergeist with a phone," who for good and evil "disappears into the Washington souk, an exotic marketplace where information is traded, character is assassinated and the air is redolent with hypocrisy."[63] An academic commentator agreed, stating that the Washington insider press elite, concerned about access, are "not fearless advocates, but supplicants willing and even eager to be manipulated."[64] A federal trial judge in the District of Columbia joined in this criticism in what the *New Yorker* columnist Jeffrey Toobin called "a cry of revulsion at cozy journalistic-source relationships in Washington."[65]

The profound implications of reporters using anonymous sources were demonstrated when *Newsweek* published an item about prisoner abuses at Guantánamo Bay. The article turned out to be wrong, though it was based on a previously reliable and anonymous source. It caused an international scandal and contributed to terrorist-caused deaths. Along with the Novak incident, it led to press reappraisal of the use of such sources.

"The press has overdone the use of unnamed sources, and that can endanger its credibility," the Pulitzer Prize–winning former *New York Times* columnist Anthony Lewis wrote in the *New York Review of Books.*[66] Al Neuharth, the founder of *USA Today,* noted that he banned anonymous sources during his regime, claiming that "most anonymous sources often tell more than they know." He called anonymous sources "the root of evil in journalism," allowing fiction to be mixed with facts.[67] Another press scholar feared the perception that reporters provide anonymity to officials engaged in political gamesmanship.[68]

The danger of using anonymous sources was pointed out by Renata Adler in an essay criticizing Bob Woodward's reliance on such sources in his books, particularly *The Brethren,* a behind-the-scenes peek at the U.S. Supreme Court. Anonymity, she noted, "makes stories almost impossible to verify. It suppresses a major element of almost every investigative story: who wanted it known." Readers need to know, Adler pointed out, why sources were talking and what their motives were—malevolent or public spirited.[69]

A Pulitzer Prize–winning journalist and a former chief of the *Los Angeles Times'* Washington, D.C., bureau described an incident that demonstrates the danger of anonymous sources.

> I was doing investigative reporting on Watergate. John Lawrence, *Los Angeles Times'* Washington bureau chief, said he knew Jeb Ma-

> gruder, a senior Nixon administration official from their days in California and could arrange an off-the-record interview. I interviewed him and promised it would be off the record.
>
> A few weeks later, as the Watergate cover-up began to unravel, it became obvious he had lied throughout the interview. In a Watergate story I wrote, I mentioned that he had lied in an interview with the *Times*. A couple of days later I ran into him, and he said, "I've got a bone to pick with you. You interviewed me off the record and then you quoted me in an article."
>
> I said, "Yes, but you lied to me."
>
> "I lied to everybody," he said.
>
> I said, "You broke our agreement on confidentiality by lying so I was no longer bound by it."[70]

The self-exposure of Deep Throat, the notorious source for the *Washington Post*'s Watergate stories, reminded the public of the potentially influential impact of anonymous sources in cases of government misconduct. Understandably, Mark Felt concluded that he could not go to prosecutors with his exposé while he was a Justice Department (FBI) official. His anonymous disclosures to Bob Woodward led to the glorification of the anonymous source and opened the door to "intrigue, chicanery, and duplicity," a recent book concludes.[71]

Some of the news media are reassessing their procedures for the use of anonymous sources, because the Department of Justice under the Bush administration has increased the number of subpoenas issued to reporters.

It may be valuable to the public that reporters have access to confidential information, the legal scholar Ronald Dworkin has noted, "but this is not a matter of anyone's right."[72] Some problems do not have complete answers, and this may be one of them. Anthony Lewis agrees: "The issue of confidential sources cannot be resolved, I fear, in a way that satisfies the needs of both journalists and the law."[73]

There is an important difference between anonymous sources and confidential sources. "All confidential sources are anonymous, but most anonymous sources are not confidential," *Time* magazine editor Norman Pearlstine noted.[74] Regularly, reporters simply decide to keep anonymous sources' names out of their publications; confidential sources have an implied or explicit contract with reporters, which reporters should go to prison to protect and honor.

On the subject of anonymity, editor Michael Kinsley wisely asks how anyone could argue that the disclosure of a covert intelligence agent's identity serves the public interest. If it doesn't serve the public interest, he continued, why exempt a journalist from his or her duty to testify in a criminal investigation? Kinsley reminds us that "in the cult of the anonymous source, worshippers visualize the object of their adoration as a noble dissident, courageously revealing malfeasance by a powerful institution that will wreak a horrible revenge if the source is uncovered. But most leaks . . . are more like this one . . . plotted by the powerful institution itself . . . for the purpose of stomping on exactly the kind of dissident who plays the hero's role in the generic leak fantasy." Kinsley observed that although leakers sometimes may be "truth-tellers exposing institutional lies," which is the justification for preserving source anonymity and reporter privilege, more often they are promoting "an institutional agenda," or "spreading lies."[75]

The morality of anonymity was noted in other contexts by Professor Wasserman. Often, sources are unsophisticated interviewees who, "encouraged by [an] affable reporter, may share observations that will make them look ridiculous—as the journalist knows." If the source does not ask for anonymity, the reporter does not provide it. Sourced information is deemed more credible because it is verifiable, journalists know. It is the "canny, high-level officials who use the press as another level of influence and who demand confidentiality" who receive it, Professor Wasserman noted. "Their need for protection is dubious, but their continuing cooperation is of great value to the journalist. So . . . they get protection." Professor Wasserman concluded: "The fact is that source protection is miles from being a paramount concern for journalists. . . . The well-being of informants, and the ways that the reporting they contribute to may rebound on their lives, are things that journalists worry about rarely, if ever."[76]

Kinsley recommended that there be guidelines to protect sources and reporters in appropriate cases. That is exactly what the Supreme Court suggested in *Branzburg*, in general policy terms as courts must do, leaving to legislatures the task of specifying what those particular limits should be.

That's what all the states that passed shield laws did. It is what Congress ought to do to cover federal cases.

Rather than leaving the matter completely to uncertainty and speculation or general subjective judicial standards or voluntary codes like *Time* magazine's, it makes sense for Congress to articulate a balanced rule. Legislation is the preferable way to do this, and most state shield laws provide exceptions in situations where the privilege would "result in a miscarriage of justice" or would be "contrary to the public interest," or if "bad faith" is involved.

Some journalists have a grandiose notion about the breadth of the First Amendment's protective shield. Decades ago, when the need for a federal shield law was considered, one famous editor argued, shortsightedly, that there was no need for one because the First Amendment provided all the protection journalists need. The argument was made again at the start of the twenty-first century that federal law should be aligned with state shield laws. A quarter century of post-*Branzburg* uncertainty and stress suggested so. As one observer noted, quite aptly, "the pilgrimage to today's definitions of freedom has not been completed without journalistic martyrs, and a treasure in litigations costs."[77]

The Reporters Committee for Freedom of the Press reported that "journalists/writers have spent time locked up—some of it very brief—in the past 22 years for not disclosing sources of information," most in the early 1990s and early twenty-first century. A few lesser-known claimants have suffered while mainstream media have used their resources to defend their reporters. Vanessa Leggett, a first-time Texas novelist, was jailed for 168 days because the local federal court did not recognize her claimed privilege and that state had no shield law. Josh Wolf, a San Francisco freelance video maker and blogger, served 224 days in jail, unsuccessfully claiming a privilege to protect his sources in a 2005 protest march he videotaped. Ultimately, he was released, and without testifying, he gave the government the information it sought. One press critic compared their dogged defiance to the "parade of marquee journalists that queued up in Washington to testify" at the Libby trial.[78]

Journalist Anthony Lewis joined the legal scholar Ronald Dworkin in concluding that a reporter's privilege is "a matter of policy rather than a constitutional right."[79] For that fundamental reason, legislation is a more precise answer. The Supreme Court has wisely outlined the constitutional design such a law must follow. State laws provide precedents demonstrating widespread popular agreement with such a balanced policy. The proper needs of news gatherers would be balanced in such a law with those of law enforcers. Law reform would be encouraged, mischief discouraged.

Anonymity is a confounding subject; it protects the weak but encourages the mischievous. In the post-Watergate era, the anonymous source was widely viewed as the whistle-blower for the public. In the wake of the Valerie Plame scandal, the perspective has changed, even within the media. Shield laws and new notions about the propriety of anonymity, rather than First Amendment litigation, must define the appropriate role of anonymity in the new century.

It is a paradox that while journalists fight for a transparent society and the right to be the medium for transferring public information, in their claim for secrecy of their sources they are insisting on a nontransparent mode of operation. The paradox is a complex one because public enlightenment may be secured by protecting secret sources, but the public can also be damaged by protecting anonymous tipsters.

A recent analysis of American newspapers pointed out the many ways in which the Internet has replaced traditional news sources. One successful Web site editor reported that he had access to "a huge amount of valuable information" that was not available to mainstream reporters who deal with "professional sources."[80] Those traditional sources, many of them off the record or confidential or anonymous, apparently are less vital to Internet journalism.

Law is power. The press-court dynamic has occurred repeatedly in the course of serious conflicts between competing legitimate rights. It is no surprise that the law has given preference to the needs of courts over those of the press. The press may, by virtue of its power, get the last public word, but the courts reserve for themselves the final action.

10

THE EFFECTS OF TECHNOLOGY ON CONFIDENTIALITY

> Technology now permits millions of important and confidential conversations to occur through a vast system of electronic networks. These advances, however, raise significant privacy concerns. We are placed in the uncomfortable position of not knowing who might have access to our personal and business e-mails, our medical and financial records, or our cordless and cellular-telephone conversations.
>
> —*Bartnicki v. Vopper* (2001) (Rehnquist, C.J., dissenting)

New Technology: The Opportunity and the Danger

Advances in technology are devised to solve specific problems; few advances do not create new problems. So it is with modern technological advances of the information age—the computer and the Internet, cell phones, techniques such as data mining, pervasive surveillance, even biometrics and genetic mapping (identifying people's voices, faces, retinas and irises, and palm prints and fingerprints, as well as their DNA)—which pose threats to confidentiality. Less well-known but more sophisticated and complicated—and inevitably more troublesome—technologies seem to evolve faster than security systems can be devised to control them: invasive imaging; roving bugs, which track and access cell phones remotely (whether phones are on or off) and subject their content to monitoring; smart dust, which consists of miniature floating sensors that can be used for surveillance and monitoring; botnets, which search for documents, steal messages, and forward them to a secret address for exploitation; sprays that make envelopes temporarily translucent and viewable; bionic ears that can pick up conversations three hundred feet away; pinhole lenses that can record conduct and conversations surreptitiously. There are reports that government agencies are developing "robobugs," insect-like high-tech drones for surveillance and live insects with computer chips on them for spyware.[1] All these gimmicks may have their advantages, but they could conceivably penetrate confidential communications and produce permanent and accessible records of them.

The scale of the problems posed by these new technologies is extraordinary. One company, Acxiom, gathers information automatically in a closed "production war room" on multiple high-speed computers. It provides corporate customers with information ("350 trillion characters of consumer data") on 196 million Americans. The information was always there, an account executive reported, but "now with the technology, you can access it. . . . It's almost unbounded."[2]

It is troubling to imagine the invasions of our privacy that these new technologies permit. The Semantic Web allows searches and collation of published documents and data and makes identity theft possible. Radio scanners can intercept cellular calls. Our cars are tracked by E-Z Pass transponders. When we visit friends, we may be photographed by security cameras on their premises before entering their apartment. When we walk the streets, enter stores, ride public transportation, we are watched. Mobile phones may be tracked with global positioning systems.[3] Innocent transactions (for example, credit-card and store purchases) are recorded, stored, and exploited without our permission. Our security may be improved, but we lose significant privacy rights in the process. We all have digital identities as well as real-world personalities.

Confidences we hold, along with those we share, are accessible by new technologies. Recent criminal cases have considered computer-based brain testing, a form of cognitive psychophysiology that measures patterns of brain activity and storage to determine if a person's stored information is consistent with guilt or innocence.[4]

One scholar fears that these evolving technologies present "the dark side of personal privacy."[5] Experts have warned that these new technologies pose fundamental threats to the commercial Internet, and could create a social crisis.[6]

An alarming exposé of the impact of computerization on privacy generally, and confidentiality specifically, detailed how employment and credit files, driving information, medical and drug records, family profiles, personal tastes and buying patterns, information on lifestyles, travel records, and psychological portraits are stored and sold. Writing in 1992, the author noted that "there are upwards of five billion records now in the United States that describe each resident's whereabouts and other personal minutiae, and information about each of us is moved from one computer to another five times a day, on average. Credit bureaus (TRW is the largest), employee information services (EIS, for example) and other data banks have access to vast amounts of information—personal as well as impersonal—which is used in unauthorized and often prejudicial ways."[7]

New technologies can penetrate cell- and cordless-phone conversations, can access phone records and bank accounts, and can track credit card use. One company reportedly advertised that it would "sell the most confidential data."[8] Employers screen employees' computer and auto records for disciplinary purposes. Insurers filter out high-risk applicants by accessing their and their families' personal histories and medical and work records. Supermarkets scan customers' records, and banks monitor customers' checks. More than half the information in government databases is screened by private and educational institutions.

Government agencies match some of their information with that of other government agencies—the Social Security Administration and the IRS, for example. But investigators often fail to use income-tax records to try to catch violations of federal law such as Medicare fraud. Technology ought to be available to properly coordinate the law-enforcement needs of various agencies. At the same time, precautions are required to prevent the misuse of information, such as that by the Pentagon's Total Information Awareness program, which was designed to collect and mine data from all government agencies for national-security purposes. That program was canceled by Congress as too intrusive. (Interestingly, the government of Singapore has adopted a version of it.) One commentator voiced criticism of the program, saying, "There is something un-American about a government program that uses secret criteria to collect dossiers on innocent people and shares that information with various agencies, all without any oversight."[9] One could make the same case against collected dossiers gathered by private commercial groups.

Although society profits from progress, privacy—and with it confidentiality—has become the victim of these advances, as relationships that historically were private and personal have become mechanized, insecure, and impersonal. Subtly and unintentionally, many of these new technologies have radically changed the confidential nature of most relationships.

A nightmarish example of the dangers of technology in a time of terrorism was disclosed in the course of a British criminal investigation and terrorism trial.[10] Islamic terrorists' stole credit cards, created computer viruses, and hacked into Web sites, which enabled them to purchase millions of dollars of explosives, instruct and incite jihadists, recruit attackers worldwide, and launder money. An innocent New Jersey woman's identity, one of thousands, was linked to this network through her E-Bay account. A Scotland Yard official reported that these are not isolated acts of craziness, but rather that investigators are finding "networks within networks, connections within connections, and links between individuals that cross local, national, and international lines."[11] None of this could have occurred without the misuse of new technologies.

A case in the federal courts deals with a troubling National Security Agency (NSA) project. With AT&T's cooperation, the NSA installed a surveillance system in a secret room in a San Francisco AT&T facility to retrieve and analyze Internet traffic. Data from sixteen Internet networks were split on fiber-optic cables, siphoned to the secure room, fed into a data analyzer, and forwarded to an NSA facility for analysis. The practice is being challenged by a privacy-rights organization.[12]

Paradoxically, we need to turn to technology itself to provide countermeasures to protect privacy. Encryption, for example, can protect confidentiality in the electronic world, but not completely. Technology offers itself—"technocountermeasures," it has been called—as the answer to questions it has created, the solution to its own problems. If electronic communications can be intercepted, steganography is a technique to bury electronic messages. Cell-phone positioning data is helpful to police and defendants when someone's whereabouts are in question. It can incriminate or exculpate a suspect. Former Supreme Court justice Sandra Day O'Connor warned that "with the benefits of more efficient law enforcement mechanisms comes the burden of corresponding constitutional responsibilities."[13] Police may enjoy the substantial advantages of new record-keeping technology systems, she admonished, but they many not rely on such systems blindly.

Even the bright side of technology has its darker side. One scholar points out that although "hyper-encryption greatly enhances privacy in the cyber world, it poses new and rather difficult barriers to public authorities as terrorists, drug lords, pedophiles, and other criminals increasingly employ new forms of encryption."[14] The opportunities created by technology impose responsibilities to control it. Technology is, one expert concluded, both the threat and the savior; it "makes things better and worse at the same time."[15] Although technologies raise new moral concerns, they also offer new possibilities for human improvement. The problem is that it is not possible to design a technology that cannot be broken or invaded or that protects confidentiality completely. There must be trade-offs and a balancing of competing interests, and a constant public awareness of the need for technological security to keep pace with every new technological advance.

The Vulnerability of Confidentiality

One aftereffect of World War II was the impact of newly available technology on what Professor Westin at the time called "the equilibrium on privacy, disclosure, and surveillance."[16] New devices with social uses in peacetime (for law enforcement, private investigations, business) brought about cultural changes as well as privacy problems. New markets were developed to capture new economic opportunities. But the use of new technology—pervasive, invasive, both necessary and abusive—had profound implications. Those opportunities and dangers were magnified later in the century and today pose serious questions about the erosion of confidentiality, privacy, and personal autonomy.

In 1977, the Supreme Court remarked on the potentially pervasive impact modern data collection has on old-fashioned, but continuing, concerns about confidentiality. Evaluating the constitutionality of a New York statute requiring the reporting of, and the collection of data regarding, certain categories of drug prescriptions, the Supreme Court acknowledged "the threat to privacy implicit in the accumulation of vast amounts of personal information in computerized data banks or other massive government files. The collection of taxes, the distribution of welfare and social security benefits, the supervision of public health, the direction of our Armed Forces, and the enforcement of the criminal laws all required the orderly preservation of great quantities of information, much of which is personal in character and potentially embarrassing or harmful if disclosed." The collection of all this information, the Court added, comes with limitations and responsibilities. "The right to collect and use such data for public purposes is typically accompanied by a concomitant statutory or regular duty to avoid unwarranted disclosures . . . in some circumstances that duty arguably has its roots in the Constitution."[17]

The amount of data collected by government agencies is vast, and so are the potential problems emanating from this collected data. The State of Ohio had to hire a security expert to secure its data-collection system when an intern from the Office of Budget and Management reported that his storage device was stolen from his car. Private information concerning sixty-four thousand state employees, over fifty-three thousand pharmacy beneficiaries, over seventy-five thousand dependents, eighty-four thousand welfare recipients, and over one thousand state vendors was contained in the purloined device. The Alabama office of the Department of Veterans Affairs lost an unencrypted computer hard drive that contained confidential information regarding 1.8 million veterans and physicians.[18]

These security problems are compounded by the vastness of the federal government. For a decade, the U.S. Census Bureau posted the Social Security numbers of sixty-three thousand people who received loans or grants, in violation of privacy laws. IRS employees have been disciplined for viewing tax returns of friends, enemies, and celebrities. In May 2006, it was disclosed that the financial and medical records of 26.5 million veterans were stolen from the home of an employee (later fired) of the Department of Veterans Affairs (one of the federal government's largest departments) who, without authorization, took home his laptop computer, hard drive, and disks containing this private information. An IRS employee traveling on a commercial flight checked his belongings and "lost an agency laptop . . . that contained sensitive personal information on 291 workers and job applicants." Days later, the *New York Times* reported that "a computer hacker stole sensitive information on 1,500 people working for the nuclear-weapons unit of the Energy Department," raising "new alarms about government's cyber security." An internal FBI report revealed that there were over one thousand instances in which data from phone calls, e-mails, and financial dealings were illegally collected by agents acting without authorization and unchecked under special national-security laws. The government agency in charge of nuclear weapons lost desktop computers with classified information about bombs.[19]

If our ship of state is springing leaks, it is not alone in this regard. Infirmities in the security of centralized databases may be unavoidable. In November 2007, the British government embarrassedly reported that two unencrypted computer disks with information pertaining to 25 million citizens (40 percent of the population) were lost in internal government mail between the tax and customs departments and the government's audit agency. Personal, insurance, and banking information was included on the lost disks. Experts called the event "potentially the most significant privacy breach of the digital era."[20]

The problem is not with government alone. Hackers invaded UCLA's database and got access to 800,000 students' private information.[21] That hacking had gone on for over a year before it was discovered. College and university databases provide an "ideal target for cyber criminals and unscrupulous insiders," according to one report. Of over 90 million records known to have been breached during a year-and-a-half period (2005–2006), 43 percent were at educational institutions. Compromised records, another data-monitoring organization reported, exceeded 136 million, "a tally so large that it has lost nearly any meaning at all."[22]

The problem exists in the corporate world as well. Aetna and Boeing, two large private organizations, recently announced thefts of personal employee records in the hundreds of thousands. A Florida class-action lawsuit involving potentially hundreds of millions of drivers nationwide disclosed that national information companies improperly used motor-vehicle records for marketing purposes. Studies in the late 1990s disclosed that there were thirty to forty thousand commercially available lists profiling over 100 million consumers. The U.S. Postal Service sells change-of-address updates to marketers and businesses. Our personal data is collected by an endless number of organizations and agencies, and as it is, we lose control over it. The immensity of this problem must not be underestimated.

A 2005 survey by the American Management Association revealed that

66 percent of businesses monitor employee computer use and 31 percent monitor outgoing phone calls. The government does more, press reports have documented. Tracking one's cash or travels may have socially beneficial purposes, but also would have given the authors Aldous Huxley and George Orwell new material for their social satires. Finding lost children and tracing criminals and recording drug sales are positive advances. But they also raise serious moral and ethical concerns.

The process of remailing, by which anonymous messages may be sent widely with no trace of their source, has positive and negative implications. The remailer reroutes the sender's message without identifying marks, and does the same with the response. The practice may assist suicide-prevention and human-rights organizations by identifying needy clients at the same time that it protects illicit and obscene vendors and irresponsible critics who do not stand behind their charges or malfeasors who anonymously purloin information.

The alarming ramifications of security breaches are vast. Some of these incidents were due to negligence; other incidents were mischievous and criminal. In an imperfect world, these invasions of confidentiality could be profound. Cybercrooks have tapped into Internet browsers and implanted connectors to "mothership" servers in Russia and China, where vast amounts of data are stored and appropriated, recent press reports disclosed. An expert on this technology was quoted condemning "the level of cunning and sophistication of the bad guys."[23]

The computer makes it easy for sophisticated offenders to invade other people's communications—one can do it anonymously, voyeuristically, mischievously, profitably.

Concerns about such invasive technologies as wiretaps are, nowadays, old-fashioned. We all use phones (cellular and portable), but more commonly and deceptively intrusive is the ubiquitous use of computers. Every time one uses a computer, a record is created, and computer use can be monitored. Users—most people—should know that there is no total security in the confidentiality of their computer use. "Anything you put online is vulnerable. . . . Don't send anything you wouldn't mind seeing widely disseminated," a privacy-rights handbook warns. "The point to remember is that "your private e-mail generally isn't private" and can be resurrected.[24] Encryption, remailing, firewalls, anonymous identities, are all imperfect protections.

Confidential electronic messages can be accessed. The White House is embroiled with Congress over House and Senate Judiciary Committee demands for staff e-mails. So is New Jersey governor Jon Corzine with his political opponents, who claim that under the state's Open Public Records Act, his e-mails must be made public if they involve government business.

The law can be an inadequate protector of technological privacy. Three recent cases challenged, on Fourth Amendment grounds, police seizures of password-protected computers. The cases involved investigations of child pornography. Third parties—an elderly father and two wives—had authorized police searches of their relatives' computers. The searches were later challenged on the ground that password-protected computers are private property, to be likened to a locked suitcase or padlocked footlocker in a bedroom. All three courts upheld as reasonable the investigating officers' belief that the parties who approved the searches had the right to authorize them and thus to legitimize their searches, an expansive deference to law enforcement and a crabbed view of the Fourth Amendment's protection.[25] The offensive nature of the defendants' pursuits may have inclined the courts to sanction the investigations.

The law is in flux. Other cases have provided e-mail messages with the same constitutional protections as telephone calls and personal papers: a warrant is required for access. In matrimonial cases, new technology has changed the nature of investigations—gone are the days of private detectives breaking into motel rooms to discover infidelities. One recent investigation described how "digital evidence like e-mail messages, traces of website visits and mobile telephone records are now permeating many contentious divorce cases. Spurned lovers steal each other's BlackBerry. Suspicious spouses hack into each other's e-mail accounts. They load surveillance software onto the family PC." Divorce lawyers interviewed reported that electronic evidence is invariably used. "It has completely changed our field."[26]

One commentator reminded lawyers that, like generals, old e-mails never die, "they just get deleted" and return to the "cyberspace graveyard."[27] Although it is acceptable for attorneys to use e-mail, she notes, there are steps worth taking to keep communications confidential—use of disclaimers are commonly found on faxes, for example. The safest course of action is not sending e-mail messages, which are often misdirected, go through third-party Internet providers, and are susceptible to hackers. At least, users should be mindful of the fact that Internet information is infinite and impossible to keep completely confidential.

A former *Time* magazine editor, Norman Pearlstine, advised: "Experienced investigative reporters, covering national security and other sensitive subjects, know to keep their sources to themselves and never to put their names in e-mails. E-mails create a permanent record, subject to legal discovery. They create far more risks for the sender than do telephone calls."[28]

In 2007, a national scandal came to public attention as a result of e-mails. When the Department of Justice fired eight U.S. attorneys, Congress unearthed over two hundred e-mails suggesting that Attorney General Gonzalez and White House political consultant Karl Rove were involved and that the dismissals had been politically motivated. In Rove's case, questions were also raised about the implications of his using two e-mail accounts—a White House account and a Republican National Committee account. The 1978 Presidential Records Act requires the archival preservation and eventual disclosure of executive decision-making deliberations. The Hatch Act prohibits the use of government property for political purposes. Did Rove violate either? Both? Or was he being scrupulously careful to violate neither? That matter is under investigation.

Digital data is hard to completely erase. "Deleting a file from a computer is therefore a concept but not a reality," a computer forensics expert reported.[29] Experts advise that "deleting a document or e-mail doesn't remove the file from a computer's hard drive, or a back-up server. The only thing erased is the address . . . indicating where the file is stored. . . . Binary computer language remains on the disk until overwritten by another file." People have the illusion that they have erased their e-mails when they delete them, but in fact the only way to delete information permanently is to "scrub the disk with special software or destroy it."[30] Do people realize the extent to which the life and afterlife of information in cyberspace may embarrass or prejudice them?

The Internet is in one sense the ultimate democratic engine of information. Theoretically, it can provide all information, unmediated by third parties, to all people for free, or make it readily available. It creates what one expert called "a new culture of interaction and participation."[31] There is no ownership—everything is in the public domain—in the new world of cyberspace. One newsletter warned that the Internet subjects people to "the same pathologies that affect our daily lives: fraud, incivility, unwelcome advertising, harassment, and even virtual rape."[32]

In today's democracy, there can be no complete privacy. Corporations by their very size raise the stakes for the misuse of collected data. For example, data from one's credit card or medical record or driver's license generates information that marketers may use to target potential sales candidates. A woman who has an abortion may receive hate mail from anti-abortion organizations. Car salesmen—and others—can discover owners of luxury cars by buying records from state licensing departments. With new technology, once information is made public, there is no way to return it to its former private state.

The conundrum about privacy and technology was described by Mark Zuckerberg, the creator of the Internet phenomenon Facebook. "People want access to all the information around them, but they also want complete control over their information," he told the *New Yorker.* Zuckerberg, who has made billions from Facebook, recognized the inherent conflict in this Internet creature. "Those two things are at odds with each other. Technologically, we could put all the information out there for everyone, but people wouldn't want that because they want to control their information."[33]

That inherent conflict of interests came to light sooner than Zuckerberg might have expected. Millions of students (and advertisers) now use the popular social-networking site. Recently, many of them formed an online protest group and complained about the site's creation of a news feed that highlighted and rebroadcast the students' information.[34] The site has privacy controls, but some students complained that their permissions were exceeded and that this additional exposure could be dangerous and embarrassing to them. Marketers also target Facebook users on the basis of their profiles, promoting products to recipients who cannot opt out of this unwanted use of their own information. Controlling disclosed information, they should have realized, is a naive notion.

How embarrassing, how down and dirty, this kind of Internet-based invasion of privacy can get was demonstrated in one case in federal court in Washington, D.C. A former senate aide, currently a law professor, sued a former girlfriend whose online diary described their sex life in lurid detail. Her diary was linked to another Web site, Wonkette.com, which spread her story and publicly humiliated the senate aide. The diary keeper reportedly claimed that she "never intended to make the blog public, but, in the information age, data is easily copied and distributed beyond its intended audience."[35]

One can question who the "intended audience" is when a blogger puts information out into public cyberspace. The federal judge hearing the case wondered "why we're here in court," but a professor of privacy rights said that he might use the case in his law-school class dealing with privacy and bloggers. Like all new technologies, the blog may be, as one communications professor labeled it, "the largest expansion of expressive capability in the history of the human race."[36] At the same time, it opens pervasive possibilities for the perversion of privacy and loss of confidentiality.

Medical security poses special problems. New technology that has received congressional support would provide an electronic storehouse of individuals' medical histories, including genomics information, test results, prescriptions, diagnoses, and doctor comments. The goal is to have a national health-care digital database network of patient records that can personalize medicine and improve research. It also raises a "nettlesome issue," as one press report noted. "It can magnify privacy problems."[37] A physician's watchdog group reported that five large companies (including Wal-Mart and Intel) have formed an organization to put employees' medical information into a "secure" database, called Dossia, if employees agree. The database will consolidate medical information from various sources—insurance companies, hospitals, doctors, pharmacies—making employees' complete medical histories available when needed. Stringent security measures are promised.[38]

In this situation again, the dangers to confidentiality are the reverse side of the coin of technological progress. Most experts agree that there are considerable economic and health-care advantages to electronic medical records—avoiding duplicate testing and preventing harmful drug interactions, for example. But without proactive privacy protections, the same click of a mouse that enables improved health care can also improperly invade personal and confidential records. Insurance companies have scanned and redlined zip codes of high-risk homosexual communities to refuse coverage and increase profits. Companies can use employee medical records to deny jobs to high-risk candidates.

The confidentiality of genetic records and the need to ensure their privacy raise troubling questions, researchers have noted, such as discrimination by employers and insurers based on this information. Suppose, for example, that among employees who are eligible for promotion, one has a genetic history putting him at risk for a debilitating disease at a relatively young age. Might the disclosure of that information disadvantage him? How could it not? The companies would argue that failing to disclose these facts would amount to fraud or gamesmanship, so they are doing nothing wrong in considering this information. The Genetic Information Nondiscrimination Act enacted in 2008 (see chapter 4) aims to address these problems.

Experts have noted the dangers of "invasion of genetic" privacy created by DNA's portrayal of people's ancestral history.[39] DNA records are being collected by law-enforcement and military agencies as well as by medical researchers and private companies. DNA gathered from discarded cigarettes and coffee cups may make interesting police-television fare, but do we want our genome gathered by less noble investigators or busybodies? Do we need, as scholars have suggested, a genetic bill of rights for the biotech age?[40]

Medical confidentiality is not the only area of privacy risks created by technology. The civil-liberties invasions by the NSA and the CIA through eavesdropping and surveillance of European banking procedures have led to congressional inquiries and prize-winning investigative journalism. Recent disclosures revealed that an antiterrorism database (Automated Targeting System, or ATS) designed to spot terrorists is being used to screen millions of American citizens who travel abroad; information in the database is maintained for forty years and may be available to governments and private contractors, but not to those citizens.[41]

The government's response to the 9/11 attacks and subsequent threats of terrorism have raised serious ends-versus-means issues, ATS being one. The use of government watch lists has been challenged as prone to abuses and justified by questionable claims of safety.[42]

Two government surveillance programs have proved controversial. One,

Echelon, is a program conducted by five friendly nations—the United States, the United Kingdom, Canada, Australia, and New Zealand—by which "satellite communications, telephone calls, faxes, e-mails and other data streams" may be intercepted by geostationary communications satellites.[43] The concern is that each country could spy on citizens of other countries where such intervention is prohibited and, on a reciprocal basis, swap pertinent data, circumventing prohibitions on domestic surveillance. One knowledgeable critic told me that it is difficult "to separate fact from urban legend" about this concern—is it myth or real?[44]

The other program, Carnivore, is an FBI technique for intercepting e-mail communications through customized "sniffers" that monitor designated subjects. Warrants are required before the intercepted material is intercepted and stored. The danger is that confidential communications could be intercepted under both of these programs, without the sender or receiver knowing it. If the communications involve a terrorist, no reasonable observer would complain. But, as with all dragnet policing techniques, others are swept into these collections and democratic values are lost in the process of protecting those very values.

In 1994 Congress passed the Communications Assistance for Law Enforcement Act (CALEA), requiring phone providers to modify and design their equipment to facilitate surveillance for law-enforcement purposes. In 2005, the Federal Communications Commission (FCC) expanded the CALEA requirement to broadband providers, ensuring government access to all Internet communications. Critics fear that innocent confidential communications will be swept into law-enforcement taps.

In England, where video surveillance is provided by over 4 million closed-circuit television cameras, some minor crimes have been deterred and serious ones solved through public surveillance. Some observers worry that "in the perennial tug of war between security and privacy, security seems to be winning."[45] When violent terrorist attacks are threatened, the public can be expected to accept, if not demand, adequate security measures.

Lawyers have been surveilled and their confidential communications monitored with the help of evolving technological gimmicks—wiretaps, special cameras and parabolic microphones, the now old-fashioned way, as Professor Westin documented.[46] Recent reports of a major investigation of illegal wiretaps in the movie community in Los Angeles indicated that lawyers have used these techniques on clients and on each other, becoming the transgressors as well as the victims of confidentiality breaches. From contentious matrimonial disputes to business transactions, attorney-client confidentiality has and continues to be violated by the improper invasive use of technology.

A recent book about the Internet search engine Google notes that "googling raises important questions of privacy and etiquette that have yet to be widely or definitively addressed." Raising the question whether there is a distinction between "harmless googling of an individual and cyber-stalking," the authors point out that this technological phenomenon "has forced people to confront and agree on new behaviors."[47] But have people confronted the issue?

Questions have been raised about Google's Gmail practices (Gmail is Google's webmail application), and some are concerned that Google can scan private e-mails for keywords that might generate advertisements—one source of Google's amazing profits. Critics have complained that Google dossiers could be more invasive than those of the government. Privacy and civil-rights groups have called for legislative controls over the company's "storage, memory, and associative ability." Google responded that its users "have no more expectation of privacy in an e-mail than you have in a postcard, or worse, a postcard you hand to a third party to carry."[48] Google also faces complaints that its map service, Street View, which provides public views of city streets, is an offensive form of Peeping Tomism.

In a recent case in which a former government scientist sued the *New York Times* because one of its columnists allegedly defamed him, internal e-mail messages by editors concerning the article were sought. The *Times* challenged the claim, and a ruling is forthcoming.[49]

Google may not have the legal power to protect the confidentiality of its users, even if it developed encryption and other technological devices to protect them. When the U.S. government demanded that Google turn over information regarding user searches, the company's lawyers protested and the ACLU supported the company's position. Other search engines—AOL, Yahoo!, MSN—acceded to the government request, stating that they saw no privacy issues.[50] The case involved child pornography, but it has implications for Patriot Act and national-security cases, trade-secrets cases, and privacy claims generally.

It takes little imagination to see the implications for confidential communications, which in modern times are commonly transmitted over the Internet. Google's lawyers conceded that it regularly responds to subpoenas in divorce and other civil and criminal cases. The *New York Times* reported that Yahoo! records helped convict a Chinese journalist of leaking state secrets.

Similar concerns are raised by radio frequency identification (RFID) devices, wireless tags that can be used to electronically identify and track people or items. RFID is more sophisticated than bar codes. RFID tags can be tiny, the size of a grain of sand, a thumbnail, or an index card, and can store a significant amount of data. The relatively new, but already widespread, technology allows for identifying and tracking goods (bar codes), documents (credit cards), cash (RFID tags are to be embedded in euros), license plates, passports, even people (ankle bracelets that record the whereabouts of parolees, for example). Like all new technological advances, RFID technology raises ethical concerns about privacy and potential invasions of confidentiality.[51] RFID tags can be infected with viruses and can potentially pass them on to databases.

A boon for retailers, the technology could also cause consumers embarrassment and annoyance. These chips can be read from a distance, by any reader, potentially allowing unauthorized people to access one's medical or financial or other personal data. What one reads, what one buys at a pharmacy, where one drives may not be facts that individuals want known—and they may not even be aware that others are tracking this information. How secure is the database in which this information is stored? Is a blocker or kill tag (comparable to a delete switch) effective? Critics have challenged the otherworldly invasive possibilities of the billions of available RFID chips whose hidden messages about us can be carried by antennae to hidden readers and video webcams. One's garbage, underwear, bank records, drug usage, and other personal records and features can be displayed in situations that may be utilitarian but also may be personally troublesome.[52]

Intrusions on privacy and invasions of intimacy are implicit in all these techniques and lead civil libertarians, to say the least, to fear a "surveillance society" with a corporate or governmental Big Brother in the wings. The problem is that the road runs two ways. In an investigation of a horrible multiple murder in New Jersey, one suspect was apprehended when police found his page on MySpace, the social-networking Website. His page included information that led the police to him and thus led to his arrest as well as the capture of another gang member.[53] Identification of information allows accountability; but at the same time, one's privacy sometimes requires anonymity. One man's intrusion may be another's protection.

Kenneth Goodman, an ethics professor, has called for a code of computer ethics to protect information confidentiality. "Not all uses enjoy equal moral warrant," he noted, so the social and political path is not clear.[54] Although there are collective benefits to new technologies like data mining, most people have not thought about the ethical and privacy problems these technologies raise. A former Department of Justice attorney who is now a computer security expert warns that "millions of Americans have become enmeshed in a vast and growing data web that is constantly being examined by a legion of Internet-era software snoops."[55]

Not everyone thinks that the reuse of information thought to be private is bad. Entrepreneurs might argue that such information sharing reflects the beneficial workings of the marketplace. If a pregnant woman is solicited out of the blue by a diaper or crib company that got her name from a "private" list of gynecological patients, she may feel that her privacy was violated. She may have been saved the trouble of finding a diaper service or crib store, but the choice was not hers.

Nor is it our choice when we are bothered by unwanted telephone solicitations during dinner. A friend told me about a cold call he received from a stockbroker soliciting his business. The stranger seemed to know information about him, and that bothered my friend.

"How did you get my name?" he asked the caller.

"You ask the wrong question," the hustling broker responded. "The question you should have asked is, 'Can I make you some money?'"

Judge Posner would probably claim that this phenomenon is an example of the cost-benefit analysis of public policy—is the harm of privacy loss greater than the service rendered? But that choice is taken from individuals when their confidential records are sold to vendors.

As we balance our conflicting interests in technology, it is vital that we be alert to the potential invasions of privacy and intrusions on confidentiality. As one data-protection expert stated to the BBC: "Where do we want the lines to be drawn? How much do we want to have surveillance changing the nature of society in a democratic nation? . . . We're not technophobes, but . . . don't forget the fundamental importance of data protection"[56] New technologies present a two-sided opportunity. The Worldwide Web offers what one scholar called "a cornucopia of information" at the same time that it offers "a fertile ground for harvesting data."[57] Data mining permits police to cull information that assists in predicting crime sites. It also allows businesses to collect, digitize, and analyze useful (if sometimes annoying) marketing information.

Some experts complain that it is already too late to undo the damage to privacy that new technologies have caused, that we have entered a transparent society and must live with all the problems it brings.[58] A futurist has referred to this phenomenon as an "anarchy" of the Internet, a chaos created by openness and availability.

The impact of new technology on private intercourse, confidential communications (patients' medical and clients' legal information), and other private secrets has changed public-policy considerations. As one prestigious study notes, "The world created by the design and deployment of novel technologies is one of our choosing."[59] It is a world we can and must control. To the tension between the search for security and the need for confidentiality must be added overarching tensions between the social and marketplace values of transparency and the individual need for confidentiality and privacy. If confidential information has become subject to surveillance, how can it be bifurcated and deemed inadmissible in a trial when it is available elsewhere? Along with technologies to control technologies that invade confidentiality is the need for rules governing the use of technologies that change the nature of confidentiality.

The European Union has a data-protection and privacy watchdog group that should be emulated in the United States. The United States and the European Union are negotiating an agreement that would allow law enforcement and security agencies to share private information about their citizens—"credit card transactions, travel histories and Internet browsing habits," the press reported in 2008.[60] One concern among negotiators is that the European Union has an independent agency to police unlawful use of this data, and the United States does not.

The European Union recently persuaded Google to modify its storage practice for search histories so that after eighteen months that information is made anonymous. The European Union was pressed by Privacy International, a London-based advocacy group, according to the *New York Times*.[61] The Organization for Economic Cooperation and Development (OECD) has pushed member nations to pass privacy-protection laws. It calls protection of stored personal data a matter of fundamental human rights.[62] Similar local, national, and international controls for information-gathering technology should be developed to monitor and enforce protective standards internationally as the new era of communication unfolds. The information highway requires policing.

In the United States, Congress is considering the Personal Data Privacy and Security Act, which would allow individuals to correct inaccurate information about themselves (in credit reports, for example) and would require companies to implement data-privacy and security programs.[63] These programs would be audited by a special office within the Federal Trade Commission (FTC). Aimed chiefly at identity theft, but also concerned with data-security risks, the proposed law acknowledges that there is a vast unregulated traffic in billions of electronic records. The Privacy Rights Clearinghouse estimates that "more than 100 million records containing personal information have been subject to some sort of security breach" since February 2005. The Office of Management and Budget estimates that the government already spends "around $5.5 billion [a year] to secure the government's information systems." Nonetheless, the bill's sponsors report that data breaches are a "persistent and pernicious threat to Americans' privacy."[64]

Other bills have been proposed in Congress, but they have not been passed. Thirty-three states have data-breach notification laws. Privacy, civil-liberties, and consumer groups are attentive to the need for countermeasures to address the new dangers to personal freedom created by new technologies.

The flood of new technology cannot and should not be resisted. But new technologies must be met with regulations designed to minimize erosions of and intrusions on privacy.

11

CONCLUSION

Summing Up

To help in understanding the seduction and illusion of confidentiality, previous chapters explored colliding ideas about secrecy, privacy, and truth.

Experience demonstrates that there are few secrets that remain secret. Eventually, information ineluctably forces its way to the surface like a natural water source emerging through the ground or a root bursting to daylight. Journalists know that information that one attempts to conceal or repress eventually finds its way to them and to the public. It is the way of the world. The more censorship is attempted, the greater the public's curiosity and the greater the pressure to circumvent it become. Anonymous sources, whistle-blowers, tipsters, insider exposés, confessional memoirs are the coin of our realm.

People know (or ought to know) that when they speak in confidence it is likely that the bearer of their secret will communicate it to someone, and that person to another. "Let me tell you something in confidence" and "Don't repeat this to a soul" are naive, hopeful pleas that are part of our common parlance. The only complete way to keep a secret is not to share it; once it is not yours alone, it is no longer a secret.

Sometimes, a breach of confidentiality is the subconscious motive of the communication, like the psychiatric patient whose confidential remarks are really a call for intervention. Sometimes, confidential communications are an unrealistic attempt to conspire with another—business adventurers seeking collaborators among their colleagues or advisers. The speakers are aware of and assume the risk that their secret will be revealed. The secret may be the desire of a person with power—governmental, business, or private—to use, exceed, or misappropriate that power; such people risk or seek exposure of their secret information.

Confidential communications are breached all the time, the philosopher Sissela Bok has noted: "In schools and in offices, at hospitals and in social gatherings," they are passed around "casually," "conveyed off the record."[1] The collective idea that communications are confidential is pervasive, even though the reality in modern life runs contrary to that mind-set. We live our lives aware of that inconsistency. Personal private communications and shared information are two concepts that modern society holds dear, though the two often are in direct conflict.

A realistic consideration of the subject of confidential communications, which is based on notions about secrets, must begin with the acknowledgment that none are inviolate or absolute. Confidentiality is a transitory state, valuable, utilitarian, respectable, often necessary, and sometimes corrupt—but not ever complete.

Confidentiality is but one part of privacy. Incomplete and impermanent, like privacy, confidentiality is relative. One's affairs are more or less private; one's communications more or less confidential. In the modern age, secrecy is harder than ever before to attain and to maintain. The current pervasiveness of the media and invasive technology conspire against confidentiality.

Privacy is a goal whose value varies from person to person. Some public personalities—authors such as J. D. Salinger or actors such as the late Greta Garbo—covet privacy. They refuse to be interviewed or to appear publicly. A new celebrity boasted, "Nobody knows who I am, so I can still enjoy my privacy." In contrast, many unknown people are quick to seek momentary notoriety. They sell or volunteer their home videos, publicly confess their troubles and sins, even display their body parts to the largest public audience in their search for a moment in the limelight. The pervasiveness of modern technology makes possible the widest publicity of traditionally private matters. So privacy is a goal, a variable and relative one, a changing one, and one newly defined by twenty-first-century practices and values. Once available, voluntarily or not, information has value. Who owns public or private information is a question with answers that vary, situation to situation, as does the value of that information.

Inherent in the analysis of confidentiality is the question, What is truth? The era of deconstruction taught that one person's perception may vary from another's, even of the same facts. Films like *Rashomon* and *Blow-Up* cleverly made that point half a century ago. Trial courts and law-school evidence classes consider this issue daily in dealing with the infirmity of eyewitness testimony. A recent survey of unjust convictions determined that the large majority were based on inaccurate eyewitness testimony. Facts are perceived, or distorted, by the eye of the beholder.

Courts, authors, all of us nonetheless seek to come as close as possible to the true assessment of facts with the imperfect tools and standards available to us. The adversary system and its rules of evidence attempt to provide reasonable routes to a relative "truth." But rules of confidentiality and of privileged communications, from the same book of rules, obscure truth or make it more elusive.

The fundamental dilemma about privileged communications is that the adversarial trial process is a search for truth, but that search may be impeded by excluding certain relevant but privileged evidence. Revered intellectuals such as John Locke and Oliver Wendell Holmes Jr. have argued that the dynamic democratic marketplace of ideas is the best place to encourage the search for truth. The adversary system and its rules of evidence are predicated on this notion. There are veteran trial lawyers who would snicker at the suggestion that what goes on in the trial system is a search for truth, rather than a partisan battle to win that may be aided by concealment and obfuscation and is justified by victory. Trial lawyers know, and cynical lay observers intuit (especially after the pervasive coverage of the O. J. Simpson case), that "truth" is what advocates may say they are after but victory is the real goal of combative trials, truth notwithstanding. The question whether the adversary system is the best process for attaining truth is the rich subject of another book. The present inquiry presumes that the adversary system—however imperfect—is the one we use for seeking truth; it is the system we have, and we are not likely to replace it.

The search-for-truth premise of trials leads to the conclusion that no privilege should be permitted, because in that search the best evidence may come from those very communications that historically have been privileged. Various forms of testimony may provide pieces of any true picture. Communications by people in confession or under psychoanalysis or in conversation with their spouses or attorneys are likely to be the best and most relevant evidence in any civil or criminal trial. Professions put people at peace so that they may reveal their truths, and they are more likely to do so than are competing attorneys in the hostile adversarial system. Yet that is the very privileged evidence that the law excludes.

A trial purports to be a search for the revelation of secrets. Witnesses are asked to swear to tell the whole truth. Discovery is aimed at disclosing facts, revealing concealments. Judges and juries are charged with discerning and uncovering facts, however painful the revelations of those facts may be to reluctant witnesses. It is deemed contemptuous of the judicial process to refuse to testify.

Some critics have claimed that the very notion of privilege is a concession to power and elitism. An authoritative and irreverent treatise advised that privilege is just that—it gives certain classes of people the special right to refuse to respond to legitimate government tribunals performing their proper functions, in order to protect their clients' secrets. For working-class folks unable to afford the attentions of these professionals, "the poor man's only privilege is perjury."[2] The most democratic rule, it has been suggested, is that no person should have the right to refuse to testify on the basis of privilege.

Another treatise concluded that "privileges give real or fancy shelter or prestige to special groups of people."[3] Thus, the hoi polloi who go to storefront tax preparers because they cannot afford accountants or attorneys, or the poor person with emotional problems who seeks lay assistance because he cannot afford a psychiatrist, are not protected if their helpers' testimony is sought. Nor is the follower of an unorthodox or unrecognized religious group protected with the sympathetic understanding provided to established churches. The allocation of privileges "tends to follow the distribution of political power in contemporary society," one commentator noted.[4] "Powerful institutions" get the privilege and their clients are the beneficiaries.

All notions about confidentiality, privacy, and truth are scrambled by new technologies. Does the use of impersonal technology by megachurches change the relation between religious leaders and their members? Does the increased use of Web sites alter expectations of confidentiality for those who seek medical or legal advice? How confidential can these technologies really be?

Technology changes reality by its pervasiveness, too. New media complicates the search for truth by overloading the input of "facts." A *New Yorker* cartoon shows a man at his computer, remarking to his wife: "I just feel fortunate to live in a world with so much disinformation at my fingertips." The psychoanalyst George Moraitis has observed that privacy is protected by ambiguity, and ambiguity is the product of too much information and misinformation. "We are now less sure about the truth than any other time in history," Moraitis believes.[5]

Moraitis's idea is reflected in cable television's practice of overcovering celebrity scandals and escapades, and high-profile trials with speculations and analyses of pseudo-experts and commentators who endlessly chew over tidbits of information and misinformation. Eventually, the public knows less of the truth—or knows a different truth than some future jury will know—by the time the trial transpires and a judicious version of the facts is established according to the rules of evidence.

In addition to the burgeoning volume of "facts" is the accessibility and transferability of facts—all facts including confidential information—created by the Internet and other advanced technologies. Previous chapters listed many of the implications of these technologies on hitherto private communications, some privileged, some confidential, others not.

Yet it is unwise to negatively characterize problematic technological innovations simply as problem causers. New technologies may be pregnant with problems, but at the same time they are filled with opportunities. So the issue invariably is how to strike the proper balance between competing interests. Resolving conflicts between competing rights is more confounding than solving conflicts between rights and wrongs.

The notions of truth, confidentiality, and privilege raise fundamental questions about the application of basic societal values. Start with Lord Chancellor Hardwicke's classic and widely quoted remark that the legal system "has a right to every man's evidence." Add the jurisprudential commitment to the adversary system's essential and democratic premise that from the give-and-take of the trial system the truth is most likely to occur. Continue the syllogism with the logic that citizens accept a duty to provide evidence at trials in order to facilitate the public dispute-resolution system. If granting exceptions to the open trial system defeats the search for truth and adds a capricious gamesmanship quality to the trial system that is antagonistic to these fundamental values, should these privileged exceptions be eliminated?

Eliminating these privileges might discourage other competing values—both pragmatic and humanistic—that are also reflective of our democratic system. Pragmatic, because they are considered necessary to encourage relationships deemed important enough to warrant incursions on the search for truth at trial. Humanistic, because they reflect a social value system that respects human autonomy and the need for zones or enclaves of privacy that are protected from invasions. The pragmatic approach has been based on a questionable behavioral assumption; the humanistic rationale is based on a valuable normative assumption.

The rationale for excluding certain classes of valuable, often crucial, evidence is that such evidence derives from relationships that supposedly could not exist if the parties to them could not be assured of the confidentiality of their revelations. That premise has been challenged by knowledgeable practicing professionals and by critics of these privileges. Sick patients will discuss their problems with their doctors, husbands will talk to wives, anonymous sources will talk to reporters, even if they know that their communications might be made public, though they would surely prefer otherwise. An experienced jurist fears that without a privilege parties will disclose facts selectively to doctors and attorneys, which will result in inappropriate treatment or advice based on incomplete data. Cynics wonder if clients and patients tell the whole truth even whey they presume that their communications are confidential.

Dean Wigmore's instrumental rationale is plausible, Professor Imwinkelried concluded, but speculative and not proved by the available anecdotal evidence.[6] The Supreme Court rejected the press's arguments about the chilling and inhibiting effect of denying the claimed journalist's privilege, calling the claim "to a great extent speculative."[7]

One can also question the humanistic rationale for privileges. Exceptions are condoned in numerous instances, so one's conclusions about what is humane is subjective and elastic. What is the harm if people in therapy or in confession or in other professional consultations were to lose the comfort of knowing that their communications would always remain confidential and had to accept that their communications could conceivably, occasionally, become public? Is that not a reasonable part of their social contract, a fair price to pay for an adversary system, a system to which they themselves may need to resort? Our social contract requires concessions, on both sides, in all policy conflicts. The claim that invasions of personal autonomy reflect an inhumane value system ignores the potential greater good that might result from disclosure. In a balanced system, confidentiality would be ensured unless a judge determined that more profound reasons were demonstrated for disclosure in that one incident.

The recent trend has been to rationalize privileges—and to qualify them—by applying the humanistic rationale. That notion is versatile, has constitutional references, and reflects modern inclinations to protect personal information as an important aspect of individual decency, human dignity, and democratic values. Privacy rights generally are a twentieth-century phenomenon, and the preservation of privileged communications on the basis of moral, humanistic grounds is part of that trend. Protecting confidentiality allows citizens to consult with experts about important life issues intelligently and independently, without fear of government intrusion. These values have roots in the Bill of Rights.

The problem with a qualified, undefined privilege created under the emerging humanistic rationale is that it loses predictability—an important value in the law. What confidential relationship is not humane and a useful part of one's autonomy? Relationships with family members, teachers, fiduciaries and agents in business, consultants of all kinds, friends, customers, banks, architects, coaches, all might qualify under such an amorphous rationale. Why protect one and not another? Foreign countries, following less democratic and more inquisitorial justice systems, have expanded their laws of privilege beyond ours—to cover families, for example. It may be viewed as impractical to have ad hoc rules, but arguably post hoc rules are just as objectionable.

The balancing required by challenges to confidentiality comes down to choosing between rights. With a clash between right and wrong, for example, between privacy and police misconduct (in Fourth Amendment cases involving wrongful searches), the choice is easier. But when the choice is between one right (the right of privacy) and another right (the right to a fair and open trial), the decision maker faces a conundrum: Which is more important—ensuring solicitude to a criminal who seeks religious or medical or legal advice, or ensuring that crimes are deterred and punished? To ask that question is to suggest its answer. As a general rule, protecting the sanctity and privacy of confidential communications is the value most people would support—but not when a palpable antisocial act is the result. Do society's interests always take precedence over the individual's?

All considerations about confidentiality contain a competing undercurrent. As much as people seek privacy and secrecy, they also require openness and transparency and communication. Those interests often intersect and create conflicts whose resolutions are at the core of the social contract.

Conflicts between secrecy and transparency are timeless; resolutions vary as cultures and times change. With changes in values, historical notions of privileged communications should be reconsidered. How relevant is the spousal privilege in a society in which so many couples (including same-sex couples) living intimately are not married and so many marriages are transitory? Is it not reasonable to hold a clergy member to account for failing to prevent a serious crime, since we separate church and state under the law? Given the realities of current "it-takes-a-village medical practice," where confidentiality is unrealistic, how can HIPAA-like rules be refined and enforced to protect against the inevitable unwarranted misuse of patient information? Are there instances in which the attorney-client privilege is applied that are dated or violative of public interests, suggesting that those protections should be limited?

On the other hand, there are many new situations in which the historical rationales for confidentiality should be applied—in families, with parents and children particularly; in the educational milieu; even with merchants in the new world of information exchange. The question is whether contested confidentiality questions should be determined politically through legislation or by judges through the judicious resolution of factual situations raised in concrete disputes. Legislators are more susceptible to the interests of powerful institutions. Trial judges might rule inconsistently. Where should the balancing power reside?

For better and worse, twenty-first-century notions of privacy differ from twentieth-century standards of privacy. Chapter 4 demonstrated how the collection and storage of a patient's medical records can save lives and improve medical care at the same time that it makes that patient's record available for commercial or mischievous purposes. Controls are required; we cannot turn away from technological advances simply because they bring problems. HIPAA regulations were conceived to control the improper dissemination of medical records, and those regulations require more aggressive enforcement.

Privacy is a general right that all people want and deserve. Confidentiality is an explicit agreement or an implicit understanding between a person and others that the confider will confide on the condition that the recipient agrees not to share the information with others. We all know that as citizens our social contract requires that our privacy be compromised under certain circumstances to achieve a greater social good. So, for example, we accept being photographed secretly on highways or at airports to protect ourselves from agreed-upon dangers. On the other hand, we do not agree explicitly or implicitly under our social contract to permit photographs of us while we are being examined by a doctor or are engaging in conjugal relations. It is understood that our privacy is elastic and may be compromised; it is hoped that there are limits to such compromises.

Although confidentiality is to be encouraged, it gives way when there are greater countervailing social policy reasons, like preventing wrongdoing or getting at the truth in a trial. If there are no total secrets and there is no complete privacy and there is no indisputable truth, how does society encourage and enforce rational rules dealing with confidentiality?

Some Answers and Recommendations

To conclude that confidentiality questions are confounding is not to suggest that there are not sensible responses to them. Some problems may be susceptible not to an acceptable all-embracing resolution, but only to a re-solution, a wise man remarked to me. That distinction is apt in considering the crosscurrents of conflicts between society's needs for confidentiality and for transparency, between its preferences for both private secrets and public openness.

A general panoramic perspective, along with specific solutions to particular questions, was suggested along the way in this book and is the focus of the remainder of this final chapter.

Confidentiality is a goal, not an absolute, and one that must be balanced against competing goals. With roots in everyday experience and the common law and expression in modern statutes and widely held value systems, confidentiality has a historic and precedential claim to respect and protection. Confidentiality also has derivative constitutional sources.

The general policy preference should be to protect, even expand and enforce, confidentiality unless it violates public policy. Sadly, a 2006 survey by the National Science Foundation found that social isolation has increased in recent decades. People reported that they have few confidants, mostly spouses, and that their circles of confidants have shrunk. "The model respondent now reports having no confidant." The importance of confidential relations must not be underestimated. Without support and confidants with whom they can discuss important matters, individuals suffer isolation, which results in a lack of well-being.[8]

Thus, the law should encourage and protect confidentiality as much as possible. Associations—professional and others—that have rules governing confidentiality should enforce them. Private confidentiality agreements, explicit or implicit under the circumstances, should be enforced unless there are overriding public-policy reasons for breaching such agreements.

On the other hand, the historical practice of affording privileges to specific classes of relations or information should be reconsidered and reformulated, and limited to the barest minimum (for example, government secrets about troop movements during wartime and identification of informants in criminal investigations). Even then, there should be no absolute privileges, as demonstrated by the abusive claims of state secrets discussed in chapter 2. I agree with Professor Imwinkelried's conclusion that "virtually any privilege can be surmounted by the accused's constitutional right to present evidence," in civil and criminal cases.[9]

This notion is implicit in widespread laws providing a qualified, not absolute, privilege for confidential communications in legal, medical, psychoanalytic, spousal, and pastoral settings and mandating that such communications be disclosed when children or others are endangered. Professor Imwinkelried's judgment should be heeded: "We should not view privilege doctrine from a narrow, legalistic perspective," because "privileges relate to broader issues of extrinsic social policy."[10]

Privileged communications have historically been a privilege of privileged groups—lawyers, doctors, the church, the state. Those groups' members should be governed by their own rules, but those rules should not necessarily take precedence in judicial proceedings or when public dangers could be prevented. The very word *privilege* connotes an undemocratic preference that is inconsistent with American values in the twenty-first century and is at war with the search for truth. Powerful institutions—the church, the state, professions—along with other institutions should be encouraged to promulgate rules and follow practices that encourage and protect confidentiality, but to rethink the issue of privilege.

The overall policy should be to encourage both professional and ordinary associations to pronounce and enforce rules of confidentiality, whether they are historical professions such as the law, evolving professions such as accounting, or newer ones such as victims' rights counseling. Professional organizations remain free to define intraorganizational codes of conduct and should be encouraged to promulgate confidentiality guidelines, as many do, to guide and govern practitioners. Agreements explicitly treating specific matters as confidential should be enforced if no public policy is violated.

Specific Reforms

In addition to those two general perspectives—respecting confidentiality and questioning privilege—specific reforms were also suggested in earlier chapters and are recapitulated below.

1a. *Government Secrets.* In no context is the balancing of competing public interests as challenging as in cases involving government secrets. In the *Morison* case, mentioned in chapter 2, a federal court ruled that the tension between the needs for information in a democracy and the "environment of physical security which a functioning democracy requires . . . is not going to abate, and the question is how a responsible balance may be achieved."[11] No balancing of interests involves more excruciating decision making. The *Morison* court analyzed the dilemma created by government secrets in a society that covets openness as a necessity for sound policy-making. Without secrecy, surveillance, and confidentiality, diplomats are hampered in their work and terrorists may be forewarned and escape retribution. Thus, if courts are not deferential to state-secrets claims, there could be grave consequences.

Nonetheless, the invocation of the words "national security" does not make the need for public debate vanish. The *Morison* court stated, "National security is public security, not government security from informed criticism. No decisions are more serious than those touching on peace and war; none are more certain to affect every member of society. Elections turn on the conduct of foreign affairs and strategies of nation defense, and the dangers of secretive government have been well documented."[12] The claim of state secrets must be adjudicated privately by judges to prevent the shield of secrecy from becoming a sword of abuse. Government secrets may be a conditional privilege; the invocation of those words should not automatically grant immunity from inquiry.

Recent studies have found that in the first six years of the Bush administration, "both the number of invocations of the privilege and the occasions on which the Administration sought to dismiss a case in its entirety increased significantly." The privilege was raised 28 percent more times than in the decade before, and in 92 percent more cases dismissals were sought.[13] A national-security-law expert referred to the state-secrets privilege claim as the "government's nuclear option when it comes to litigation" and faulted the government for "misapplying and misusing the state secret privilege."[14]

There should be an end to absolute judicial deference to government claims of privilege. Rather, courts must engage in a balancing process and exercise judgment in these cases, as in all others. Outright dismissal of the case, rather than a prudent and fair excision of truly necessary secret documents, must be a rare last resort.[15] The use of experts to aid courts in discerning the validity of the need for secrets, reference to Congress for standards and criteria for protecting secrets, and the use of special courts or in camera proceedings are examples of alternatives to the draconian dismissal of cases that should be used in all but the rarest case. Proposed federal legislation that would ensure in camera, independent judicial review of executive assertions of the state-secrets privilege should be enacted.

The trend to overstate the defense of state secrets and the trend to increase classification and decrease declassification of government records both must be reversed dramatically. The spirit of openness reflected by FOIA but neglected in practice must be revived. A major reform of classification practices by government agencies is required, as prestigious investigations have repeatedly suggested. FOIA should be modified as well, to meld with classification and declassification laws and ensure a new policy and presumption of openness.

Government records should not be classified unless it can be demonstrated that making such records publicly available would create clear and present dangers. Those records that are unnecessarily classified should be declassified. Classified records should be the rare exception, not the general rule. Such a policy does not ignore the need for secrecy in limited cases. However, government secrets should be protected only when required by law and, if the classification decision is contested, when a court determines in camera that demonstrated exigencies require confidentiality and that the claim is not being asserted improperly.

1b. *Law Enforcement.* Law-enforcement officers protect their anonymous sources as a matter of life and death. The witness protection program is the extreme example. But everyday law-enforcement practices are premised on the value of anonymous informants. Police and prosecutorial officials rely on citizen informants, criminal informants, and paid informants. Law-enforcement officers control the anonymity of their sources. Their sources cooperate and tell the truth, or they can be "burned" (exposed). The value of anonymity in these situations is that it is necessary to induce the source to impart the information, except for the good citizen who is helpful because he or she is motivated by civic responsibility (though he or she may or may not wish to be identified). The identity of the informant, not the information imparted by the informant, is protected.

That noted, informants are used excessively, they are notoriously unreliable, and their evidence often leads to wrongful convictions and official corruption, Congress was recently informed.[16] Intervention by a judicious party is appropriate to guard against abuses by confidential informants.

2. *Contracted Confidentiality.* Confidentiality agreements are proper and should be enforced like all other contracts. They are matters of venerable contract law and of personal honor. However, they should not be en-

forced in a public litigation when in the judgment of the presiding judge countervailing public-policy considerations warrant disclosure. If a marital settlement or employment arrangement includes a confidentiality clause, for example, it should be enforced like any other contractual agreement. Parties may agree to maintain the privacy of their personal affairs. If, however, for reasons of public policy—for example, if sexual deviancy or child molestation was involved—that fact should not be shrouded in secrecy.

The element of confidentiality in settlement agreements can have positive and negative public-policy effects. It is appropriate to encourage settlements, which reduce the public costs of trials, in individual cases. But in cases where there may be multiple claims involving the same issue—for example, cases involving product defects—it is against the public interest to permit confidential settlements and to hide the fact that a defect exists. In those instances, although individual claimants may be willing to agree to a confidentiality clause, the public suffers because a public defect is hidden and overall litigation costs escalate. Statutes or court rules requiring judicial review and the disclosure of settlements when there is a clear public interest in the matter are wise. Where they do not exist already they should be passed and govern. As long as there is no public interest violated by maintaining the confidentiality as a matter of contract, there is an ethical basis for encouraging private communications.

3. *Medical Confidentiality.* HIPAA recognizes that medical confidentiality is an endangered species in the modern world. The act attempts to control abuses and unnecessary uses of medical information. Courts and legislatures should focus on containment of medical records. Expectations of privacy should be realistic and balanced. Confidentiality protection need not be "meager and feckless," as one scholar described it;[17] confidentiality should be aggressively enforced in all meritorious cases.

Good laws do not solve social problems unless they are policed and enforced. Aggressive enforcement of HIPAA regulations—not presently the case—is needed. Medical professionals must rigorously maintain the confidentiality of patients' information as a general rule; medical records should remain confidential unless a strong public interest demands disclosure—as in cases of a serious communicable disease, for example. Violations of medical confidentiality by third parties, as well as by participants, warrant swift and certain penalties.

The element of confidentiality is not always designed to conceal problems; it can be part of reform efforts as well. A bill introduced in 2005, the National Medical Error Disclosure and Compensation Act (or the National MEDiC Act) uses confidentiality to encourage the settlement of contentious medical-malpractice cases. By creating a mediatory agent to facilitate the negotiation of medical-malpractice cases, as some programs in the United States do, the bill aims to decrease the costs of malpractice litigation without hiding problems.[18] This model should be replicated in other appropriate situations.

4. *Extensions of Confidentiality Protection.* Confidentiality protection should be extended to families and educational institutions, under the same rationales that have historically been applied to other relationships. The presumption of confidentiality may be overcome when greater public interests so command. Notions about what constitutes a spouse or family should conform to modern realities. If the law recognizes and protects the confidentiality of spousal relations, the same protection should apply in comparable legal partnerships (even if they are considered "unorthodox"). If schools offer confidential settings for valuable educational purposes—counseling, for example—those commitments should be respected unless overriding public interests are involved.

The fear that extending confidentiality protections to other relationships is like pulling a ball of thread is specious. Why not honor all serious agreements to keep communications confidential?

5. *Separating Church and State—the Pastoral Privilege.* The absolute clerical privilege, which has permitted injustices and repeated crimes of violence and predation, should not be recognized under secular law. Church rules should be respected, but when they violate important rules of the secular state, society's higher interest must prevail. Megachurches and small independent congregations should be encouraged to provide voluntary confidential counseling, but participants should be advised that future court proceedings could potentially require disclosure in limited instances. Confidential counseling should remain so, whether the counselor is a clergy member or a layperson acting in a clerical capacity. Again, the distinction between confidentiality and privilege should govern all these situations.

6. *Shield Laws.* Following most state practices, Congress should pass a

qualified federal shield law, one that balances press and court needs. Promising anonymity to sources may be a useful general practice, but reporters' communications should not be privileged when there is an overriding public interest in the identity of a reporter's source. Judges should determine, according to rational standards that already exist, the rare instances in which anonymity must be preserved. The media must develop and follow better, more balanced specific rules on promising anonymity.

7. *Relaxing the Attorney-Client Privilege.* There should be a more expansive and balanced approach to the attorney-client privilege. There are other appropriate exceptions to the privilege beyond the traditional crime-fraud and will-contest exceptions. When a client is deceased, and when there are strong policy reasons to make an exception to attorney-client confidentiality, courts should be able to do so. The media adviser in litigation should be held by the parties to the agreed-upon standard of confidentiality and should be accountable for breaking that promise. He or she ought not to be able to claim privilege under some stretched attorney-client claim. Corporate and other institutional attorneys should be free to disclose criminal acts without fearing self-incrimination, and stockholders and others should have access to evidence of insider misconduct by corporate managers.

Bar rules regarding confidentiality codify important professional norms. But they should not be absolute. When the interests of justice manifestly warrant it, exceptions should be made by the presiding courts. There is no reason that a citizen should be exposed to unjust adjudication (the adjudication of capital punishment, for example), as in the Virginia case discussed in chapter 3, because rules—even wise general rules—are not open to appropriate exceptions.

The Supreme Court has stated that disclosing allegedly privileged materials to a trial court to determine the merits of a claim of privilege does not end the privilege. In camera inspection is a common judicial practice. In this context, and in many others such as claims of state secrets, it preserves the essence of claims of confidentiality and privilege at the same time as it controls excessive and improper claims.[19]

8. *Confidentiality in the Corporate Setting.* Increasingly, old notions about confidential communications evolve and change, and new ones emerge. The era of corporate scandals has given rise to well-intended legal

requirements for internal mechanisms of reform. Complaints were made that regulatory-agency requirements for "up the ladder" and "noisy withdrawal" reporting by corporate lawyers conducting in-house corporate investigations put them in the position of being whistle-blowers rather than counselors. Critics feared that rather than serving salutary prophylactic functions, this reformative requirement might make responsible corporate officials reluctant to share secrets with counsel and thus reluctant to correct problems.[20]

Organizations can be forgiven for feeling whipsawed when they are pressed to expose themselves to culpability in attempting to right wrongs. Under post-Enron federal regulations, attorneys—in-house lawyers (and accountants) or outside counsel—who investigate financial chicanery in corporations find themselves at the "scene of the crime." They are uncertain what is confidential, who the client is, who the culprit is, and whether they are counselors (legal advisers) or investigator-enforcers (not protected by rules of confidentiality). Attorneys worry that in advising corporate clients how to conform to the law, their confidential advice could become public—to their and their clients' embarrassment.[21]

The public interest would favor more transparency in corporate management than protective privileges suggest in these situations. Bar rules should permit, and encourage, attorneys to honor confidentiality as a general rule but should also allow attorneys to seek release from general rules of confidentiality where the public interest would be served by disclosure. If everyone knew of this risk of disclosure, no one could complain about being betrayed by counsel.

9. *Dealing with New Technology.* Torts and crimes by users of technology must be defined and penalties for their breaches enforced to inhibit violations of confidentiality. The very notion of confidentiality is threatened and altered by the reality of new technology. Ironically, although new technologies like the computer and cell phone expand people's contacts, it has been reported that people feel more isolated and have fewer close interpersonal relationships.

Technology experts have argued that new electronic encryption technologies will enhance privacy by ensuring secrecy—noting that the two concepts are not the same. Privacy is not secrecy. People wish to reveal selectively or not at all. Anonymity protects privacy; only noncommunication protects secrecy. Benjamin Franklin and Carlos Marcello were right: "If I tell you, I'll have to kill you" is the wry version of their perspective.

The United Kingdom has a data-protection law implementing an E.U. convention that restricts what organizations may do with collected data, to whom data may be disclosed, how long it may be kept, and for what purposes it may be used. Legislation in the United States dealing with the impact of technology on confidentiality should be a priority, and it should coordinate enforcement procedures here with those of agencies abroad.

Some wise observers have concluded that it may already be too late to prevent the essential loss of confidentiality. The surveillance arms race is over, they fear, and a skilled technological elite will prevail, leaving only a world of "shared transparency" as an alternative, with ubiquitous personal data available to everyone. The prolific author-jurist Richard Posner posits that in a cost-benefit analysis, personal privacy is low on the public-value scale.[22] Confidentiality is quick to be given away and is used to conceal unpleasant or embarrassing facts. The more progressive approach is advanced by other scholars who are more hopeful and have outlined protective measures that would contain the loss of privacy.[23]

The resolution of confidentiality questions and the development of wise social policies must be based on the realities of the evolving sophisticated technological world we inhabit. Experts have demonstrated that complete confidentiality is an illusion. Banking records, student records, medical records, employer records, pharmacy records, all are called "confidential." But they are not. Legally and illegally, these records are available and exploitable by government agencies, businesses and marketers, law-enforcement agencies, and technological invaders.[24] "This document is confidential" and "Your call may be monitored for quality purposes" are admonitions that we've all heard but few of us believe.

Vast nationwide organizations collect data on pharmacy prescriptions. Insurance companies collect health records that are coded for various medical conditions. Access to these records is not limited to the patients' physicians. Government agencies—the federal Government Printing Office and many state departments and agencies—make their lists available to marketers. Credit organizations gather information about people and evaluate their credit risk on the basis of it. Machines may analyze information about people, such as recent purchases they have made, and tell them what books (Amazon) or movies (Netflix) they might like. Privacy expert Marc Rotenberg refers to this growing phenomenon as the "extraction of self."[25] Refinement and enforcement of confidentiality laws must be high on the American reform agenda.

A progressive society and a vital marketplace can encourage new technologies to protect anonymity in an open society and to protect privacy in the electronic era.[26]

Finding the Right Balance

Most days bring to the public's attention engaging and confounding dilemmas caused by clashes between demands for confidentiality and opposing concerns. These issues present exquisite philosophical and jurisprudential conflicts. How disputes between competing rights, each based on important, fundamental social values, are resolved is reflective of a society's basic nature and its fundamental value system. In almost every instance in which the protection of confidentiality is an issue, there is an equally important countervailing demand to make the information public. Solomonic decision making is needed.

There is an old Yiddish tale about a wise old rabbi from a small rural village who was asked to mediate a bitter disagreement between a husband and wife. To the irate wife's complaint, he replied, "You are right." Then to the contrite husband's rejoinder, he again replied, "You are right." To their mutual plea that his inconsistent advice was not solving their problem, he replied, "You both are right." The rabbi's Socratic technique surfaced the parties' conflicting points, but he offered no judgment. Judges must make decisions in conflicts before them.

That fictional dilemma might be repeated endlessly if resort to judges was necessitated whenever the adversarial rights of litigants to or the public interest in information is brought into conflict with claims of confidentiality. It is common and natural that people seek confidentiality in their daily dealings, especially with professional advisers. But in conflicts, their adversaries may also reasonably claim that the interests of confidentiality sometimes must bow to the search for truth when there is an overriding public interest in discovering that truth. When two rights collide, a judicial reckoning—one more decisive than that of the apocryphal rabbi—is required to resolve the conflict.

In his analysis of the proper balancing of privacy and confidentiality with public safety, Professor Etzioni suggests four criteria to guide decision makers. They are not unlike other judicial balancing formulas adopted by courts in other situations—the *Branzburg* rule for invoking the journalist's claim of privilege, for example. Professor Etzioni asks (1) "Is there a compelling need for corrective actions?" (2) Can the goal be reached "without recalibrating the public good"? (3) Is the intervention "minimally intrusive"? and (4) Have the changes in policies dealt adequately with "the undesirable side effects of the needed interventions"? He concedes that "one cannot pinpoint with complete precision the perfect balanced solution."[27]

Professor Etzioni has more faith in the restraint of government and has fewer worries about the loss of privacy than I do. Nevertheless, the idea of striking a balance between competing socially valuable interests and assessing the import of these interests is the key solution to evolving questions of confidentiality in the emerging century.

Not only is confidentiality confounding, but it is also ephemeral and insecure. Every privilege has exceptions, so courts are regularly asked to strike a proper balance between valuable but competing interests. In a Massachusetts case in 2002, the headmaster of a private school was told that students had been sexually abused at the school. He promptly conducted an internal investigation with the help of the school's attorney. When the matter became public, and a state investigation began, school officials refused to turn over their investigation records to the grand jury. School officials claimed that they needed to have a "frank disclosure of the facts" with their attorney so that they could comply with applicable regulatory laws. Why should they be penalized for their attempts to conform to the law and perform their responsibilities under it? Their argument was the essential argument underlying the venerable attorney-client privilege.

But the court did not buy the argument. When the law mandates disclosure, as it did in cases of child abuse, there can be no expectation of confidentiality. The officials were immune from claims of breaching confidentiality in such cases, the court concluded. Since the grand jury proceeding is secret, the disclosures before it would remain secret. The attorney-client privilege is subject to a crime-fraud exception, so the facts had to become public. Nonetheless, the school officials' concerns were reasonable. As the court recognized, in a time when "today's increasingly dense regulatory terrain" makes conformity with the law complex, internal investigations to correct problems are in the public interest.[28]

Objections to demands for evidence may be based on claims of confidentiality. But ultimately, when there is a conflict, the decision is not for the parties to make but should be made by the presiding judge; it should not be based on some rule of privilege that takes the decision out of the decision-making process. The guiding principle should be whether the overriding public interest requires the protection of confidentiality or the disclosure of the testimony or documents in contention. A model for such an approach is found in the D.C. statute mentioned in chapter 7 that permits judges to decide when the interests of public justice warrant protecting a witness from legal process.

It is a wise policy, if not always a wholly satisfactory one, to leave disputes over confidentiality to judges. Many collateral issues can be cumbersome in a trial system that is already slow and expensive and confrontational. What happened in my shield-law case (see chapter 9) was a wise and judicious resolution. But the result was uncertain, expensive, and stressful.

The argument that a clear legislative yes or no is a better resolution of claimed privileges has its limitations as well. Legislatures cannot envision and resolve every potential situation. Even the application of statutorily created privileges is subject to judicial interpretations: Are there applicable exceptions (and is the particular case one of them)? Is the person claiming the privilege the correct party to invoke it? Has the privilege been waived? Is the situation one in which the privilege is meant to apply? Thus, it is impossible to avoid disputed issues about privileged communications in the course of litigation. That reality breeds inevitable uncertainty about the perpetuity and totality of privileged communications.

The D.C. privilege statute applies to situations involving abused spouses and physicians and mental-health professionals. It permits judges to allow these people to disclose confidential information in cases when it is in the public interest to do so, even if the confidential information was acquired in their professional capacity or in a marital setting. The disqualification from testifying is deemed not to apply if "disclosure is required in the interests of public justice" and the evidence is required in a criminal case where the accused is charged with causing the death of or inflicting injuries on another human being. The D.C. balancing-the-interests-of-justice test deals judiciously with the tensions between claims of privilege and duties to disclose.[29]

This judicious balancing of competing interests is reminiscent of Justice Powell's suggested balancing test in *Branzburg* (see chapter 9). Under the D.C. statute, prior permission of the court would be required before one could subpoena medical records protected by the doctor-patient privilege.[30] A court must interpret the broad and imprecise language of the public-interest exception in making its decision. Courts did so in several recent cases noted in chapter 7, on the spousal privilege. They do so in countless cases every day—it is the nature of the judicial process.

Because the scales of justice may tip in different directions depending on the facts of each case, categorical rules like those historically allowing privileges are not the best answer. There may be more exceptions than rules, and the exceptions are too indefinite to define. If the power of the judiciary is decisive in conflicts over profound competing interests, as the ruling was in the case involving President Nixon, why should it not be the appropriate last resort in more common disputes?

Technology

As to the concerns about the impact of technology, there are trade-offs and a philosophical answer. In a metaphorical way, as well as on our calendars, 1984 has come and passed. Orwellian days have led to Kafkaesque impositions on personal autonomy. There is power in data, and the information age has created the most data-drenched society of all time. In his 1966 report, Professor Westin voiced concerns about the impact of the thirty thousand digital computers that existed at the time. Today, there are almost *100 million* host computers and a growing array of phones and cameras and other commonly used, and abused, techniques for information gathering and communication by individuals, organizations, corporations, and the government. Data security is elusive; perhaps ultimately it is apocryphal. Anonymity, solitude, privacy are quaint notions in the twenty-first century. Confidentiality is a protection everyone seeks, but it is one few people are able to find and maintain.

Is this recurring war between the need for confidentiality and the need for access to information a tragedy? Surely, it is a loss of the innocence of a calmer, simpler time. But we have gained both enlightenment about relationships as a result of changing values, and amenities as a result of new technology. The best society is one that understands the inevitability of necessary trade-offs, encourages and protects confidentiality in as many appropriate relations as possible, and opens itself for the public's interests.

We have learned from experiences under totalitarian regimes how sterile and inhuman life can become when confidences are not permitted and people's private moments and confidential relationships, speech, and conduct are surveilled by government. The German film *The Lives of Others,* winner of the 2007 Oscar for the best foreign-language film, portrayed such a state and the deadening conditions that the Stasi (which aspired "to know everything") wrought upon its citizens. Such regimes still exist, to varying degrees, and we have witnessed troubling examples of the propensity to use surveillance to gain power in the United States. As elusive and besieged as confidentiality is in the early twenty-first century, it is an important human value, a part of evolving standards of individual privacy. It is worthy of understanding and respect.

In the conflict between openness, accountability, and transparency on one hand and privacy, anonymity, sanctuary, and confidentiality on the other, there should be no winners or losers, only wise compromises. We face neither the end of privacy and confidentiality nor the beginnings of a totally transparent society. We should be open to an end of privileged communications and to the protection of confidentiality through the expansion of a *Branzburg*-like jurisprudence of balanced values. This dynamic reality does not make for easy or formulaic answers. Judgments must be made, trade-offs managed. Our complex society requires only wise answers that strike the right balance between important competing values.

NOTES

Introduction

1. *Couch v. United States*, 409 U.S. 322, 341 (1973).

2. Alessandro Manzoni, *The Betrothed* 155 (Archibald Colquhoun trans., Dutton 1956) (1827).

3. Gerald J. Margolis, *The Psychology of Keeping Secrets*, 1 Intl Rev. Psycho-Analysis 291, 291 (1974).

4. Emilio Mordini, *Confidentiality in Child Psychiatry* (research paper, Psychoanalytic Institute for Social Research), *available at* http://www.bioethics.it/pdf/pc_2/confidentiality_in_child_psych.pdf.

5. André Malraux, *The Human Condition* (1933).

6. Xaviera Hollander, *The Happy Hooker's Code of Ethics*, Wash. Post, May 6, 2007, Outlook, at B5.

7. *Id.*

8. Mario Puzo, *The Godfather* 326 (Fawcett 1969); *The Assassination of President John F. Kennedy and Organized Crime, Report of Ralph Salerno, Consultant to the Select Committee on Assassinations* para. 285, *in Appendix to Hearings before the Select Committee on Assassinations of the U.S. House of Representatives*, 95th Cong., vol. 9, at 58 (1979).

9. Marc Lamont Hill, *The Barbershop Notebooks: Damned If You Do, Damned If You Don't*, PopMatters, Feb. 24, 2006, http://www.popmatters.com/columns/hill/060224-1.shtml.

10. David Kocieniewski, *Scared Silent: In Prosecution of Gang, a Chilling Adversary: The Code of the Streets*, N.Y. Times, Sept. 19, 2007, at A23.

11. Adam Liptak, *Web Sites Expose Informants*, N.Y. Times, May 22, 2007, at A1.

12. Bruce M. Landesman, *Confidentiality and the Lawyer-Client Relationship*, 1980 Utah L. Rev. 765.

13. Albert Camus, *Notebooks 1935–1942* 4 (Philip Thody trans., Alfred A. Knopf 1963).

14. François, duc de la Rochefoucauld, *Moral Maxims and Reflections* no. 477 (English trans., London, 1706).

15. Ted Gup, *Nation of Secrets: The Threat to Democracy and the American Way of Life* 48 (2007).

16. Kim Lane Scheppele, *Legal Secrets: Equality and Efficiency in the Common Law* 302–303 (1988).

17. Jeffrey Rothfeder, *Privacy for Sale: How Computerization Has Made Everyone's Private Life an Open Secret* 29 (1992).

18. Peter Gay, *Freud: A Life for Our Time* (1997).

19. Margolis, *supra* note 3, at 291.

20. Personal correspondence with George Moraitis.

21. 3 *The Writings of Melanie Klein* (R. E. Money-Kyrle et al. eds., Hogworth Press 1975); Ronald Britton, *Belief and Imagination: Explorations in Psychoanalysis* (New Library of Psychoanalysis No. 31, 1998).

22. Nancy Kulish, *Female Sexuality: The Pleasure of Secrets and the Secret of Pleasure,* 57 Psychoanalytic Study of the Child 151, 158 (2002).

23. Thomas J. Cottle, *Children's Secrets* 1–8 (1980).

24. Anemona Hartocollis, *Remain Silent? Some in Custody Spell It All Out,* N.Y. Times, Jan. 5, 2007, at A1.

25. 2 Friedrich Nietzsche, *Sämtliche Werke: Kritische Studienausgabe* 333 (Giorgio Colli & Mazzino Montinari eds., de Gruyter 1980).

26. Louis Menand, *Lives of Others,* New Yorker, Aug. 6, 2007, at 64.

27. *All Things Considered* (NPR radio broadcast Mar. 30, 2005); Cameron W. Barr, *For Md. Postcard Artist, Mystery's in the Mail,* Wash. Post, Mar. 17, 2005, at B3.

28. C. P. Snow, *Science and Government* 72 (1961).

29. Scheppele, *supra* note 16.

30. *Plunkett v. Hamilton,* 136 Ga. 72 (1911).

31. Eric Lichtblau, *Bank Data Is Sifted by U.S. in Secret to Block Terror,* N.Y. Times, June 23, 2006, at A1; Stacey Stowe, *Witness Says Cadet Made Her Have Sex to Keep a Secret,* N.Y. Times, June 23, 2006; Adam Liptak, *Prosecutors Can't Keep a Secret in Case on Steroid Use,* N.Y. Times, June 23, 2006; Shankar Vedantam, *Social Isolation Growing in U.S., Study Says,* Wash. Post, June 23, 2006, at A3.

32. Nikki Waller, *Embalming of Smith's Body Hits Snag,* Miami Herald, Feb. 18, 2007, at B1; Trenton Daniel & Jennifer Piedra, *After Delays, Smith's Body Is Treated,* Miami Herald, Feb. 18, 2007, at B1.

33. Lawrence Van Gelder, *Arts, Briefly: J. Lo's Ex Won't Take No for an Answer,* N.Y. Times, Dec. 4, 2006, at B2; Lawrence Van Gelder, *Arts, Briefly: Postscripts to Marriage,* N.Y. Times, July 4, 2006, at B2.

34. *Pennsylvania v. Ritchie,* 480 U.S. 39 (1987); Edward J. Imwinkelried, *The New Wigmore: A Treatise on Evidence; Evidentiary Privileges* § 11.4.2, at 1329 (Richard D. Friedman ed., 2002).

35. Robert Roy Reed & Jay Szklut, *The Anonymous Community: Queries and Comments,* 90 Am. Anthropologist 689 (1988).

36. Associated Press, *Saban Praises, Offers Support to Troubled Williams,* ESPN, Feb. 24, 2006, http://sports.espn.go.com/nfl/news/story?id=2343790.

37. *United States v. Arthur Young & Co.,* 104 S. Ct. 1495 (1984). How far should the law go in enforcing professional codes? About one-third of the states have some accountant's privilege, so the status of professional privilege is in flux. *See* John R. Robinson & Clyde D. Stoltenberg, *Privilege and Accountants' Workpapers,* 68 A.B.A. J. 1248 (1982).

38. Scheppele, *supra* note 16, at 159, 172.

39. Amitai Etzioni, *The Limits of Privacy* (1999).

40. Richard A. Posner, *Not a Suicide Pact* 142, 144 (2006).

41. Alan F. Westin, *Privacy and Freedom* 20 (1967).

42. Menand, *supra* note 26, at 64.

43. John Schwartz, *DNA Pioneer's Genome Blurs Race Lines,* N.Y. Times, Dec. 12, 2007, at A24.

Chapter 1

1. University of Miami, Miller School of Medicine, Privacy/Data Protection Project, privacy and confidentiality, http://privacy.med.miami.edu/glossary/xd_privacy_basicdef.htm.

2. Samuel D. Warren & Louis D. Brandeis, *The Right to Privacy,* 4 Harvard L. Rev. 193 (1890).

3. *Id.* at 220.

4. Exploring Constitutional Conflicts: The Right of Privacy, http://www.law.umkc.edu/faculty/projects/ftrials/conlaw/rightofprivacy.html

5. Ken Gormley, *One Hundred Years of Privacy,* 1992 Wis. L. Rev. 1335, 1336–1337.

6. Philip Kurland, *The Private I,* U. Chi. Mag., Autumn 1976, at 7, 8.

7. Ellen Alderman & Caroline Kennedy, *The Right to Privacy* (1995).

8. University of Miami, Miller School of Medicine, Privacy/Data Protection Project, http://privacy.med.miami.edu/index.htm.

9. Alan F. Westin, *Privacy and Freedom* (1967).

10. Beth Givens, *The Privacy Rights Handbook* (1997).

11. *Encyclopedia of Bioethics* 1356–1363 (Warren T. Reich ed., 1978) (entry on privacy).

12. *In re Cusumano,* 162 F.3d 708 (1998); *see also* Judith Shelling, *A Scholar's Privilege,* 40 Jurimetrics J. 517 (2000).

13. *Duchess of Kingston's Trial,* (1776) 20 How. St. Tr. 355, 587 (Eng.).

14. Edward D. Cosden Jr., *The Physician-Patient Privilege in Oklahoma,* 7 Tulsa L.J. 157, 159 (1971).

15. Arthur Garwin, *Confidentiality and Its Relationships to the Attorney-Client Privilege, in Attorney-Client Privilege in Civil Litigation* 31, 32 (Vincent S. Walkowiak ed., 3d ed. 2004).

16. *Countess of Shrewsbury's Trial,* (1612) 2 How. St. Tr. 769, 778 (Eng.), *quoted in*

4 John Henry Wigmore, *A Treatise on the System of Evidence in Trials at Common Law* § 2190, at 2963 (1905).

17. 12 *Cobbett's Parliamentary History* 693 (London, T. C. Hansard 1812).

18. *Blair v. United States,* 250 U.S. 273 (1919); 4 Wigmore, *supra* note 16, §§ 2190–2192.

19. Edward J. Imwinkelried, *The New Wigmore: A Treatise on Evidence; Evidentiary Privileges* (Richard D. Friedman ed., 2002); *see also* Michael H. Graham, *Handbook of Federal Evidence* (2d ed. 1986); Michael H. Graham & Edward Ohlbaum, *Courtroom Evidence* (National Institute of Trial Advocacy 1997); Simon Greenleaf, *Treatise of Evidence* (Boston, Little, Brown, 1899); David M. Greenwald et. al., *Testimonial Privileges* (3d ed. 2005); *McCormick on Evidence* (John William Strong ed., 5th ed. 1999); *Moore's Federal Rules Pamphlets,* Part 2, *Federal Rules of Evidence* (1996); Edmund M. Morgan & Jack B. Weinstein, *Basic Problems of State and Federal Evidence* (5th ed. 1976); *Weinstein's Federal Evidence* (Joseph M. McLaughlin ed., 2d ed. 2006).

20. *Russell v. Jackson,* (1851) 9 Hare 387, 391 (Eng.).

21. 4 John Henry Wigmore, *A Treatise on the System of Evidence in Trials at Common Law* § 2286, at 3186 (1905).

22. Imwinkelried, *supra* note 19, § 2.2.

23. Imwinkelried, *supra* note 19.

24. *Id.*

25. 23 Charles Alan Wright & Kenneth W. Graham Jr., *Federal Practice and Procedure: Evidence* § 5422.1 (Supp. 2000).

26. 5 Jeremy Bentham, *Rationale of Judicial Evidence passim* (London, Hunt and Clarke, 1827).

27. Sissela Bok, *Secrets: On the Ethics of Concealment and Revelation* (1982).

28. Council of the Bars and Law Societies of the European Union, *The Professional Secret, Confidentiality, and Legal Professional Privilege in Europe* (2003), *available at* http://www.ccbe.eu/fileadmin/user_upload/NTCdocument/update_edwards_report_1182333982.pdf.

29. Javier H. Rubinstein, *International Commercial Arbitration: Reflections at the Crossroads of the Common Law and Civil Law Traditions,* 5 Chi. J. Int'l L., 303 (2004).

30. *Krolikowski v. Univ. of Mass.* 150 F. Supp. 246 (2001).

31. *Univ. of Pa. v. EEOC,* 493 U.S. 182, 194 (1990).

32. *Syposs v. United States,* 63 F. Supp. 2d 301 (1999).

33. Robert H. McLaughlin, *From the Field to the Courthouse: Should Social Science Research Be Privileged?* 24 Law & Soc. Inquiry 927 (1999).

34. *See* Rachel Callanan, *My Lips Are Sealed: The Need for a Testimonial Privilege and Confidentiality for Victim-Advocates,* 18 Hamline J. Pub. L. & Pol'y 226 (1996).

35. Amee A. Shah, *The Parent-Child Testimonial Privilege—Has the Time for It Finally Arrived?* 47 Clev. St. L. Rev. 41 (1999).

36. Confidence in the Family Act, H.R. 3577, 105th Cong. (1998).

37. *Jaffee v. Redmond,* 518 U.S. 1, 32 n.4 (Scalia, J., dissenting).

38. Bok, *supra* note 27, at 115.

39. Imwinkelried, *supra* note 19, at 127–128.

40. *Developments in the Law: Privileged Communications,* 98 Harv. L. Rev. 1450, 1493 (1985).

41. Raymond F. Miller, *Creating Evidentiary Privileges: An Argument for the Judicial Approach,* 31 Conn. L. Rev. 771, 778 (1999).

42. Imwinkelried, *supra* note 19, at l.

43. Miller, *supra* note 41, at 774.

Chapter 2

1. Alan Westin, *Privacy and Freedom* (1967); Sissela Bok, *Secrets: On the Ethics of Concealment and Revelation* (1982); Woodrow Wilson, *The New Freedom* 114 (1913).

2. *EEOC v. Notre Dame Du Lac,* 715 F.2d 331, 336 (7th Cir. 1983).

3. *Kennedy v. Mendoza-Martinez,* 372 U.S. 144, 160 (1963); *Terminiello v. Chicago,* 337 U.S. 1, 37 (1949) (Jackson, J., dissenting).

4. Ted Gup, *Nation of Secrets: The Threat to Democracy and the American Way of Life* 48 (2007).

5. Erwin N. Griswold, *Secrets Not Worth Keeping,* Wash. Post, Feb. 15, 1989, at A25.

6. 26 Charles Alan Wright & Kenneth W. Graham Jr., *Federal Practice and Procedure: Evidence* § 5664 (1986 & Supp. 2006).

7. Paul Freund, *On Presidential Privilege,* 88 Harv. L. Rev. 13 (1974).

8. *United States v. Reynolds,* 345 U.S.1 (1953).

9. William G. Weaver & Robert M. Pallitto, *State Secrets and Executive Power,* 120 Pol. Sci. Q. 85 (2005).

10. *Trial of Maha Rajah Nundocomar,* (1775) 20 How. St. Tr. 924, 1057 (India), *quoted in* 4 John Henry Wigmore, *A Treatise on the System of Evidence in Trials at Common Law* § 2193, at 2969 (1905) .

11. *Beatson v. Skene,* (1860) 5 Hurst and N. 838, 853 (Eng.), *cited in* 4 Wigmore, *supra* note 10, § 2375, at 3335 n.1, 3341.

12. *Duncan v. Cammell, Laird & Co.,* [1942] A.C. 624, 644 (Eng.), *noted in* Weaver & Pallitto, *supra* note 9, at 98.

13. *United States v. Burr,* 25 F. Cas. 30 (No. 14692d) (C.C.D. Va. 1807).

14. *Totten v. United States,* 92 U.S. 105 (1875).

15. *Tenet v. Doe,* 544 U.S. 1, 11 (2005).

16. *United States v. Reynolds,* 345 U.S. 1 (1953).

17. *See* Constitution Project, *Reforming the State Secrets Privilege* (2007), *available at* http://www.constitutionproject.org/pdf/Reforming_the_State_Secrets_Privilege_Statement1.pdf.

18. Constitution Project, Panel Discussion on the State-Secrets Privilege at the National Press Club 6–8 (Jan. 24, 2008) [hereinafter Constitution Project Discussion on State-Secrets Privilege] (statement of Judy Loether), *available at* http://www.constitutionproject.org/pdf/Transcript_State_Secrets_Panel_at_NPC_January_24_2008.pdf.

19. *See, e.g., Al-Haramain Islamic Found. v. Bush,* 451 F. Supp. 2d 1215 (D. Or. 2006), *rev'd and remanded,* 507 F.3d 1190 (9th Cir. 2007); *Hepting v. AT&T Corp.,* 439 F. Supp. 2d 974 (N.D. Cal. 2006), *appeal docketed,* Nos. 06-17132, 06-17137 (9th Cir. Nov. 9, 2006).

20. Barry Siegel, *Claim of Privilege* (2008); *see also* Louis Fisher, *In the Name of National Security: Unchecked Presidential Power and the* Reynolds *Case* (2006); Constitution Project, *supra* note 17.

21. 4 Wigmore, *supra* note 10, § 2375, at 3341–3342, § 2376, at 3345; *Gugy v. Maguire,* [1863] 13 L.C.R. 33, 38 (Mondelet, J.) (Can.), *quoted in* 4 Wigmore, *supra* note 10, § 2376, at 3346.

22. *Jane Doe v. CIA,* No. 05 Civ. 7939 (S.D.N.Y. Jan. 4, 2007), *available at* http://www.fas.org/sgp/jud/statesec/doe010407.pdf; *Fitzgerald v. Penthouse Int'l, Ltd.,* 776 F.2d 1236 (4th Cir. 1985).

23. *El-Masri v. United States,* 479 F.3d 296 (4th Cir. 2007).

24. *Id.* at 304.

25. Constitution Project Discussion on State-Secrets Privilege, *supra* note 18, at 11–12 (statement of Ben Wizner).

26. *Sterling v. Tenet,* 416 F.3d 338, 348 (4th Cir. 2005).

27. *Kasza v. Browner,* 133 F.3d 1159, 1166 (9th Cir. 1998) (quoting *Halkin v Helms,* 598 F.2d 1, 8 (D.C. Cir 1978)).

28. *Maxwell v. First Nat'l Bank of Md.,* 143 F.R.D. 590 (D. Md. 1991).

29. Weaver & Pallitto, *supra* note 9, at 105.

30. Karl Vick, *Judges Skeptical of State-Secrets Claim,* Wash. Post, Aug. 16, 2007, at A4.

31. *United States v. Morison,* 844 F.2d 1057 (1988).

32. Aliya Sternstein, *NASA Researchers Balk at Background Checks,* Nat'l J.'s Tech. Daily, Sept. 4, 2007, *available at* http://govexec.com/dailyfed/0907/090407tdpm1.htm.

33. Scott Shane, *F.B.I. Is Warned over Its Misuse of Data Collection,* N.Y. Times, Mar. 21, 2007; David Stout, *F.B.I. Head Admits Mistakes in Use of Security Act,* N.Y. Times, Mar. 10, 2007.

34. *Al-Haramain Islamic Found. v. Bush,* 451 F. Supp. 2d 1215 (D. Or. 2006), *rev'd and remanded,* 507 F.3d 1190 (9th Cir. 2007); *see also Hepting v. AT&T Corp.,* 439 F. Supp. 2d 974 (N.D. Cal. 2006), *appeal docketed,* Nos. 06-17132, 06-17137 (9th Cir. Nov. 9, 2006). The government surveillance program at issue in the *Hepting* case is discussed briefly in chapter 10. Approximately fifty other cases challenging the government's surveillance efforts have been consolidated and are pending before Judge Vaughn Walker of the U.S. District Court for the District of Northern California.

35. Nicole Hallett, *Protecting National Security or Covering Up Malfeasance: The Modern State Secrets Privilege and Its Alternatives,* 117 Yale L.J. Pocket Part 82 (2007), http://thepocketpart.org/2007/10/01/hallett.html.

36. S. 2533, 110th Cong. (2008); Press Release, Senator Edward M. Kennedy, Kennedy Introduces State Secrets Protection Act (Jan. 22, 2008), *available at* http:

//kennedy.senate.gov/newsroom/press_release.cfm?id=C56BD1D0-7AD3-46EA-9D30-A77317F28B70.

37. David Kay & Michael German, *Abusing the Secrets Shield,* Wash. Post, June 18, 2007, at A17.

38. See the ABA resolution on the state-secrets privilege and the accompanying report (Revised Report 116A), available at http://www.abanet.org/adminlaw/annual2007/State-Secrets-Report-Full-HOD.pdf.

39. Weaver & Pallitto, *supra* note 9, at 87.

40. Exec. Order No. 13,292, 3 C.F.R. 196 (2004), *reprinted as amended in* 50 U.S.C. § 435 (Supp. 2003).

41. *Report to the Secretary of Defense by the Committee on Classified Information* (Coolidge Committee) (1956); *Report of the Commission on Government Security* (Wright Commission) (1957); House Special Subcommittee on Government Information (Moss Subcommittee) (1958); *Report of the Defense Science Board Task Force on Secrecy* (Seitz Task Force) (1970); *Keeping the Nation's Secrets: A Report to the Secretary of Defense by the Commission to Review Department of Defense Security Policies and Practices* (Stillwell Commission) (1985); Joint Security Commission, *Redefining Security: A Report to the Secretary of Defense and the Director of Central Intelligence* (1994).

42. *Report of the Commission on Protecting and Reducing Government Secrecy,* S. Doc No. 105-2 (1997).

43. Gup, *supra* note 4, at 9.

44. 5 U.S.C § 552a(b)(1).

45. *NLRB v. Robbins Tire & Rubber Co.,* 437 U.S. 214, 242 (1978).

46. *Dep't of the Air Force v. Rose,* 425 U.S. 352, 361 (1976).

47. Catherine Nielsen, *40 Years of FOIA, 20 Years of Delay: The Knight Open Government Survey* (2007), *available at* http://www.gwu.edu/~nsarchiv/NSAEBB/NSAEBB224/ten_oldest_report.pdf.

48. Open FOIA Act, S. 2746, 110th Cong. (2008); Coalition of Journalists for Open Government, *Still Waiting after All These Years? An In-Depth Analysis of FOIA Performance from 1998 to 2006, available at* http://www.cjog.net/documents/Still_Waiting_Narrative_and_Charts.pdf.

49. Editorial, *Classifying Toothpaste,* Wash. Post, Feb. 27, 2006, at A14.

50. Dan Eggen, *White House Declares Office Off-Limits,* Wash. Post, Aug. 23, 2007, at A4.

51. Harold C. Relyea, *Security Classified and Controlled Information: History, Status, and Emerging Management Issues* (CRS Report RL33494, 2006; updated 2008), *available at* http://assets.opencrs.com/rpts/RL33494_20080211.pdf.

52. Eleanor Randolph, *Is U.S. Keeping Too Many Secrets?* L.A. Times, May 17, 1997, at A1.

53. Editorial, *The Must-Do List,* N.Y. Times, Mar. 4, 2007, Week in Review, at 11.

54. Norman Pearlstine, *Off the Record: The Press, the Government, and the War over Anonymous Sources* (2007).

55. Robert G. Kaiser, Op-Ed., *Public Secrets,* Wash. Post, June 11, 2006, at B1.

56. Michael A. Fletcher, *Cheney's Mystery Visitors,* Wash. Post, June 4, 2007, at A13.

57. Peter Baker, *Cheney Defiant on Classified Material,* Wash. Post, June 22, 2007, at A1.

58. Flynt Leverett & Hillary Mann, Op-Ed, *What We Wanted to Tell You about Iran,* N.Y. Times, Dec. 22, 2006, at A31.

59. Edward J. Imwinkelried, *The New Wigmore: A Treatise on Evidence; Evidentiary Privileges* § 8.4.2 (Richard D. Friedman ed., 2002).

60. *Earl of Stafford's Trial,* (1640) 3 How. St. Tr. 1427, 1441 (Eng.); *Hennessy v. Wright,* (1888) 21 Q.B.D. 509, 512 (Eng.).

61. 4 Wigmore, *supra* note 10, § 2367, at 3320–3321, § 2375, at 3340.

62. *Hartranft's Appeal,* 86 Pa. 433, 458 (1877).

63. See the cases cited in Imwinkelried, *supra* note 59, at 1108.

64. *Clark v. United States,* 289 U.S. 1, 13, 16 (1933).

65. Imwinkelried, *supra* note 59, § 7.6.1, at 1083 (referring to *Marbury v. Madison,* 5 U.S. (1 Cranch) 137 (1803)).

66. *United States v. Nixon,* 418 U.S. 683 (1974).

67. *Coastal States Gas Corp. v. Dep't of Energy,* 617 F.2d 854 (D.C. Cir. 1980).

68. *Judicial Watch v. Dep't of Justice,* 432 F.3d 366, 372 (D.C. Cir. 2005).

69. *Nixon,* 418 U.S. at 711.

70. *Id.* at 705

71. *In re Sealed Case,* 116 F.3d 550 (D.C. Cir. 1997).

72. *Williams v. Mercer,* 783 F.2d 1488, 1519–1520 (11th Cir. 1986).

73. *N.Y. Times Co. v. United States,* 403 U.S. 713, 752 n.3 (1971) (Burger, C.J., dissenting).

74. *United States v. Hooker Chemicals & Plastics Corp.,* 114 F.R.D. 100, 102 (W.D.N.Y. 1987).

75. Imwinkelried, *supra* note 59, § 7.7.1, at 1641.

76. *Ballard v. Comm'r of Internal Revenue,* 544 U.S. 40 (2005).

77. *Boehner v. McDermott,* 484 F.3d 573 (D.C. Cir. 2007).

78. *Gugy v. Maguire,* [1863] 13 L.C.R. 33, 38 (Mondelet, J.) (Can.).

79. Quoted in Bok, *supra* note 1, at 150 (citing *Lord Acton and His Circle* 166 (Abbot Gasquet ed., 1906).

80. *Detroit Free Press v. Ashcroft,* 303 F.3d 681 (6th Cir. 2002).

Chapter 3

1. 4 John Henry Wigmore, *A Treatise on the System of Evidence in Trials at Common Law,* § 2290, at 3194 (1905).

2. *Hatton v. Robinson,* 31 Mass. (14 Pick.) 416, 422 (1833).

3. *Chirac v. Reinicker,* 24 U.S. 280 (1826); *see also Hunt v. Blackburn,* 128 U.S. 464, 470 (1888); *United States v. United Shoe Mach. Corp.,* 89 F. Supp. 357, 357–359 (D. Mass. 1950).

4. *United States v. Hodge & Zweig,* 548 F.2d 1347, 1355 (9th Cir. 1977).

5. 4 Wigmore, *supra* note 1, § 2192, at 2965; Edward J. Imwinkelried, *The New Wigmore: A Treatise on Evidence; Evidentiary Privileges* § 2.5, at 113 (Richard D. Friedman ed., 2002); Edward J. Imwinkelried, *Draft Article V of the Federal Rules of Evidence on Privileges, One of the Most Influential Pieces of Legislation Never Enacted: The Strength of the Ingroup Loyalty of the Federal Judiciary,* 58 Ala. L. Rev. 41, 46 (2006).

6. 5 Jeremy Bentham, *Rationale of Judicial Evidence* 325 (London, Hunt and Clarke, 1827), *quoted in* 4 Wigmore, *supra* note 1, § 2291, at 3201.

7. *Id.* at 323, *quoted in* Wigmore, *supra* note 1, § 2291, at 3199.

8. 4 Wigmore, *supra* note 1, § 2290.

9. C., *On the Production of Cases Prepared for the Opinion of Counsel,* 17 Law Magazine 51, 68 (1837), *quoted in* 4 Wigmore, *supra* note 1, § 2291, at 3198.

10. *United States v. Liebman,* 742 F.2d. 807 (3d Cir. 1984).

11. *Restatement (Third) of the Laws Governing Lawyers* § 87 (2000).

12. *United States v. Bauer,* 132 F.3d 504, 510 (9th Cir. 1997).

13. *Upjohn Co. v. United States,* 449 U.S. 383 (1981).

14. Marjorie Cohen, *The Evisceration of the Attorney-Client Privilege in the Wake of September 11, 2001,* 71 Fordham L. Rev. 1233 (2003).

15. *Model Rules of Prof'l Conduct* R. 1.6 (2003); *Restatement (Third) of the Laws Governing Lawyers* ch. 5.

16. *Restatement (Third) of the Laws Governing Lawyers* § 59; *United States v. Stepney,* 246 F. Supp. 2d 1069, 1074 (N.D. Cal. 2003).

17. 4 Wigmore, *supra* note 1, § 2298, at 3217.

18. *In re Grand Jury Investigation,* 772 N.E.2d 9, 20 (Mass. 2002).

19. *Clark v. United States,* 289 U.S.1, 15 (1933).

20. *United States v. Hodge & Zweig,* 548 F.2d 1347, 1355 (9th Cir. 1977).

21. *Ethics and the Legal Profession* (Michael Davis & Frederick Elliston eds., 1986).

22. 23 Charles Alan Wright & Kenneth W. Graham Jr., *Federal Practice and Procedure: Evidence* § 5422.1, at 407 (Supp. 2000).

23. David A. Green, *Lawyers as Tattletales,* 20 Ga. St. U. L. Rev. 617, 640 (2004).

24. William H. Simon, *The Confidentiality Fetish,* Atlantic Monthly, Dec. 2004, at 113.

25. Alexis Anderson et al., *Ethics in Externships: Confidentiality, Conflicts, and Competence Issues in the Field and in the Classroom,* 10 Clinical L. Rev. 473 (2004).

26. Theo S. Liebman, *Confidentiality, Consultation, and the Child Client,* 75 Temp. L. Rev. 821 (2002).

27. Julie Creswell, *Law Firms Are Starting to Adopt Outsourcing,* N.Y. Times, Oct. 27, 2006, at C3.

28. *FTC v. TRW, Inc.,* 628 F.2d. 207, 212 (D.C. Cir. 1980).

29. *In re Grand Jury Subpoenas,* 995 F. Supp. 332 (E.D.N.Y. 1998).

30. Robert H. Aronson, *Attorney-Client Confidentiality and the Assessment of Claimants Who Allege PTSD,* 766 Wash. L. Rev. 313 (2001).

31. *United States v. Kendrick,* 331 F.2d 110, 114 (4th Cir. 1964).

32. *Arizona v. Macumber,* 544 P.2d 1084 (Ariz. 1976).

33. Paul Rosenzweig, Testimony before the American Bar Association Task Force on the Attorney-Client Privilege (Feb. 11, 2005), *available at* http://www.heritage.org/research/legalissues/tst021105a.cfm.

34. *von Bulow v. von Bulow*, 828 F.2d 94 (2d Cir. 1987).

35. *Swidler & Berlin v. United States*, 524 U.S. 399 (1998).

36. *In re Sealed Case*, 124 F.3d 230 (D.C. Cir. 1997), *rev'd*, *Swidler & Berlin v. United States*, 524 U.S. 399 (1998); *see also* Paul R. Rice, *Attorney-Client Privilege in the United States* § 8:1 (2d ed 1999).

37. Adam Liptak, *Lawyer Reveals Secret, Toppling Death Sentence*, N.Y. Times, Jan. 19, 2008, at A1.

38. Adam Liptak, *When Law Prevents Righting a Wrong*, New York Times, May 4, 2008, Week in Review, at 4.

39. *People v. Belge*, 372 N.Y.S.2d 798 (Cty. Ct. 1975).

40. *Ethics on Trial* (WETA-TV documentary 1986).

41. Leslie C. Griffin, *The Lawyer's Dirty Hands*, 8 Geo. J. Legal Ethics 219 (1995).

42. Ann M. Murphy, *Spin Control and the High-Profile Client*, 55 Syracuse L. Rev. 545 (2005).

43. *Haugh v. Schroder Inv. Mgmt. N. Am., Inc.*, 92 Fair Empl. Prac. Cas. (BNA) 1043 (S.D.N.Y. 2003).

44. Personal correspondence with Lanny Davis.

45. *Hickman v. Taylor*, 329 U.S. 495, 510–511 (1947).

46. *See* Edward J. Imwinkelried, *The New Wigmore: A Treatise on Evidence; Evidentiary Privileges* § *1.3.11* (Richard D. Friedman ed., 2002).

47. *McCormick on Evidence* 388 (John William Strong ed., 5th ed. 1999).

48. *Hickman*, 329 U.S. at 516 (Jackson, J., concurring).

49. Charles P. Cercone, *The War against Work Product Abuse*, 64 U. Pitt. L. Rev. 639 (2003).

50. *Hickman*, 329 U. S. 495.

51. *Upjohn Co. v. United States*, 449 U. S. 383 (1981).

52. Mitchel L. Winick et al., *Playing I Spy with Client Confidences: Confidentiality, Privilege, and Electronic Communications*, 31 Tex. Tech. L. Rev. 1225, 1227 (2000); *see also* Stephen M. Johnson, *The Internet Changes Everything: Revolutionizing Public Participation and Access to Government Information through the Internet*, 50 Admin. L. Rev. 277, 331 (1998).

53. Maureen B. Collins, *E-mail and Attorney-Client Communications*, 88 Ill. B.J. 541 (2000).

54. Sheryl Gay Stolberg, *Senator Insists Bush Aides Testify Publicly*, N.Y. Times, Mar. 19, 2007, at A1.

55. *Garner v. Wolfinbarger*, 430 F.2d 1093 (5th Cir. 1970).

56. Rice, *supra* note 36, §§ 8:19–22.

57. *U.S. Postal Service v. Phelps Dodge Refining Corp.*, 852 F. Supp. 156 (E.D.N.Y. 1994).

58. Jack B. Weinstein, *Evidence* § 503(a)(3)[01], at 31–38 (1993).

59. Thomas F. O'Neil III & Adam H. Charnes, *The Embryonic Self-Evaluative Privilege: A Primer for Health Care Lawyers,* 5 Annals Health L. 33 (1996).

60. Memorandum from Larry D. Thompson, Deputy Attorney General, to Heads of Department Components, U.S. Attorneys: Principles of Federal Prosecution of Business Organizations (Jan. 20, 2003), *available at* http://www.usdoj.gov/dag/cftf/corporate_guidelines.htm; *see also* Memorandum from Eric Holder Jr., Deputy Attorney General, to the Heads of Department Components, U.S. Attorneys (June 16, 1999), *reprinted in* 66 Crim. L. Rep. (BNA) 189 (1999).

61. See, for example, the ABA resolution, sponsored by the ABA Task Force on Attorney-Client Privilege and adopted on August 9, 2005, opposing this practice [hereinafter ABA Resolution]. http://www.abanet.org/poladv/documents/report111.pdf.

62. Sarbanes-Oxley Act of 2002, Pub. L. No. 107-204, 116 Stat. 745.

63. *ABA Report Regarding Proposed Amendments to Federal Sentencing Guidelines for Organizations* 7 (2004), *available at* http://www.abanet.org/poladv/documents/report303.pdf.

64. Charles Duhigg, *Poisoned by Scandal, Craving an Antidote,* N.Y. Times, Dec. 10, 2006, Business, at 1.

65. Ryan D. O'Dell, *Federal Court Positively Adopts a Federal Common Law Testimonial Privilege for Mediation: Is It Justified?* 1999 J. Disp. Resol. 203, 213.

66. Pamela A. Kentra, *Hear No Evil, See No Evil, Speak No Evil: The Intolerable Conflict for Attorney-Mediators between the Duty to Maintain Mediation Confidentiality and the Duty to Report Fellow Attorney Misconduct,* 1997 BYU L. Rev. 715, 717.

67. *Folb v. Motion Picture Indus. Pension & Health Plans,* 16 F. Supp. 2d 1164 (C.D. Cal. 1998).

68. *Lake Utopia Paper Ltd v. Connelly Containers, Inc.,* 608 F.2d 928 (2d Cir. 1979).

69. Justin Kelly, *Court Upholds Mediation Confidentiality in Key Civil Case,* ADRWorld.com, Jan. 27, 2006, http://www.adrworld.com/sp.asp?id=39417 (site requires registration), *also available at* http://www.massuma.net/confidentiality.pdf.

70. *Rojas v. Superior Court,* 33 Cal. 4th 407 (2004).

71. Laura A. Miles, *Absolute Mediation Privilege, Promoting or Destroying Mediation by Rewarding Sharp Practice and Driving Away Smart Lawyers,* 25 Whittier L. Rev. 617 (2004).

72. *Restatement (Third) of the Laws Governing Lawyers* § 73 (2000); *see also Upjohn Co. v. United States,* 449 U.S. 383 (1981).

73. Anthony Alfieri, Op-Ed., *Lessons on Ethics for Lawyers,* Miami Herald, Feb. 10, 2006, at A25.

74. Personal correspondence with Stanley Alpert.

75. ABA Resolution, *supra* note 61.

76. Carole Basri & Irving Kagan, *Corporate Legal Departments* ch. 9 (PLI 2004).

77. Josephine Carr, *Are Your Internal Communications Protected?* ACC Docket, Nov./Dec. 1996, at 32.

78. Case 155/79, *Australian Mining & Smelting Europe Ltd. v. Comm'n,* 2

C.M.L.R. 264 (1982); *see also* Commission Decision 85/79 (John Deere), 1984 O.J. (L 35) 58 (EC).

79. Peter E. Nahmias, *Two Lawyers for the Price of One,* ACC Docket, June 2003, at 102.

80. Javier H. Rubinstein, *International Commercial Arbitration: Reflections at the Crossroads of the Common Law and Civil Law Traditions,* 5 Chi. J. Int'l L.303 (2004).

81. *Greenough v. Gaskell,* (1833) 1 Mylne & Keen 98, 103 (Eng.).

82. Daniel R. Fiskel, *Lawyers and Confidentiality,* 65 U. Chi. L. Rev. 1, 10 (1998).

83. Simon, *supra* note 24, at 113.

84. *Spaulding v. Zimmerman,* 116 N.W.2d 704 (Minn. 1962).

Chapter 4

1. 4 John Henry Wigmore, *A Treatise on the System of Evidence in Trials at Common Law* § 2380, at 3347 (1905).

2. *Duchess of Kingston's Trial,* (1776) 20 How. St. Tr. 355, 573 (Eng.), *quoted in* 4 Wigmore, *supra* note 1, § 2380, at 3347.

3. Alfred Swaine Taylor, *Principles and Practice of Medical Jurisprudence* 21–23 (10th ed. 1948).

4. Joseph C. Stetler & Alan R. Moritz, *Doctor and Patient and the Law* ch. 14 (4th ed. 1962).

5. Charles Tilford McCormick, *McCormick's Handbook of the Law of Evidence* 227 n.95 (Edward W. Cleary ed., 2d ed. 1972).

6. *Centrillo v. Syntex Laboratories,* 1478 Ill. App. 3d 581 (App. Ct. 1986).

7. *Hammonds v. Aetna Casualty & Surety Co.,* 243 F. Supp. 793 (N.D. Ohio 1965).

8. Mark Siegler, *Confidentiality in Medicine—A Decrepit Concept,* 307 New Eng. J. Med. 1518 (1982).

9. Milt Freudenheim, *Company Clinics Cut Health Costs,* N.Y. Times, Jan. 14, 2007.

10. Jeffrey Rothfeder, *Privacy for Sale: How Computerization Has Made Everyone's Private Life an Open Secret* 180 (1992); Gina Kolata, *When Patients' Records Are Commodities for Sale,* N.Y. Times, Nov. 15, 1995, at B1.

11. Siegler, *supra* note 8, at 1518.

12. Robert Klitzman, Essay, *The Quest for Privacy Can Make Us Thieves,* N.Y. Times, May 9, 2006.

13. Amy Harmon, *Insurance Fears Lead Many to Shun DNA Tests,* N.Y. Times, Feb. 24, 2008, at A1.

14. Pub. L. No. 110-233, 122 Stat. 881 (2008).

15. Sheri A. Alpert, *Health Care Information: Access, Confidentiality, and Good Practice, in Ethics, Computing, and Medicine* 75, 91 (Kenneth W. Goodman ed., 1998).

16. *Limbaugh v. State,* 887 So. 2d 387 (Fla. Dist. Ct. App. 2004); Peter Whoriskey, *Rush Limbaugh Turns Himself In on Fraud Charge in Rx Drug Probe,* Wash. Post, Apr. 29, 2006, at C1.

17. *In re O.L.*, 584 A.2d 1230 (D.C. 1990).

18. *In re D.H., discussed in In re O.L.*, 584 A.2d 1230.

19. *In re N.H.*, 569 A.2d 1179 (D.C. 1990).

20. William J. Ellos, *Ethical Practice in Clinical Medicine* (1990).

21. Personal correspondence with Dr. H. M. Rosenwasser.

22. Matt Hayes, *DOJ Dismisses Doctor-Patient Privilege,* Fox News.Com, March 22, 2005, http://www.foxnews.com/story/0,2933,150664,00.html.

23. John M. Carroll, *Confidential Information Sources, Public and Private* ch. 8 (2d ed. 1991).

24. Ronald H. Uscinski, The Shaken Baby Syndrome: Reflections of a Neurosurgeon (unpublished memo, on file with author); personal correspondence with Ronald H. Uscinski.

25. Gina Kolata, *States and V.A. at Odds on Cancer Data,* N.Y. Times, Oct. 10, 2007, at A20.

26. Ian Urbina & Ron Nixon, *Disuse of System Is Cited in Gaps in Soldiers' Care,* N.Y. Times, Mar. 30, 2007, at A1.

27. *Whalen v. Roe,* 429 U.S. 589 (1977).

28. Applied Digital Solutions.

29. Royal College of General Practitioners, *The Value of General Practice* 6 (2006), *available at* http://www.rcgp.org.uk/pdf/iss_info_06_valuegenprac.pdf.

30. Milt Freudenheim & Robert Pear, *Health Hazard: Computers Spilling Your History, N.Y. Times, Dec. 3, 2006* (quoting Representative John D. Dingell); Christopher Lee, *Doctors Slow to Adopt E-Records for Patients,* Wash. Post, Oct. 12, 2006, at A10.

31. Amitai Etzioni, *The Limits of Privacy* ch. 5 (1999).

32. National Committee on Vital Health and Statistics, *Health Privacy and Confidentiality Recommendations* (1997), *available at* http://www.ncvhs.hhs.gov/privrecs.htm.

33. Judith Wagner DeCew, *The Priority of Privacy for Medical Information, in The Right to Privacy* 213, 214 (Ellen Frankel Paul et al. eds., 2000); *see also* Judith Wagner DeCew, *In Pursuit of Privacy: Law, Ethics, and the Rise of Technology* (1997).

34. Editorial, *Safeguarding Private Medical Data,* N.Y. Times, Mar. 26, 2008, at A22.

35. Batami Sadan, *Patient Data Confidentiality and Patient Rights,* 62 Int'l J. Med. Informatics 41 (2001).

36. Lisa Seachrist, *Shalala's Medical Privacy Report Gets Mixed Reviews,* Bioworld Today, Sept. 15, 1997.

37. Rob Stein, *Medical Privacy Law Nets No Fines,* Wash. Post, June 5, 2006, at A1.

38. Bruce Lambert & Nate Schweber, *Hospital Workers Punished for Peeking at Clooney File,* N.Y. Times, Oct. 10, 2007.

39. Jennifer Steinhauer, California *Hospital Faces Sanctions after Workers Wrongly Looked at Patient Records,* N.Y. Times, Apr. 8, 2008, at A16.

40. Privacy Rights Clearinghouse, Fact Sheet 8: Medical Records Privacy, http://www.privacyrights.org/fs/fs8-med.htm (last visited May 29, 2008).

41. Robert Pear, *Warnings over Privacy of U.S. Health Network,* N.Y. Times, Feb. 18, 2007, at A16.

42. Simson Garfinkel, *Database Nation: The Death of Privacy in the 21st Century* 129 (2000).

43. S. Rodatà, *Tecnologie e Diritti* (1996), *quoted in* Emilio Mordini, *Confidentiality in Child Psychiatry* 3–4 (research paper, Psychoanalytic Institute for Social Research), *available at* http://www.bioethics.it/pdf/pc_2/confidentiality_in_child_psych.pdf.

44. Zechariah Chafee Jr., *Privileged Communications: Is Justice Served or Obstructed by Closing the Doctor's Mouth on the Witness Stand?* 52 Yale L.J. 607, 616 (1943).

Chapter 5

1. Zechariah Chafee Jr., *Privileged Communications: Is Justice Served or Obstructed by Closing the Doctor's Mouth on the Witness Stand?* 52 Yale L.J. 607, 611 (1943).

2. *Ethics Case Book of the American Psychoanalytic Association* 21 (Paul A. Dewald & Rita W. Clark eds., 2001).

3. 25 Charles Alan Wright & Kenneth W. Graham Jr., *Federal Practice and Procedure: Evidence* § 5522, at 8 (2005).

4. 12 Sigmund Freud, *On Beginning the Treatment, in The Standard Edition of the Complete Psychological Works of Sigmund Freud* 121, 135 (James Strachey ed. and trans., 1958).

5. Deborah Serani, *Understanding Psychoanalysis,* 4 Participant-Observer 4 (2002).

6. *Caesar v. Mountanos,* 542 F.2d 1064, 1072 (9th Cir. 1976) (citing *Taylor v. United States,* 222 F.2d 398, 401 (D.C. Cir. 1955)).

7. Jocelyn Noveck, Associated Press, *Real-Life Shrinks Debate Ethical Lapses on "Sopranos,"* USA Today, June 6, 2007 (quoting Dr. Jan Van Schaik, chair of the Ethics Committee at the Wisconsin Psychoanalytic Institute), http://www.usatoday.com/life/television/news/2007-06-06-sopranos-therapists_N.htm.

8. Henri F. Ellenberger, *The Discovery of the Unconscious* (1970).

9. Paul W. Mosher, *Psychotherapist-Patient Privilege: The History and Significance of the United States Supreme Court's Decision in the Case of* Jaffee v. Redmond, *in Confidential Relationships: Psychoanalytic, Ethical, and Legal Contexts* 177 (Christine M. Koggel et al. eds., 2003).

10. Manfred S. Guttmacher & Henry Weihofen, *Psychiatry and the Law* (1952); Mosher, *supra* note 9; *see also* Ralph Slovenko, *The Physician and Privileged Communications,* 110 J. La. St. Med. Soc'y 39 (1958); Ralph Slovenko, *Psychiatry and a Second Look at the Medical Privilege,* 6 Wayne L. Rev. 175 (1960); Ralph Slovenko & Gene L. Usdin, *The Psychiatrist and Privileged Communication,* 4 Archives Gen. Psychiatry 431 (1961); Ralph Slovenko, *Psychotherapist-Patient Testimonial Privilege: A Picture of Misguided Hope,* 23 Cath. U. L. Rev. 649 (1974); Ralph Slovenko, *On Testimonial Privilege,* 11 Contemp. Psychoanalysis 188 (1975); Ralph Slovenko, *The Psychotherapist-Patient Testimonial Privilege,* 57 Am. J. Psychoanalysis 63 (1997); Ralph Slovenko, *Psychotherapy and Confidentiality: Testimonial Privileged Communication, Breach of Confidentiality, and Reporting Duties* (1998).

11. *Binder v. Ruvell*, No. 52C-2535 (Ill. Cir. Ct., Cook County June 24, 1952).

12. Mosher, *supra* note 9, at 187.

13. Ralph Slovenko, *Psychotherapy and Confidentiality*, 24 Clev. St. L. Rev. 375, 381 (1975).

14. Mosher, *supra* note 9, at 193; *see also* Carolyn Peddy Courville, *Rationales for the Confidentiality of Psychotherapist-Patient Communications*, 35 Hous. L. Rev. 187, 197 (1998).

15. David J. Lynn & George E. Vaillant, *Anonymity, Neutrality, and Confidentiality in the Actual Methods of Sigmund Freud: A Review of Forty-three Cases, 1907–1939*, 155 Am. J. Psychiatry163, 169 (1998).

16. Lore Reich Rubin, *Wilhelm Reich and Anna Freud*, 12 Int'l F. Psychoanalysis 108 (2003).

17. Brenda Maddox, *Freud's Wizard* 104 (2007).

18. 25 Wright & Graham, *supra* note 3, § 5222.

19. Mary Kay O'Neil, *Confidentiality, Privacy, and the Facilitating Role of Psychoanalytic Organizations*, 88 Int'l J. Psychoanalysis 691 (2007).

20. Allannah Furlong, *Confidentiality with Respect to Third Parties*, 86 Int'l J. Psychoanalysis 375 (2005).

21. *Jaffee v. Redmond*, 518 U.S. 1, 7 n.5, 10 (1996).

22. *Id.* at 11.

23. Martin L. Gross, *The Psychological Society* 8 (1978).

24. Edward J. Imwinkelried, *The New Wigmore: A Treatise on Evidence; Evidentiary Privileges* § 2.5, at 113 (Richard D. Friedman ed., 2002).

25. *Jaffee*, 518 U.S. at 18–19 (Scalia, J., dissenting).

26. Edward J. Imwinkelried, *Draft Article V of the Federal Rules of Evidence on Privileges, One of the Most Influential Pieces of Legislation Never Enacted: The Strength of the Ingroup Loyalty of the Federal Judiciary*, 58 Ala. L. Rev. 41, 51 (2006) (quoting Representative William L. Hungate).

27. *Univ. of Pa. v. EEOC*, 493 U.S. 182, 193 (1990).

28. *Jaffee*, 518 U.S. at 19–36 (Scalia, J., dissenting).

29. *Id.* at 22.

30. *Graham v. United States*, 746 A.2d 289 (D.C. 2000).

31. D.C. Code § 14-307(b)(1) (2001).

32. John Springer, *Former Classmate Says Skakel Confessed to Killing Martha Moxley*, CourtTV.com, May 16, 2001 (quoting John Higgins), http://www.courttv.com/trials/moxley/051602_ctv.html.

33. Thomas J. Reed, *The Futile Fifth Step: Compulsory Disclosure of Confidential Communication among Alcoholics Anonymous Members*, 70 St. John's L. Rev. 693 (1996).

34. *State v. Boobar*, 637 A.2d 1162 (Me. 1994); Joseph Berger, *Alcoholic Said He Killed, Colleagues Testify*, N.Y. Times, June 7, 1994, at B1 (discussing *People v. Cox*); an Hoffman, *Faith in Confidentiality of Therapy Is Shaken*, N.Y. Times, June 15, 1994, at A1; *Retrial Begins in Murder Case Tied to Confession to A.A. Group*, N.Y. Times, Nov. 3, 1994, at B7.

35. Judith Kohler, *Military Judge Issues Arrest Warrant for Rape Counselor,* San Angelo Standard-Times, May 27, 2005.

36. *Tarasoff v. Regents of Univ. of Cal.,* 17 Cal. 3d 425 (1976).

37. *Id.* at 431.

38. Jerome S. Beigler, *The New Informants: The Betrayal of Confidentiality in Psychoanalysis and Psychotherapy, by Christopher Bollas and David Sundelson,* 45 J. Am. Psychoanalytic Ass'n, 627 (1997) (book review).

39. *Barefoot v. Estelle,* 463 U.S. 880, 896–899 (1983).

40. *Id.* at 437; *see also* John G. Fleming & Bruce Maximov, *The Patient or His Victim: The Therapist's Dilemma,* 62 Cal. L. Rev. 1025, 1030 (1974).

41. *Tarasoff,* 17 Cal. 3d at 451, 460, 463 (Mosk, J., concurring and dissenting).

42. *In re Estate of Votteler,* 327 N.W.2d 759 (Iowa 1982).

43. *Tarasoff,* 17 Cal. 3d at 442.

44. *Lipari v. Sears, Roebuck & Co.,* 497 F. Supp. 185 (D. Neb. 1980).

45. *McIntosh v. Milano,* 168 N.J. Super. 466 (Super. Ct. Law Div. 1979).

46. *Md. State Bd. of Physicians v. Eist,* 176 Md. App. 82 (Ct. Spec. App. 2007); Bob Pyles, *Absolute Power: The* Eist *Case,* Am. Psychoanalyst, Winter/Spring 2008, at 10; Bob Pyles, *The Height of Arrogance,* Am. Psychoanalyst, Winter/Spring 2007, at 22.

47. *Pate v. Threlkel,* 661 So. 2d 278 (Fla. 1995).

48. *Safer v. Estate of Pack,* 677 A.2d 118 (N.J. Super. Ct. App. Div. 1996).

49. M. Gregg Bloche, *Psychotherapy and Confidentiality: Testimonial Privileged Communication, Breach of Confidentiality, and Reporting Duties, by Ralph Slovenko,* 340 New Eng. J. Med. 820 (1999) (book review).

50. Beigler, *supra* note 38, at 627.

51. Glen Gabbard & Paul Williams, *Preserving Confidentiality in the Writing of Case Reports,* 82 Int'l J. Psychoanalysis 1067 (2001).

52. *In re Lifschutz,* 2 Cal. 3d 415, 438 (1970).

Chapter 6

1. J. N. D. Kelley, *Early Christian Doctrines* (Prince Press rev. ed. 2003).

2. Oscar Wilde, *The Picture of Dorian Gray* ch. 8 (1891).

3. *Caesar v. Mountanos,* 542 F.2d 1064 (9th Cir. 1976).

4. *In re Lifschutz,* 2 Cal. 3d 415, 427 (1970).

5. William Harold Tiemann & John C. Bush, *The Right to Silence: Privileged Clergy Communication and the Law* ch. 10 (2d ed. 1983).

6. Tiemann & Bush, *supra* note 5.

7. William Harold Tiemann, *The Right to Silence: Privileged Communication and the Pastor* 19, 34 (1964).

8. 4 Jeremy Bentham, *Rationale of Judicial Evidence* 586–592 (London, Hunt and Clarke, 1827), *quoted in* 4 John Henry Wigmore, *A Treatise on the System of Evidence in Trials at Common Law* § 2396, at 3364 (1905).

9. *Dictionnaire de Droit Canonique* 41 (R. Naz ed., 3d ed. 1957).

10. Tiemann & Bush, *supra* note 5, at 21.

11. Anthony Cardinal Bevilacqua, *Confidentiality Obligation of Clergy from the Perspective of Roman Catholic Priests,* 29 Loy. L.A. L. Rev. 1733, 1741 (1996).

12. *Echo of an Ancient Rite,* Time, Jan. 9, 1984.

13. 4 Wigmore, *supra* note 8, § 2394.

14. *People v. Phillips* (N.Y. Ct. Gen. Sess. 1813), *reprinted in Privileged Communications to Clergymen,* 1 Cath. Law. 199, 203 (1955).

15. *People v. Smith,* 2 City Hall Rec. (Rogers) 77 (N.Y. Ct. Oyer & Terminer 1817), *reprinted in* 1 Cath. Law. 199, 209 (1955).

16. *Trammel v. United States* 445 U.S. 40, 51 (1980).

17. *Mullen v. United States,* 263 F.2d 275 (D.C. Cir. 1959).

18. General Convention of the Episcopal Church, Memorandum on Privileged Communications in the Episcopal Church, *quoted in* Tiemann & Bush, *supra* note 5, at 56.

19. Phil Hirschkorn, *Court Hears Priest's Testimony in Murder Case Appeal,* CNN .com, July 18, 2001, http://archives.cnn.com/2001/LAW/07/18/priest.confession; *see also* Michael M. Martin, *Clergy-Penitent Privilege: New Ground Broken,* 226 N.Y. L.J. 3 (2001); Jim Dwyer, *Testimony of Priest and Lawyer Frees Man Jailed for '87 Murder,* N.Y. Times, July 25, 2001.

20. Associated Press, *Talk with Chaplain Leads to Murder Charges,* N.Y. Times, Dec. 12, 1982.

21. Tiemann & Bush, *supra* note 5, at 167.

22. *Church of Jesus Christ of Latter-Day Saints v. Superior Court,* 764 P.2d 759 (Ariz. Ct. App. 1988).

23. Shannon O'Malley, *Mandatory Child Abuse Reporting Statutes and the Clergy-Communicant Privilege,* 21 Rev. Litig. 701 (2002).

24. Lennard K Whittaker, *The Priest-Penitent Privilege: Its Constitutionality and Doctrine,* 13 Regent U. L. Rev. 145, 166 n.168 (2000).

25. Frank Keating, Op-Ed., *Finding Hope in My Faith,* N.Y. Times, June 19, 2003.

26. Office of the Attorney General, *Report on the Investigation of the Diocese of Manchester* (2003), *available at* http://doj.nh.gov/publications/nreleases/3303diocese .html.

27. Timothy D. Lytton, *Holding Bishops Accountable: How Lawsuits Helped the Catholic Church Confront Clergy Sexual Abuse* (2008).

28. Laurie Goodstein, *Deal Reported in Abuse Cases in Los Angeles,* N.Y. Times, July 15, 2007, at A1; *see also* Randal C. Archibold, *San Diego Diocese Settles Lawsuit for $200 Million,* N.Y. Times, Sept. 8, 2007, at A8.

29. Goodstein, *supra* note 28, at A1.

30. Randal C. Archibold, *Archdiocese Loses Case to Keep Former Priests' Records Secret,* N.Y. Times, Apr. 18, 2006 (quoting Professor Marci A. Hamilton).

31. Leon J. Podles, *Sacrilege: Sexual Abuse in the Catholic Church* 516 (2008).

32. U.S. Conference of Catholic Bishops, *Charter for the Protection of Children and Young People* arts. 1–4 (2005), *available at* http://www.usccb.org/ocyp/charter .shtml.

33. *In re Swenson,* 237 N.W. 589, 591 (Minn. 1931).

34. Whittaker, *supra* note 24, at 152.

35. Associated Press, *Texas Supreme Court Backs Pastor over His Publicizing of Affair,* N.Y. Times, June 30, 2007.

36. *Id.*

37. Christopher B. Mueller & Laird C. Kirkpatrick, *Federal Evidence* § 211 (3d ed. 2007) cites various examples. *See also* Claudia L. Catalano, *Who Are Clergy?* 101 A.L.R.5th 619 (2006); 1 David M. Greenwald et al., *Testimonial Privileges,* § 6:14 (3d ed. 2005).

38. James Callahan & Richard Mills, *Historical Inquiry into the Priest-Penitent Privilege,* 81 U. Det. Mercy L. Rev. 705 (2004).

39. Mueller & Kirkpatrick, *supra* note 37, ch. 5.

40. Michael A. Riccardi, *Rabbi's Disclosure Ruled Not a Breach of Duty,* 224 N.Y. J.L. 1 (2000).

41. Personal correspondence with Rabbi Roger Herst.

42. Child Welfare Information Gateway, *Clergy as Mandatory Reporters of Child Abuse and Neglect* (2008), *available at* http://www.childwelfare.gov/systemwide/laws_policies/statutes/clergymandated.pdf.

43. Norman Abrams, *Addressing the Tension between the Clergy-Communicant Privilege and the Duty to Report Child Abuse in State Statutes,* 44 B.C. L. Rev. 1127 (2003).

44. Christopher R. Pudelski, *The Constitutional Fate of Mandatory Reporting Statutes and the Clergy-Communicant Privilege in a Post-*Smith *World,* 98 Nw. U. L. Rev. 703 (2004); Abrams, *supra* note 43; 1 Greenwald, *supra* note 37, § 6:14.

45. Abrams, *supra* note 43, at 1142.

46. *People v. Hodges,* 13 Cal. Rptr. 2d 412 (Cal. App. Dep't Super. Ct. 1992).

47. Nancy Blodgett, *Confidentiality vs. Doctrine: Jehovah's Witness Lawyers, Workers Face Dilemma,* A.B.A.J., Feb. 1, 1988, at 16.

48. *Doe 2 v. Superior Court (Calkins),* 34 Cal. Rptr. 458 (Ct. App. 2005).

49. *Id.* at 469 (quoting *Trammel v. United States,* 445 U.S. 40, 51 (1980)).

50. *Doe 1 v. Superior Court,* 34 Cal. Rptr. 3d 248 (Ct. App. 2005).

51. *Landeros v. Flood,* 551 P.2d 389 (Cal. 1976).

52. Pudelski, *supra* note 44.

53. 1 Greenwald, *supra* note 37, ch. 6.

54. Andrew A. Beerworth, *Treating Spiritual and Legal Counselors Differently: Mandatory Reporting Laws and the Limitations of Current Free Exercise Doctrine,* 10 Roger Williams U. L. Rev. 121 (2004).

55. Abrams, *supra* note 43, at 1138–1139; *see also* Seth C. Kalichman, *Mandated Reporting of Suspected Child Abuse: Ethics, Law, and Policy* (2d ed. 1999).

56. *See* Tiemann, *supra* note 7, at 22.

57. Tiemann & Bush, *supra* note 5, at 73.

58. Azizah al-Hibri, *The Muslim Perspective on the Clergy-Penitent Privilege,* 29 Loy. L.A. L. Rev. 1723 (1996).

59. Whittaker, *supra* note 24, at 152.

60. *People v. Hodges,* 13 Cal. Rptr. 2d 412 (Cal. App. Dep't Super. Ct. 1992) (citing *Reynolds v. United States,* 98 U.S. 145 (1878)).

61. *Lemon v. Kurtzman,* 403 U.S. 602, 612–613 (1971).

62. *Everson v. Bd. of Educ.,* 330 U.S. 1, 18 (1947).

63. *Minersville School Dist. Bd. of Educ. v. Gobitis,* 310 U.S. 586, 594–595 (1940).

64. *Reynolds v. United States,* 98 U.S. 145 (1878).

65. *Employment Div. v. Smith,* 494 U.S. 872 (1990).

66. *Id.* at 878, 887, 906.

67. Stephen Gottschalk, *Spiritual Healing on Trial: A Christian Scientist Reports,* Christian Century, June 22–29, 1988, at 602.

68. *Commonwealth v. Twitchell,* 416 Mass. 114 (1993).

69. 42 U.S.C. §§ 2000bb *et seq.*

70. *Gonzales v. O Centro Espirita Beneficente Uniao do Vegetal,* 546 U.S. 418, 423 (2006).

71. *Freeman v. Dep't of Highway Safety & Motor Vehicles,* 924 So. 2d. 48 (Fla. Dist. Ct. App. 2006).

72. *Braunfeld v. Brown,* 366 U.S. 599 (1961).

73. R. Michael Cassidy, *Sharing Sacred Secrets: Is It (Past) Time for a Dangerous Person Exception to the Clergy-Penitent Privilege?* 44 Wm. & Mary L. Rev. 1627 (2003).

Chapter 7

1. *Trammel v. United States,* 445 U.S. 40, 44 (1980).

2. 1 William Blackstone, *Commentaries on the Laws of England* *442, at 441 (by Thomas M. Cooley, Callaghan & Co. 2d ed. 1872).

3. 4 John Henry Wigmore, *A Treatise on the System of Evidence in Trials at Common Law* § 2228, at 3038 (1905) (quoting Lord Chancellor Hardwicke in *Barker v. Dixie*).

4. *Id.* § 2332, at 3257 (quoting *Commissioners on Common Law Procedure* (2d report 1853)).

5. *Id.* (quoting *State v. McAuley,* 4 Heisk. 424, 432 (1871)); *id.* § 2336, at 3261 (quoting *Robin v. King,* 2 Leigh 140, 144 (1830) and *Hester v. Hester,* 4 Dev. 228, 230 (1833)); *Stein v. Bowman,* 38 U.S. (13 Pet.) 209, 223 (1839).

6. *McCormick on Evidence* § 86, at 340–341 (John William Strong ed., 5th ed. 1999).

7. *United States v. Mitchell,* 137 F.2d 1006, 1008 (2d Cir. 1943).

8. *Wyatt v. United States,* 362 U.S. 525, 536 n.5 (1960) (Warren, C. J., dissenting) (quoting 8 John Henry Wigmore, *Evidence in Trials at Common Law* 332 (McNaughton rev. ed. 1961)).

9. 5 Jeremy Bentham, *Rationale of Judicial Evidence* 338, 340, 343–344 (London, Hunt and Clarke, 1827)

10. *Stein v. Bowman,* 38 U.S. (13 Pet.) 209, 223 (1839).

11. *Blau v. United States,* 340 U.S. 332 (1951).

12. *See, e.g., Marvin v. Marvin,* 18 Cal. 3d 660 (1976).

13. National Marriage Project, *The State of Our Unions: The Social Health of Mar-*

riage in America (2005), *available at* http://marriage.rutgers.edu/Publications/SOOU/TEXTSOOU2005.htm.

14. Stephanie Coontz, Op-Ed., *Marriage, a History: How Love Conquered Marriage; Taking Marriage Private,* N.Y. Times, Nov. 26, 2007, at A27.

15. *United States v. Mitchell,* 137 F.2d 1006, 1008 (2d Cir. 1943).

16. *Hawkins v. United States,* 358 U.S. 74, 81 (1958) (Stewart, J., concurring).

17. *State v. Drury,* 110 Ariz. 447, 451, 453–454 (1974).

18. *United States v. Acker,* 52 F.3d 509, 515 (4th Cir. 1995).

19. *Stein v. Bowman,* 38 U.S. (13 Pet.) 209, 223 (1839).

20. *Wyatt v. United States,* 362 U.S. 525, 527 (1960).

21. *Pappas v. United States,* 241 F. 665 (9th Cir. 1917).

22. *United States v. Mitchell,* 137 F.2d 1006 (2d Cir. 1943).

23. *Johnson v. United States,* 616 A.2d 1216 (D.C. 1992); *see also Wyatt v. United States,* 362 U.S. 525 (1960); *Morgan v. United States,* 363 A.2d 999 (D.C. 1976).

24. *Trammel v. United States,* 445 U.S. 40 (1980).

25. Kimberly Ann Connor, *A Critique of the Marital Privileges,* 36 Val. U. L. Rev. 119, 179 (2001).

26. *Troxel v. Granville,* 530 U.S. 57, 98 (Kennedy, J., dissenting) (2000).

27. General Accounting Office, *Defense of Marriage Act: Update to Prior Report* (GAO-04-353R 2004).

28. John Bowe, *Gay Donor or Gay Dad?* N.Y. Times Magazine, Nov. 19, 2006, at 70 (quoting Arthur Leonard).

29. *Greenwald v. H & P 29th St. Associates,* 241 A.D. 2d 307 (N.Y. App. Div. 1997).

30. David Blankenhorn, *The Future of Marriage* (2007).

31. Committee on Lesbian and Gay Rights et al., Association of the Bar of the City of New York, *Marriage Rights for Same-Sex Couples in New York* (2001), *available at* http://www.abcny.org/pdf/report/samesex_marriage.pdf; National Gay and Lesbian Task Force, *Why Civil Unions Are Not Enough* (2005), *available at* http://www.thetaskforce.org/downloads/reports/fact_sheets/WhyCivilUnionsAreNotEnough.pdf; National Marriage Project, *supra* note 13; *see also* Edward J. Imwinkelried, *The New Wigmore: A Treatise on Evidence; Evidentiary Privileges* § 6.7.3, at 665 (Richard D. Friedman ed., 2002); Wikipedia, Same-Sex Marriage in the United States, http://en.wikipedia.org/wiki/Same-sex_marriage_in_the_US (last visited June 27, 2008). Because it is so new and uncertain, I do not report current news about gay marriage, at issue in some state courts and legislatures.

32. *See* Elizabeth Kimberly Penfil, *In the Light of Reason and Experience: Should Federal Evidence Law Protect Confidential Communications Between Same-Sex Partners?* 88 Marq. L. Rev. 815 (2005).

33. *Troxel v. Granville,* 530 U.S. 57, 63–64 (2000).

34. Elizabeth Marquardt, Op-Ed., *When 3 Really Is a Crowd,* N.Y. Times, July 16, 2007.

35. National Marriage Project, *supra* note 13.

36. National Gay and Lesbian Task Force, *2000 Census and Same-Sex Households: A*

User's Guide (2002), *available at* http://www.thetaskforce.org/downloads/reports/reports/2000Census.pdf.

37. Kevin Schlosser, *Litigation Review: Limitations on Marital Privilege,* N.Y. L.J., Jan. 24, 2006 (discussing *People v. Signorelli*).

38. *Rosie O'Donnell Heads to San Fran to Wed,* ABC News, Feb. 26, 2004, http://abcnews.go.com/WNT/Story?id=131678&page=2.

39. National Gay and Lesbian Task Force, *supra* note 31.

40. 4 Wigmore, *supra* note 3, § 2337, at 3265.

41. Imwinkelried, *supra* note 31, at 454–456.

42. Amee A. Shah, *The Parent-Child Testimonial Privilege—Has the Time for It Finally Arrived?* 47 Clev. St. L. Rev. 41, 46 (1999).

43. Penfil, *supra* note 32, at 830.

44. *Id.*

Chapter 8

1. Professor Imwinkelried lists illustrative cases in Edward J. Imwinkelried, *The New Wigmore: A Treatise on Evidence; Evidentiary Privileges* 1185–1186 (Richard D. Friedman ed., 2002).

2. Alan F. Westin, *Privacy and Freedom* 104 (1967).

3. Sheri A. Alpert, *Health Care Information: Access, Confidentiality, and Good Practice, in Ethics, Computing, and Medicine* 75, 92 (Kenneth W. Goodman ed., 1998).

4. Andrew Ross Sorkin & Richard Pérez Peña, *Why Wall St. Journal Editors Held News of Murdoch Bid,* N.Y. Times, May 8, 2007, Business, at 1.

5. Ellen Nakashima, *Calif. Examining HP's Media-Leak Probe, Firm Says,* Wash. Post, Sept. 7, 2006, at D1; Damon Darlin, Leak, Inquiry and Resignation Rock a Boardroom, N.Y. Times, Sept. 7, 2006, at A1.

6. Viet D. Dinh, Op-Ed., *Dunn and Dusted,* Wall St. J., Sept. 26, 2006, at A14.

7. Steve Karnowski, *Star Tribune Publisher Says He Took Data from Former Employer,* Associated Press, June 25, 2007, http://apexchange.typepad.com/industry_news/2007/06/star-tribune-pu.html; Richard Pérez Peña, *Publisher Is Ordered to Leave Job for a Year,* N.Y. Times, Sept. 19, 2007, at C10.

8. MetLife, Customer Privacy Policy, http://www.metlife.com/Applications/Corporate/WPS/CDA/PageGenerator/0,4773,P560,00.html?FILTERNAME=@URL%FILTERVALUE=/WPS/%IMAGE2.X=0%IMAGE2.Y=0 (last visited June 27, 2008).

9. Carol Vogel, *Arts, Briefly; A Former Curator Cries Foul,* N.Y. Times, Dec. 30, 2006.

10. Edward Wyatt, *Smithsonian Agreement Angers Filmmakers,* N.Y. Times, Apr. 1, 2006, at A1.

11. Sharon Waxman, *The Lawsuit Over Producer Credit for 'Crash' Gets Personal,* N.Y. Times, Mar. 9, 2006, at B7.

12. Ann Zimmerman, *Inside Wal-Mart's "Threat Research" Operation,* Wall St. J., Apr. 4, 2007; *see also* Marcus Kabel, *Wal-Mart Defends Security Tactics,* Miami Herald, Apr. 5, 2007, at C1.

13. Kurt Eichenwald, *International Business: Reuters Unit Puts 3 Executives on Paid Leave,* N.Y. Times, Jan. 31, 1998, at A1.

14. American Institute of Architects, *Code of Ethics and Professional Conduct* ethical std. 3.4, R. 3.401 & cmt. (2007), *available at* http://www.aia.org/SiteObjects/files/Hyperlinked_2007_CodeforWeb%20page.pdf.

15. John Uff, *Engineering Ethics: Some Current Issues,* Ingenia, Aug. 2002, at 47, *available at* http://www.ingenia.org.uk/ingenia/issues/issue13/Uff.pdf; the case, *Holger Hjortsvang v. San Francisco Bay Area Rapid Transit District,* was settled, and is not reported.

16. *Funds of Funds Ltd. v. Arthur Anderson & Co.,* 545 F. Supp. 1314 (S.D.N.Y. 1982).

17. American Institute of Certified Public Accountants, *Code of Professional Conduct* R. 301, *available at* http://www.aicpa.org/about/code/index.html.

18. *Couch v. United States,* 409 U.S. 322, 335 (1973).

19. *United States v. Doe,* 465 U.S. 605, 611 (1984).

20. *Couch,* 409 U.S. at 341 (Douglas, J., dissenting).

21. *Id.* at 343–344.

22. *See* John R. Robinson & Clyde D. Stoltenberg, *Privilege and Accountants' Workpapers,* 68 A.B.A. J. 1248 (1982).

23. Internal Revenue Restructuring and Reform Act of 1998 § 3411, I.R.C. § 7525.

24. Sarbanes-Oxley Act of 2002 § 404, 15 U.S.C. § 7262.

25. *Merrill Lynch & Co. v. Allegheny Energy,* No. 02 Civ. 7689(HB), 2004 US Dist. LEXIS 21543 (S.D.N.Y. Oct. 26, 2004) (asserting that accountants should not be forced to be "conduits" for their adversaries and citing *In re Pfizer Inc. Sec. Litig.,* 1993 WL 561125 (S.D.N.Y. Dec. 23, 1993), *Gutter v. E.I. DuPont de Nemours & Co.,* 1998 WL 2017926 (S.D. Fla. May 18, 1998), and *Gramm v. Horsehead Industries, Inc.,* 1990 U.S. Dist. LEXIS 773 (S.D.N.Y. Jan. 25, 1990)).

26. *Doe v. KPMG, LLP,* 325 F. Supp. 2d 746 (N.D. Tex. 2004).

27. *United States v. KPMG, LLP,* 316 F. Supp. 2d 30 (D.D.C. 2004).

28. *Merrill Lynch & Co.,* 2004 U.S. Dist. LEXIS 21543.

29. William H. Simon, *The Confidentiality Fetish,* Atlantic Monthly, Dec. 2004, at 113, 115.

30. *Restatement (Second) of Agency,* § 395 (1958).

31. *Restatement (Third) of Agency,* § 8.05 (2005).

32. Francis B. Tiffany, *Handbook of the Law of Principal and Agent* (2d ed. 1924).

33. Kim Lane Scheppele, *Legal Secrets: Equality and Efficiency in the Common Law* ch. 7 (1988).

34. *Civil Justice Roundtable Discussion* 5 (2004), *available at* http://www.ojp.usdoj.gov/bjs/pub/pdf/cjrd.pdf.

35. Ted Gup, *Nation of Secrets: The Threat to Democracy and the American Way of Life* 219 (2007).

36. Laurie Kratky Doré, *Secrecy by Consent: The Use and Limits of Confidentiality in the Pursuit of Settlement,* 74 Notre Dame L. Rev. 283 (1999); *see also* Laurie Kratky Doré, *The Confidentiality Debate and the Push to Regulate Secrecy in Civil Litigation, Report of the 2000 Forum for State Court Judges, Roscoe Pound Foundation* (2000) [hereinafter Doré, *Confidentiality Debate*].

37. John Eligon, *Coria Settles with Company He Claims Made a Bad Pill,* N.Y. Times, June 21, 2007, Sports.

38. Owen Fiss, Comment, *Against Settlement,* 93 Yale L. J. 1073, 1075–1076 (1984).

39. Aseem Mehta, *Resolving Environmental Disputes in the Hush-Hush World of Mediation: A Guide for Confidentiality,* 120 Geo. J. Legal Ethics 521, 522–523 (1997).

40. Dan Christensen & Patrick Danner, *High Court Prohibits Lawsuit Secrecy,* Miami Herald, Apr. 6, 2007, at A1.

41. *Comments of the Silha Center for the Study of Media Ethics and Law on the Proposed Amendment to Local Rule 5.03: United States District Court for the District of South Carolina* (2002) [hereinafter *Silha Center Report*], *available at* http://www.silha.umn.edu/Resource%20Documents/sccomments.pdf.

42. S.C. R. Civ. P. 41.1.

43. *Silha Center Report, supra* note 41, at 2 (citing *Nixon v. Warner Commc'ns, Inc.,* 435 U.S. 589, 597 (1978)); *In re Knight Publ'g Co.,* 743 F.2d 231 (4th Cir. 1989); *Brown v. Advantage Eng'g, Inc.,* 960 F.2d 1013 (11th Cir. 1992); *Proctor & Gamble Co. v. Bankers Trust Co.,* 78 F.3d 219 (6th Cir. 1996); *Bank of Am. Nat'l Trust & Savings Ass'n v. Hotel Rittenhouse Assoc.,* 800 F.2d 339 (3d Cir. 1986).

44. *Brown & Williamson Tobacco Corp. v. FTC,* 710 F.2d 1165, 1180 (6th Cir. 1983); *see also Cipollone v. Liggett Group, Inc.,* 106 F.R.D. 573, 577 (D.N.J. 1985); *Silha Center Report, supra* note 41.

45. Richard Zitrin, *Legal Ethics: The Case against Secret Settlements (or, What You Don't Know Can Hurt You),* 2 J. Inst. Stud. Legal Ethics 115 (1999).

46. Doré, *Confidentiality Debate, supra* note 36, at 16.

47. *Id.*

48. *See* Frank M. Baglione, Note, *Title VII and the Tenure Decision: The Need for a Qualified Academic Freedom Privilege Protecting Confidential Peer Review Materials in University Employment Discrimination Cases,* 21 Suffolk U. L. Rev. 691, 694 (1987).

49. Robert H. McLaughlin, *From the Field to the Courthouse: Should Social Science Research Be Privileged?* 24 Law & Soc. Inquiry 927, 935 (1999); *see also* Judith Shelling, *A Researcher's Privilege:* In re Cusumano, 40 Jurimetrics J. 517 (2000).

50. S. 1437, 106th Cong. (1999); *see also* Felice J. Levine & John M. Kennedy, *Promoting a Scholar's Privilege: Accelerating the Pace,* 24 Law & Soc. Inquiry 967 (1999).

51. Imwinkelried, *supra* note 1, at 102.

52. U.S. Dep't of Education, Nat'l Center for Education Statistics, *Projections of Education Statistics to 2014* (2005), *available at* http://nces.ed.gov/pubs2005/2005074.pdf.

53. Gup, *supra* note 35, at 186–187.

54. *Krolikowski v. Univ. of Mass.,* 150 F. Supp. 2d 246, 248 (D. Mass. 2001).

55. *EEOC v. Univ. of Notre Dame Du Lac*, 715 F.2d 331, 336 (7th Cir. 1983); *see also EEOC v. Franklin & Marshall College*, 775 F.2d 110 (3d Cir. 1985).

56. *Barnhill v. Bd. of Regents*, 166 Wis. 2d 395 (1992).

57. *Univ. of Pa. v. EEOC*, 493 U.S. 182 (1990).

58. Imwinkelried, *supra* note 1, at 87.

59. Kabel, *supra* note 12, at C1.

Chapter 9

1. *Diaz v. Eighth Judicial District Court*, 993 P.2d 50 (Nev. 2000).

2. Michiko Kakutani, *Barry Bonds and Baseball's Steroids Scandal*, N.Y. Times, Mar. 23, 2006, at B1 (reviewing Mark Fainaru-Wada & Lance Williams, *Game of Shadows* (2006)).

3. Edward Wasserman, *Good Stories from Bad Sources*, Miami Herald, Mar. 5, 2007, at A27.

4. Jeffrey Toobin, *Name That Source*, New Yorker, Jan. 16, 2006, at 30, 34 (quoting Rodney Smolla).

5. Gilbert Cranberg, Letter to the Editor, *Judith Miller Leaves*, N.Y. Times, Nov. 11, 2005.

6. *People v. Fancher*, 4 Thomp. & C. (N.Y.) 467, 471 (1874); *People v. Durant*, 116 Cal. 179, 220 (1897); *Rogers v. State*, 88 Miss. 38, 44 (1906); *Plunkett v. Hamilton*, 70 S.E. 781, 784 (Ga. 1911).

7. 23 Charles Alan Wright & Kenneth W. Graham Jr., *Federal Practice and Procedure: Evidence*, § 5426, at 715–716 (1980).

8. Will E. Messer, *Open Season on the Journalist's Privilege*, 94 Ky. L.J. 421, 424 (2005/2006); *see also* Project for Excellence in Journalism, *Journalists and the Jail Cell* (2006), *available at* http://journalism.org/node/2514.

9. *Garland v. Torre*, 259 F.2d 545, 549 (2d Cir. 1958).

10. *Bridges v. California*, 314 U.S. 252, 291 (1941) (Frankfurter, J., dissenting).

11. *In re Goodfader*, 45 Haw. 317 (1961).

12. *Grosjean v. Am. Press Co.*, 297 U.S. 233, 250 (1936).

13. *Bridges*, 314 U.S. at 265.

14. *Associated Press v. United States*, 326 U.S. 1, 51 (1945).

15. *Blackmer v. United States*, 284 U.S. 421, 438 (1932).

16. Editorial, *Shielding a Basic Freedom*, N.Y. Times, Sept. 12, 2005.

17. Vincent Blasi, *The Newsman's Privilege: An Empirical Study*, 70 U. Mich. L. Rev. 229 (1971).

18. *Branzburg v. Hayes*, 408 U.S. 665 (1972).

19. *Id.* at 682, 696.

20. *Id.* at 725 (Stewart, J., dissenting).

21. *Id.* at 709–711 (Powell, J., concurring).

22. *Id.* at 725 (Stewart, J., dissenting).

23. Romualdo P. Eclavea, Annotation, *Privilege of Newsgatherer against Disclosure of Confidential Sources or Information*, 99 A.L.R.3d 37 (1980).

24. Norman Pearlstine, *Off the Record: The Press, the Government, and the War over Anonymous Sources*, at 79 (2007).

25. Toobin, *supra* note 4, at 30 (quoting Rodney Smolla).

26. *In re Grand Jury Subpoena (Miller)*, 397 F.3d 964, 997–998 (D.C. Cir. 2005) (Tatel, J., concurring).

27. *McKevitt v. Pallasch*, 339 F.3d 530, 533 (7th Cir. 2003).

28. H.R. 2102, 110th Cong. (passed by House Oct. 16, 2007); S. 2035, 110th Cong. (2007).

29. James C. Goodale et al., *Reporter's Privilege Cases, in Communications Law* (PLI Patents, Copyrights, Trademarks and Literary Property, Course Handbook Series, Order No. G4-3945, 1995), includes 264 pages of such cases. *See also* Eclavea, *supra* note 23, at 37.

30. Ronald Goldfarb, *Reporter's Privileges and Responsibilities*, Wash. Law., Sept. 2005.

31. Marie Brenner, *Lies and Consequences: Sixteen Words That Changed the World*, Vanity Fair, Apr. 2006, at 206.

32. Pearlstine, *supra* note 24, at 174, 240.

33. *In re Grand Jury Subpoena (Miller)*, 397 F.3d 964, 981 (D.C. Cir. 2005).

34. *Id.* at 986 (Tatel, J., concurring).

35. David Carr, *Subpoenas and the Press*, N.Y. Times, Nov. 27, 2006, at C1.

36. Karl H. Schmid, *Journalist's Privilege in Criminal Proceedings: An Analysis of United States Courts of Appeals' Decisions from 1973 to 1999*, 39 Am. Crim. L. Rev. 1441, 1443 (2002).

37. Carr, *supra* note 35, at C9.

38. *O'Grady v. Superior Court*, 139 Cal. App. 4th 1423 (Cal. Ct. App. 2006).

39. Jonathan Glater, *At a Suit's Core: Are Bloggers Reporters, Too?* N.Y. Times, Mar. 7, 2005, at C1.

40. Jacques Steinberg, *For New Journalists, All Bets, but Not Mikes, Are Off*, N.Y. Times, June 8, 2007, Week in Review.

41. Eric Alterman, *Out of Print*, New Yorker, Mar. 31, 2008, at 48, 55.

42. *Branzburg v. Hayes*, 408 U.S. 665, 704 (1972).

43. Scott Shane, *For Bloggers, Libby Trial Is Fun and Fodder*, N.Y. Times, Feb. 15, 2007, at A1.

44. Scott Gant, *We're All Journalists Now: The Transformation of the Press and Reshaping of the Law in the Internet Age* (2007).

45. Howard Kurtz, *Got A Camera? You, Too, Can Be a Network Reporter*, Wash. Post, Sept. 24, 2007, at C7.

46. David D. Kirkpatrick, *Feeding Frenzy for a Big Story, Even if It's False*, N.Y. Times, Jan. 29, 2007, at A1.

47. *Cusumano v. Microsoft Corp.*, 162 F.3d 708 (5th Cir. 1998).

48. Judith Shelling, *A Researcher's Privilege:* In re Cusumano, 40 Jurimetrics J. 517 (2000).

49. Ronald Dworkin, *The Rights of Myron Farber*, N.Y. Rev. Books, Oct. 26, 1978.

50. Raymond F. Miller, *Creating Evidentiary Privileges: An Argument for the Judicial Approach*, 31 Conn. L. Rev. 771, 773 (1999).

51. Clark Hoyt, The Public Editor, *Culling the Anonymous Sources*, N.Y. Times, June 8, 2008 (quoting Bill Keller).

52. Personal correspondence with W. Hodding Carter III.

53. Edward Wasserman, Op-Ed., *The Vanishing Art of Standing Firm*, Miami Herald, Feb. 20, 2007, at A27.

54. Michael Brick, *How the Murder Case against a Former F.B.I. Supervisor Collapsed*, N.Y. Times, Nov. 2, 2007, at A20; *see also* Robin Shulman, *Mobster Girlfriend's Decade-Old Interview Undercuts Murder Case*, Wash. Post, Nov. 2, 2007, at A13.

55. Toobin, *supra* note 4, at 35 (quoting Walter Pincus).

56. *In re Caldwell*, 311 F. Supp. 358 (N.D. Cal. 1970).

57. *Branzburg v. Hayes*, 408 U.S. 665, 695 (1972).

58. Geneva Overholser, Op-Ed., *The Journalist and the Whistle-Blower*, N.Y. Times, Feb. 6, 2004.

59. Max Frankel, *The Washington Back Channel*, N.Y. Times Magazine, Mar. 25, 2007, at 42.

60. Personal correspondence with W. Hodding Carter III.

61. Edward Wasserman, Op-Ed., *Reporters Can't Be Fried or Foe of Sources*, Miami Herald, Jan. 8, 2007, at A23; Edward Wasserman, Op-Ed., *Media Sources: Confidentiality Vow Should Not Be Easily Surrendered*, Miami Herald, Mar. 19, 2007, at A21.

62. Toobin, *supra* note 4, at 32 (quoting Martin Kaplan).

63. Richard Cohen, Op-Ed., *Oozing Hypocrisy over a Leak*, Wash. Post, Oct. 2, 2003, at A23.

64. Adam Liptak, *After Libby Trial, New Era for Government and Press*, N.Y. Times, Mar. 8, 2007, at A17.

65. Toobin, *supra* note 4, at 33.

66. Anthony Lewis, *Privilege and the Press*, N.Y. Rev. Books, July 14, 2005, at 4, 8 (reviewing Floyd Abrams, *Speaking Freely: Trials of the First Amendment* (2005)).

67. Al Neuharth, Op-Ed., *Evil of Journalism: Anonymous Sources*, USA Today, Jan. 15, 2004, http://www.usatoday.com/news/opinion/columnist/neuharth/2004-01-16-neuharth_x.htm.

68. Matt Apuzzo, Associated Press, *Journalists May Testify in CIA Leak Case*, Wash. Post, Jan. 1, 2007, http://www.washingtonpost.com/wp-dyn/content/article/2007/01/01/AR2007010100463.html (referring to comments by Roy Peter Clark, of the Poynter Institute).

69. Alicia C. Shepard, *Life after Watergate*, Washingtonian, Nov. 2006, at 47 (quoting Renata Adler).

70. Personal correspondence with Jack Nelson.

71. Ted Gup, *Nation of Secrets: The Threat to Democracy and the American Way of Life* 174 (2007).

72. Dworkin, *supra* note 49.

73. Lewis, *supra* note 66, at 8.

74. Pearlstine, *supra* note 24, at 2.

75. Michael Kinsley, Op-Ed., *Sources Worth Protecting?* Wash. Post, Oct. 10, 2004, at B7.

76. Edward Wasserman, *The Ironies of Source Protection,* Miami Herald, Dec. 12, 2005 at A29.

77. J. Edward Gerald, *News of Crime: Courts and Press in Conflict* 150 (1983); *see also* David E. Kendall, *News of Crime: Courts and Press in Conflict,* 37 Vand. L. Rev. 647, 658 (1984) (book review).

78. Wasserman, *supra* note 53, at A27.

79. Lewis, *supra* note 66, at 8; Dworkin, *supra* note 49.

80. Alterman, *supra* note 41, at 56; *see generally* Gant, *supra* note 44.

Chapter 10

1. Rick Weiss, *Dragonfly or Insect Spy? Scientists at Work on Robobugs,* Wash. Post, Oct. 9, 2007, at A3.

2. Reg Whitaker, *The End of Privacy: How Total Surveillance Is Becoming a Reality* 132 (1999); *see also* Nina Bernstein, *Personal Files via Computer Offer Money and Pose Threat,* N.Y. Times, June 12, 1997, at A1.

3. Loopt and Buddy Beacon are examples of such tracking systems. *See* Laura M. Holson, *These Phones Can Find You,* N.Y. Times, Oct. 23, 2007, at A1.

4. *Harrington v. Iowa,* 659 N.W.2d 509 (Iowa 2003).

5. A. Michael Froomkin, *The Death of Privacy?* 52 Stan. L. Rev. 1461, 1501 (2000).

6. Neal Stephenson, *The Diamond Age* (1995); David Brin, *The Transparent Society: Will Technology Force Us to Choose between Privacy and Freedom?* (1998).

7. Jeffrey Rothfeder, *Privacy for Sale: How Computerization Has Made Everyone's Private Life an Open Secret* 17 (1992).

8. *Id.* at 85.

9. Bruce Schneier, *How to Not Catch Terrorists,* Forbes, March 26, 2007, http://www.forbes.com/security/2007/03/23/terrorism-security-database-tech-security-cx_bs_0326security.html.

10. Brian Krebs, *Three Worked the Web to Help Terrorists,* Wash. Post, July 6, 2007, at D1.

11. Sarah Lyall, *Britain Convicts 4 in Separate Terrorism Trials,* N.Y. Times, July 6, 2007, at A6.

12. *Hepting v. AT&T Corp.,* 439 F. Supp. 2d 974 (N.D. Cal. 2006), *appeal docketed,* Nos. 06-17132, 06-17137 (9th Cir. Nov. 9, 2006); Karl Vick, *Judges Skeptical of State Secrets Claim,* Wash. Post, Aug. 16, 2007, at A4; Editorial, *Sense on Secrecy,* Wash. Post, Aug. 15, 2007, at A10. A number of lawsuits have been filed against other telecom companies, and approximately fifty cases challenging the government's surveillance efforts have been consolidated and are pending before Judge Vaughn Walker of the U.S. District Court for the District of Northern California.

13. *Arizona v. Evans,* 514 U.S. 1, 17–18 (1995).

14. Amitai Etzioni, *The Limits of Privacy* 76 (1999).

15. Deborah G. Johnson, *Computer Ethics* 5, 21 (3d ed. 2001).

16. Alan F. Westin, *Privacy and Freedom* 67 (1967).

17. *Whalen v. Roe,* 429 U.S. 589, 605 (1977) (citing Barry B. Boyer, *Computerized Medical Records and the Right to Privacy: The Emerging Federal Response,* 25 Buff. L. Rev. 37 (1975); Arthur R. Miller, *Computers, Data Banks, and Individual Privacy: An Overview,* 4 Colum. Hum. Rts. L. Rev. 1 (1972); Arthur R. Miller, *The Assault on Privacy* (1971)).

18. Associated Press, *Alabama: Hospital Data Is Missing,* N.Y. Times, Feb. 13, 2007, at A19.

19. Ellen Nakashima, *U.S. Exposed Personal Data,* Wash. Post, Apr. 21, 2007, at A5; David Stout, *Veterans Chief Voices Anger on Data Theft,* N.Y. Times, May 25, 2006, at A16; Christopher Lee, *IRS Laptop Lost with Data on 291 People,* Wash. Post, June 8, 2006, at A4; David Stout, *Data Theft at Nuclear Agency Went Unreported for 9 Months,* N.Y. Times, June 10, 2006, at A11; John Solomon, *FBI Finds It Frequently Overstepped in Collecting Data,* Wash. Post, June 14, 2007, at A1; Matthew L. Wald, *Inspector Lists Computers with Atomic Secrets as Missing,* N.Y. Times, Apr. 1, 2007.

20. Eric Pfanner, *Data Leak in Britain Affects 25 Million,* N.Y. Times, Nov. 22, 2007.

21. Brad Stone, *800,000 Affected by Data Breach, U.C.L.A. Says,* N.Y. Times, Dec. 13, 2006, at A24.

22. Tom Zeller Jr., *An Ominous Milestone: 100 Million Data Leaks,* N.Y. Times, Dec. 18, 2006, at C3.

23. Jon Swartz & Byron Acohido, *Hackers Set Traps on Broad Websites,* USA Today, May 1, 2007 (quoting Roger Thompson), http://www.usatoday.com/tech/news/computersecurity/2007-05-01-malware_N.htm.

24. Beth Givens, *The Privacy Rights Handbook* 169, 171 (1997).

25. *United States v. Buckner,* 473 F.3d 551 (4th Cir. 2007); *United States v. Morgan,* 435 F.3d 660 (6th Cir. 2006); *United States v. Andrews,* 383 F.3d. 374 (6th Cir. 2004); Pamela A. MacLean, *Courts Grapple with Computer Searches,* Nat'l L.J., May 14, 2007.

26. Brad Stone, *Tell-All PCs and Phones Transforming Divorce,* N.Y. Times, Sept. 15, 2007, at A1.

27. Maureen B. Collins, *E-mail and Attorney-Client Communications,* 88 Ill. B. J. 541 (2000).

28. Norman Pearlstine, *Off the Record: The Press, the Government, and the War over Anonymous Sources* 25 (2007).

29. Eric Taub, *Deleting May Be Easy, but Your Hard Drive Still Tells All,* N.Y. Times, Apr. 5, 2006.

30. Robert S. Boyd, *Deleted Messages Usually Can Be Retrieved,* Miami Herald, Apr. 14, 2007, at A2.

31. Kevin Kelly, *Scan This Book,* N.Y. Times Magazine, May 14, 2006, at 43, 48.

32. Esther Dyson, *Daily Life on the Net: Net Vignettes,* Release 1.0, Dec. 31, 1993, *available at* http://cachefly.oreilly.com/radar/r1/12-93.pdf.

33. John Cassidy, *Me Media: How Hanging Out on the Internet Became Big Business,* New Yorker, May 15, 2006, at 50, 54.

34. Susan Kinzie & Yuki Noguchi, *In Online Social Club, Sharing Is the Point Until It Goes Too Far,* Wash. Post, Sept. 7, 2006, at A1.

35. Matt Apuzzo, *Washingtonienne Sex Blog Headed to Court,* Miami Herald, Dec. 29, 2006, at A11.

36. *Id.* at A11.

37. Steve Lohr, *Smart Care via a Mouse, but What Will It Cost?* N.Y. Times, Aug. 20, 2006.

38. *Large Companies to Give Employees Online Access to Personal Health Information,* Physician's First Watch, Dec. 7, 2006, http://firstwatch.jwatch.org/cgi/content/short/2006/1207/2.

39. Patricia A. Roche & George J. Annas, *DNA Testing, Banking, and Genetic Privacy,* 355 New Eng. J. Med. 545 (2006).

40. *See Why We Need a Genetic Bill of Rights: Rights and Liberties in the Biotech Age* (Sheldon Krimsky & Peter Shorett eds., 2005).

41. Michael J. Sniffen, *Senator Vows to Examine Screening System,* Miami Herald, Dec. 2, 2006, at A6.

42. Constitution Project, *Promoting Accuracy and Fairness in the Use of Government Watch Lists: Statement of the Constitution Project's Liberty and Security Initiative* (2006), *available at* http://www.constitutionproject.org/pdf/Watch_Lists_Statement_12-5-061.pdf.

43. Wikipedia, ECHELON, http://en.wikipedia.org/wiki/ECHELON; *see also* Wikipedia, Carnivore (software), http://en.wikipedia.org/wiki/Carnivore_%28software%29.

44. Personal correspondence with Eric Lichtblau, author of *Bush's Law: The Remaking of American Justice,* and a Pulitzer Prize–winning reporter with the *New York Times.*

45. Mark Landler, *Where Little Is Left Outside the Camera's Eye,* N.Y. Times, July 8, 2007, Week in Review, at 7.

46. Westin, *supra* note 16, at 109–110.

47. David A. Vise & Mark Malseed, *The Google Story* 147 (2005).

48. *Id.,* at 158–162; *see also* Press Release, Privacy Rights Clearinghouse, Thirty-One Privacy and Civil Liberties Organizations Urge Google to Suspend Gmail (updated Apr. 19, 2004), *available at* http://www.privacyrights.org/ar/GmailLetter.htm.

49. Neil A. Lewis, *Editor's E-Mail May Be Used in Suit against the Times,* N.Y. Times, Jan. 6, 2007, at A12.

50. Adam Liptak, *In Case about Google's Secrets, Yours Are Safe,* N.Y. Times, Jan. 26, 2006, at A19.

51. Kenneth W. Goodman, *Moral Foundations of Data Mining,* in *Encyclopedia of Data Warehousing and Mining* 832 (John Wang ed., 2005); *see also* Kenneth W. Goodman, *Ethics, Computing, and Medicine: Informatics and the Transformation of Health Care* (1998); Dara J. Glasser et al., *Chips, Tags and Scanners: Ethical Challenges for Radio Frequency Identification,* 9 Ethics & Info. Tech. 101 (2007).

52. Katherine Albrecht & Liz McIntyre, *Spychips: How Major Corporations and Government Plan to Track Your Every Move with RFID* (2005).

53. Nikita Stewart, *Alleged Leader in N.J. Slayings Heads to Court Today,* Wash. Post, Aug. 20, 2007, at B2.

54. Goodman, *supra* note 51, at 833.

55. John Markoff, *Taking Spying to Higher Level, Agencies Look for More Ways to Mine Data,* N.Y. Times, Jan. 6, 2007, at A11.

56. *Britain Is "Surveillance Society,"* BBC News, Nov. 2, 2006, http://news.bbc.co.uk/1/hi/uk/6108496.stm (quoting Richard Thomas).

57. Froomkin, *supra* note 5, at 1486.

58. Brin, *supra* note 6; Stephenson, *supra* note 6.

59. Royal Academy of Engineering, *Dilemmas of Privacy and Surveillance: Challenges of Technological Change* 19 (2007), *available at* http://www.raeng.org.uk/policy/reports/pdf/dilemmas_of_privacy_and_surveillance_report.pdf.

60. Charlie Savage, *U.S. and Europe Near Agreement on Private Data,* N.Y. Times, June 28, 2008, at A1.

61. Thomas Crampton, *Google to Reduce History of Personal Searches,* N.Y. Times, June 13, 2007, at C3.

62. *See OECD Guidelines on the Protection of Privacy and Transborder Flows of Personal Data, available at* http://www.oecd.org/document/18/0,2340,en_2649_34255_1815186_1_1_1_1,00.html.

63. S. 495, 110th Cong. (2007).

64. Press Release, Senator Patrick Leahy, Leahy, Sanders Introduce Personal Data Privacy and Security Act of 2007, S. 495 (Feb. 6, 2007), *available at* http://leahy.senate.gov/press/200702/020607.html; Congressional Budget Office, *Cost Estimate: S. 2321; E-Government Reauthorization Act of 2007* (2007), *available at* http://www.cbo.gov/ftpdocs/88xx/doc8873/s2321.pdf.

Chapter 11

1. Sissela Bok, *Secrets: On the Ethics of Concealment and Revelation* 123 (1983).

2. 23 Charles Alan Wright & Kenneth W Graham Jr., *Federal Practice and Procedure: Evidence* § 5422, at 667–677 (1990).

3. Charles T. McCormick, *Handbook of the Law of Evidence* § 81 (1954).

4. 23 Wright & Graham, *supra* note 2, § 5422.

5. Personal correspondence with George Moraitis.

6. Edward J. Imwinkelried, *The New Wigmore: A Treatise on Evidence; Evidentiary Privileges* 278–279, 289 (Richard D. Friedman ed., 2002).

7. *Branzburg v. Hayes,* 408 U.S. 665, 693–694 (1972).

8. Miller McPherson et al., *Social Isolation in America: Changes in Core Discussion Networks over Two Decades,* 71 Am. Soc. Rev. 353 (2006).

9. Imwinkelried, *supra* note 6, at 1337–1338, 1351.

10. *Id.* at l.

11. *United States v. Morison,* 844 F.2d 1057, 1082 (1988).

12. *Id.* at 1081.

13. Amanda Frost, *The State Secrets Privilege and the Separation of Powers,* 75 Fordham L. Rev. 1931, 1939 (2007).

14. Carrie Newton Lyons, *The State Secrets Privilege: Expanding Its Scope through Government Misuse,* 11 Lewis & Clark L. Rev. 99, 100, 111 (2007) (citing Bill Conroy, *DEA Agent's Whistleblower Case Exposes the "War on Drugs" as a "War of Pretense,"* Narco News Bull., Sept. 7, 2004).

15. *See* Robert M. Chesney, *State Secrets and the Limits of National Security Litigation,* 75 Geo. Wash. L. Rev. 1249 (2007).

16. *Joint Oversight Hearing on Law Enforcement Confidential Informant Practices before the Subcommittee on Crime, Terrorism, and Homeland Security and the Subcommittee on the Constitution, Civil Rights, and Civil Liberties of the House Committee on the Judiciary,* 110th Cong. (2007); *Snitching in the Spotlight: House Committee Holds Hearing on Informant Abuses,* Drug War Chron., Aug. 3, 2007, http://www.november.org/stayinfo/breaking07/SnitchSpotlight.html (discussing testimony of Professor Alexandra Natapoff).

17. Sheri A. Alpert, *Health Care Information: Access, Confidentiality, and Good Practice, in Ethics, Computing, and Medicine* 75, 75 (Kenneth W. Goodman ed., 1998).

18. S. 1784, 109th Cong. (2005); Hillary Rodham Clinton & Barack Obama, *Making Patient Safety the Centerpiece of Medical Liability Reform,* 354 New Eng. J. Med. 2205 (2006).

19. *United States v. Zolin,* 491 U.S. 554, 568–569 (1989).

20. *See* John Paul Lucci, *4th and 205: How a Rush of Global Comments Blocked the SEC's First Attempted Punt of Attorney-Client Privilege under Sarbanes-Oxley,* 20 Touro L. Rev. 363 (2004).

21. James W. Semple, *The Effect of the Sarbanes-Oxley Act on the Attorney-Client Privilege,* 53 Fed'n Def. & Corp. Couns. 419 (2003).

22. Richard Posner, *The Right of Privacy,* 12 Ga. L. Rev. 393 (1978).

23. A. Michael Froomkin, *The Death of Privacy?* 52 Stan. L. Rev. 1461 (2000).

24. Robert Gellman, *The Myth of Patient Confidentiality,* iMP Magazine, Nov. 1999, *available at* http://lists.essential.org/med-privacy/msg00449.html.

25. Henry Fountain, *Worry. But Don't Stress Out,* N.Y. Times, June 26, 2005, Week in Review (quoting Marc Rotenberg).

26. David Brin, *The Transparent Society: Will Technology Force Us to Choose between Privacy and Freedom?* 195 (1998) (quoting Erich Hughes, *Cypherpunk Manifesto*).

27. Amitai Etzioni, *The Limits of Privacy* 184–186 (1999).

28. *In re Grand Jury Investigation,* 772 N.E.2d 9 (Mass. 2002).

29. D.C. Code § 14-307(b); *Graham v. United States,* 746 A.2d 289 (D.C. 2000).

30. *Brown v. United States,* 567 A.2d 426 (D.C. 1989).

ACKNOWLEDGMENTS

Many people helped me prepare this book and think through the various issues touched upon in it.

My colleague Charles Younger managed all my work in his everyday professional and helpful style and manner. Michael O'Malley was the perfect empathetic editor, start to finish. Karen Schoen was a scrupulous copy editor.

Drs. George Moraitis and Harvey Rosenwasser read and reread the manuscript and made many helpful suggestions. Specialists read various chapters and offered useful critiques: Drs. Howard Hurtig and Lanny Gardner; Judge Earl Johnson; journalists Hodding Carter and David Vise; Professor Jane Kirtley; ethicists Dr. Ken Goodman and Dr. Ernest Wallwork; analyst Sharon Alperovitz; attorney and privacy expert Marc Rotenberg; Rabbi Roger Herst; the late Father Robert Drinan; and my wife, Joanne Goldfarb.

Student interns found me what I sought and expedited my research; particularly helpful were Cathy Barnard, Caroline Sand, and Rosty Shiller.

INDEX